TALES FROM THE
VANDERBILT COMMODORES

TALES FROM THE
VANDERBILT COMMODORES

A COLLECTION OF THE GREATEST
COMMODORE STORIES EVER TOLD

CHRIS LEE

SPORTS
PUBLISHING

Sports Publishing books may be purchased in bulk at special discounts for sales promotion, corporate gifts, fund-raising, or educational purposes. Special editions can also be created to specifications. For details, contact the Special Sales Department, Sports Publishing, 307 West 36th Street, 11th Floor, New York, NY 10018 or sportspubbooks@skyhorsepublishing.com.

Sports Publishing® is a registered trademark of Skyhorse Publishing, Inc.®, a Delaware corporation.

Visit our website at www.sportspubbooks.com.

10 9 8 7 6 5 4 3 2 1

Library of Congress Cataloging-in-Publication Data is available on file.

Series design by Tom Lau
Cover photo credit: AP Images

Print ISBN: 978-161321-712-2
Ebook ISBN: 978-1-61321-750-4

Printed in the United States of America

Contents

Introduction

I'd always wanted to be a sportswriter, and yet in 2003, I was just some guy with two business degrees working in college admissions when a good friend, Brent High, called me with the opportunity to help him start a Vanderbilt website at an up-and-coming company named Rivals.com. Let me be honest: the invitation was more about my willingness to put in the time—Brent knew I'd grown up following Vandy closely—than my qualifications, because covering Vanderbilt seemed to be a virtual dead-end. Mitch Light and Bill Trocchi, both excellent writers, had run a wonderful little newspaper entitled *The Commodore Report* a few years prior, but it wasn't financially viable.

Anyway, once I said "yes" to Brent, I then spent two years writing off losses on my taxes, which is tough to do when your only expenses are an Internet connection and gas to and from games.

Few cared about Vanderbilt sports then. Football was a perpetual wasteland and the men's basketball team, which had once been the only good thing going in Vanderbilt athletics, was in the midst of an 11–18 campaign. Baseball wasn't even an afterthought, which was probably good because Vandy fans had enough misery in their lives already. If you'd told me in January 2003 that I'd one day be planning my holidays around bowl games and using phrases like "top-ranked Vanderbilt" in the stories I wrote, I'd have never believed you. Nor would I have believed that Vanderbilt would become a big-enough deal in sports that I could launch two radio shows around it. Of course, that was never the reason I did it to begin with; Vanderbilt fans were so beaten down and starving for coverage that I felt they deserved something, and I had a chance to do that.

Meanwhile, change was happening behind the scenes that would lead to unprecedented success for Vandy's three major men's programs. Fifteen months after starting, I'd be at the Georgia Dome furiously cranking out stories at 2 a.m. after the Commodores beat a top five Mississippi State team. A scrawny freshman quarterback named Jay Cutler started the football program on a better trajectory, and in my third year of running the site, Vandy did the unthinkable and beat Tennessee in Knoxville in football.

The best story, though, was being one of the few with a front-row seat while Tim Corbin took the baseball program from the scrap heap into national prominence, and eventually on to a national title, in a matter of about a decade.

Once Vanderbilt's athletic success came, the one regret I had always had was not being able to tell some of the stories I witnessed in longer form. In the fall of 2013, I got another one of those phone calls when Skyhorse Publishing asked me if I would write a book on Vanderbilt sports. As with Brent, they had me at "hello."

The task then became two things: finding the time and deciding what to write about. Thanks to an understanding wife, I spent plenty of late nights in my home office knocking it out. As for the second, I had to determine on which aspects of Vanderbilt's athletics history I would focus. Upon deciding that, I chose to write about the twelve most significant teams I'd covered. From there, the biggest challenge of all was deciding what *not* to write, because had it not been for editorial direction, the book would have been twice this big. I regret I couldn't write more, but I think I hit the high points.

Anyway . . . this book could have never happened either directly or indirectly without several people.

Thanks to Julie Ganz at Skyhorse for working with me, and to my friend Mitch Light, now at *Athlon's,* for recommending me for the job.

Thanks to the subscribers at VandySports.com for their support. When I lost my full-time job in 2011, many of you kept telling me that I needed to write full-time and I can guarantee you that without that encouragement, I would have never had the confidence to make the leap. It was easily the best decision of my professional career.

I also can't thank my co-publishers Jesse Johnson and Mike Rapp at VandySports enough for similar encouragement. The two of you have become dear friends through our decade of doing this.

Thanks also to Mike for the use of several outstanding photos for this book.

On that note, thank you also to my good friend Jimmy Jones for not only sharing a number of unforgettable road trips with me, but also for letting me use his photos.

The life of a full-time freelancer can be more than a little scary when you have a wife and two kids and don't know exactly how much is coming in from month to month. Thanks especially to Steve Brumfield at *Sports and Entertainment Nashville Magazine* and Corey Chavous at *DraftNasty* for giving me opportunities with their respective publications.

On the radio side, I am so grateful to John Ingram and the folks at Currey Ingram Academy and to my friend and sometimes-cohost at VandySports.com Radio, Jovan Haye, and his company PostShare, for their support of my endeavors there.

Thanks to Vanderbilt sports information directors (SIDs) Andy Boggs, Larry Leathers, and Kyle Parkinson for their help over the years. I also owe a special thank-you to former baseball SID Thomas Samuel, who went out of his way to help me and also became a dear friend.

Thanks to Brett Hait, who worked at the now-defunct *Nashville City Paper*. Brett was kind enough to, in the nicest possible way, pull me aside and show me where my writing was lacking, and then show me how to improve it. I also value Brett as a close friend.

I also owe a special thanks to Tim Corbin for going above and beyond to help me over the years, and especially as we were in the process of publishing this book. It is not often that a writer is privileged to deal with a coach as successful as Corbin, and yet one who is so humble and gracious with his time.

Thanks to my parents Arthur and Jimmie Lou Lee for their unfailing love and support . . . and, of course, for taking me to countless Vanderbilt athletic contests.

Thanks to my wife, Kristin, for her support, for giving up most of her almost nonexistent free time to help make sure I got this done; to my daughter, Isabella, who had to hear, "Daddy's working," a lot more than she liked; and to my son, David, who must be the least-demanding infant in human history.

And, of course, thanks to Brent, now an associate athletic director at Lipscomb University, without whose prompting in the beginning none of this would have ever happened.

Anchor down, and happy reading!

Chris

PART I:
FOOTBALL

2008 Football: Going bowling out of nowhere

Coach Bobby Johnson was the latest in a long line of supposed saviors for a floundering Vanderbilt football program, but on the eve of the 2008 season, it looked as if Johnson would leave as yet another coach to fail to get VU to a single bowl. And if the end were on the horizon for Johnson, no one would say Vanderbilt had been unfair to him.

Hired out of Furman in 2001 to replace Woody Widenhofer, Johnson started his career with four straight two-win seasons. However, everyone also realized what a mess Johnson had inherited; Widenhofer's last team had been out-scored by 176 points that season. With the help of defensive coordinator Bruce Fowler, Johnson, a guy who liked to put his best athletes on defense, had chipped away and made the Commodores competent there. Vandy had given up 36.5 points per game in Widenhofer's last season. That number decreased every year but one, and by 2007, the 'Dores were giving up just 22.6 per contest.

But there were two problems. With the exception of the 2007 season, the 'Dores couldn't score. For four years, Johnson had rocket-armed quarterback Jay Cutler[1] except that Johnson

---

1 Cutler was a first-round NFL Draft pick and went on to a successful NFL career. He's still starting for the Chicago Bears as of this book's publication.

Bobby Johnson patrols the sidelines at Dudley Field. (Jimmy Jones)

Quarterback Jay Cutler, the 2005 Southeastern Conference Offensive Player of the Year, laid a lot of the groundwork that led to the 2008 bowl season. (Mike Rapp)

treated him like Morris Peterson's Ferrari, barely taking him out of the garage for a drive. Once he did, Vanderbilt darn near broke a twenty-three-year bowl drought, going 5–6 in 2005. Fortunately for Johnson, one of those wins snapped a twenty-three-year losing streak against Tennessee.

Johnson had followed up with 4–8 and 5–7 campaigns, but the second problem was this: most of those players were now gone. Earl Bennett, who had just become the Southeastern Conference's all-time record holder for career catches, bolted a year early for the NFL and was taken by the Chicago Bears. He was one of nine starters gone after that season; that number included VU's entire offensive line and most importantly, left tackle Chris Williams, who was the Bears' first-round pick. Five defensive starters were gone, including linebacker Jonathan Goff, who was now with the New York Giants.

The probability of a turn around had started to fade. A return to the 2–10 days seemed a lot more likely than did a bowl.

Chris Williams, wearing No. 74 here for the Chicago Bears, was a first-round pick in the 2007 NFL Draft. (Jimmy Jones)

A stunning start

The outlook was bad enough that the Commodores, who opened the year at Ohio's Miami University, were three-point underdogs to a squad that had gone 6–7 in the previous season, and 2–10 the year before that.[2] On a Thursday night in front of an ESPN audience, the year started well. Vanderbilt led 27–10 at the half, thanks to a pair of touchdown runs and a TD throw from Chris Nickson. Cornerback D.J. Moore helped greatly, returning a punt 91 yards to the Miami 1 to set up one score and also paved the way for a Bryant Hahnfeldt field goal with an interception.

Thanks to a defense that picked off three passes, the 'Dores didn't need to do much in the second half. They cruised to a 34–13 win, due in large part to Nickson's 20 carries for 166 yards and another 91 through the air.

Any road victory for Vanderbilt was a big win, but 24th-ranked South Carolina would be a lot tougher in the home opener the next week. Vanderbilt had ruined the Gamecocks' season the previous year. Carolina had been 5–0 and ranked sixth in the national polls, but Vandy came to Columbia and beat the 'Cocks there. Since then, Carolina had been making a lot of noise about the game being a fluke.

The extra motivation certainly did not hurt, nor did a break that was about to come. Trailing 10–3 in the third quarter, Vandy's Brett Upson bounced a punt near the Vanderbilt sideline. It hit a Gamecock blocker and safety Ryan Hamilton bounced on it, giving VU the ball at the USC 31. On the next play, Nickson rolled right and saw tight end Brandon Barden open, and the Virginia Tech transfer used a big height advantage on All-Southeastern Conference defensive back Captain Munnerlyn to haul it in at the 4 and take it for the score.

Vandy's Greg Billinger blocked a Ryan Succop field goal, and John Stokes ran it to the Vandy 42. From there, Nickson led Vandy

---

2 Another sign of how down the program was: the fact that Southeastern Conference schools rarely, until that game, played road games at Mid-American Conference schools.

on a drive to inside the Carolina 1, and he scored on a quarterback sneak for a 17–10 lead. A 13-yard scoring run from Jared Hawkins made the lead 14 after Bryant Hahnfeldt's extra point. Carolina countered with Chris Smelley's touchdown pass, and Carolina punted late in the game, pinning Vandy back at its 5 with 2:16 to play in hopes that the 'Dores would have to punt it back. Instead, Hawkins gained 24 yards on five carries and the 'Dores ran out the clock.

Carolina coach Steve Spurrier had often made disparaging comments about Vanderbilt when he'd been the coach at Florida. But Spurrier had always been honest, and even though Carolina outgained VU by a 325–225 margin, he pulled no punches that Thursday night.

"Last year's [loss] was just as stunning and it sort of irritated me that our players tried to say we weren't ready. We were ready to play, we just got our tails kicked. I'm sure those Vanderbilt players are wondering what kind of excuses those Carolina guys have now. We don't have excuses, they just beat us," Spurrier said.

Rice University and its up-tempo, high-scoring offense visited Nashville next. The teams traded scores throughout the first half, and went to the break tied 21-all. After Rice shanked a punt on the first possession of the second half, receiver Jamie Graham took an end around and ran 27 yards for a score, giving VU its first lead.

The defense had stiffened by then. Hahnfeldt added a 48-yard field goal and Moore, who already had an interception and two rushes for 37 yards, made a big special teams play when he returned a punt to the Rice 1, where Nickson scored to increase the lead to 38–21.

It certainly wasn't how the night had started. The Owls, fresh off scoring 98 points in their first two games, had 148 first-quarter yards that Saturday evening. Johnson spoke of what the Commodore staff did at halftime to help the defense.

"We quit trying to make so many adjustments. We were trying to match up every little thing that they were doing and we started to make fewer adjustments in the second half. We went to a more basic defense and just tried to put more pressure on the quarterback," he said.

Vanderbilt was an eight-point underdog at Ole Miss the next weekend. It was a talented Rebel team, one that would go 9–4 and beat Texas Tech in the Cotton Bowl. Ole Miss looked as if it would roll over the 'Dores early. Leading 3–0, Rebel defensive lineman Peria Jerry then picked up a fumble and rumbled 13 yards for a touchdown.

That started a crazy succession of plays; Vandy fumbled its next snap, but Ole Miss's Jevan Snead immediately threw an interception to Vandy's Hamilton, who raced 79 yards for a touchdown. On the ensuing kickoff, Ole Miss's Mike Wallace ran it back 98 yards for a score and after the dust had settled, Ole Miss led 17–7.

Near the end of the first quarter, Hawkins caught a 9-yard touchdown pass from Nickson. The game settled into an exchange of punts for most of the rest of the quarter, but another interception by Hamilton and a 23-yard return set up a Hahnfeldt 34-yard field goal. At half, the game was tied at 17.

Ole Miss moved the ball on Vanderbilt throughout the second half, but Hamilton was a one-man wrecking crew when it counted. The Rebels drove 12 plays and 78 yards to the VU 1 to open the second half, but he made a touchdown-saving tackle on Cordera Eason on a fourth-and-inches play. Later in the third, he recovered a fumble on a punt. Reshard Langford also got in on the action, intercepting Snead midway through the fourth quarter.

But all Vandy could manage was a Hahnfeldt field goal just 12 seconds into the fourth. The Rebels got the ball back with 5:10 left and went 87 yards in six plays when Dexter McCluster was about to score the go-ahead touchdown, but freshman linebacker Chris Marve, a developing star, forced a fumble that gave Vandy the ball back at the 20 with 2:40 to play.

The Commodores had barely moved the ball that night—202 total yards—but their timing was impeccable. Vandy went 57 yards in six plays, and with 31 seconds left, Hahnfeldt hit a huge 40-yard field goal for a six-point lead. The Rebels ran the kickoff back to their 47, putting Snead potentially in the position to win the game. Again, Hamilton picked him at the Vandy 14 on the game's last play.

The 'Dores were now 4–0 for the first time since 2005 and would be ranked on Monday for the first time since a 4–0 start in 1984.

"It was a wild game. A lot of crazy things happened in the first quarter and went all the way through to the end. I am extremely proud of our guys for playing hard. We had a bunch of guys get hurt. We had some guys come in who had not played before," Johnson said.

Vandy's remarkable season was starting to attract attention. Not only was VU ranked 19th in next week's poll, but ESPN decided to also host its renowned *GameDay* show from Nashville for the Auburn game.

"It think it's great for our university, our fans, and our players and coaches," Johnson said. "It's definitely going to add to the excitement as we prepare for our game."

The crew of Chris Fowler, Lee Corso, Kirk Herbstreit, and Desmond Howard set up on campus in The Commons area (that's where some new dorms had just been built to house first-year students) that morning of October 4 and thousands of fans flocked to the set. By the time the game kicked off that night with the 13th-ranked Tigers, fan excitement was at a fever pitch.

Auburn, four-point favorites, jumped out to a 13–0 early lead on two Chris Todd touchdown passes. It could have been worse; the Tigers had the ball first-and-goal at the Vandy 4 on their first drive and gave it to future Houston Texan Ben Tate four straight times, but the VU defense, led by linebacker Patrick Benoist, stuffed him on each attempt. Auburn's Wes Byrum also clanked an extra point off the right upright, an error that would cost the Tigers dearly later in the evening.

"I was proud of the way our guys hung in there. The first quarter was kind of scary, but we came fighting back," Johnson said.

Nickson had chronic shoulder problems, and after he started 3-for-8 for four yards with an interception, Johnson replaced him with Mackenzi Adams midway through the second quarter. Adams had mixed success throughout his Commodore career, but he'd led Vandy to the huge upset in Columbia the previous year and Johnson banked on catching lightning in a bottle that night.

It was the right move. After Moore returned a punt 25 yards to the Auburn 30, Adams hit Sean Walker for 11, Barden for 12, and Barden again for 3. That put Vandy second-and-goal at the 5 with under two minutes in the half, but the Tigers sacked Adams back at the 15. Adams, though, hit Justin Wheeler between a pair of AU defenders with 39 seconds left for a score, and Vandy went to the locker room down just six.

The defense had stiffened in that second quarter, allowing just 20 yards in the period after Tate ran all over the Commodores in the first quarter. Tate had 27 carries for 108 yards that night, but mysteriously, Auburn coach Tommy Tuberville gave him the ball just six times (for 12 yards) after halftime.

Meanwhile, Todd, who also had shoulder issues, struggled to move the ball with any consistency; he'd finish just 8-of-16 for 70 yards. Tuberville inserted Kodi Burns late in the third quarter and the Tigers had a first-and-10 at the VU 28, but penalties and three incompletions knocked Auburn back 11 yards before it punted.

At that point, Vandy had the ball at its 32 with 10:01 left in the third. Adams converted a big third-down throw to Wheeler for 13, and later, a first-down toss to him that went for 18. Adams also had a big 12-yard run that accounted for another first down and moved the Commodores into Auburn territory. A 9-yard throw to George Smith got Vandy to the 1, and on the next play, Adams found Barden for a touchdown.

Vandy now led 14–13 after Hahnfeldt's PAT, but the Commodores were also having trouble moving the ball. The teams traded punts for the rest of the evening. With 6:33 left, Auburn got the ball at its 21 and Tate converted a fourth-and-1 at the Auburn 31 to keep the drive alive. But Todd, now back in, threw an incompletion and then was sacked on successive plays by Benoist and Steven Stone.

Auburn punted back to Vandy with 2:51 left, and if Vandy could run the clock out, it had a win. Thanks to the fact that Auburn had used all three time-outs, Vandy couldn't run the clock out, and punted from its 42, where Brett Upson hammered one that Alan Strong caught on the fly and downed on the Auburn 3. The Tigers had 2:16 left, and when Todd attempted a long throw across the field toward the Vanderbilt sideline, cornerback Myron Lewis picked it.

The crowd went crazy. With Auburn out of time-outs, VU only needed to kneel on the ball three times. The defense had been fantastic, sacking Auburn five times, and for the third-straight game, had not allowed a second-half point.

"We couldn't run it. We tried both quarterbacks and they played us a little in the second half, got in our face, gave us bad plays . . . We're not making any excuses. We lost this game. I did," Tuberville said.

Vanderbilt was now just a win away from clinching bowl eligibility. The Commodores moved all the way up to 13th in the polls on Monday and prepared for a trip to 1–4 Mississippi State.

The swoon

As great a story as the start had been, this team had some big holes. Teams with gaudy records usually dominate the stat sheets; Vanderbilt was gaining just 279 yards per game and giving up 333. Vanderbilt had also gained 14 turnovers and lost just five; those numbers tend to even out over time.

The Commodores were unlikely to end up on the plus-23 pace in turnover margin they were on.[3] If they went to a bowl game, that meant that the offense would have to start moving the ball more effectively. With Nickson's balky shoulder, Adams's inconsistency, and a running game that lacked a standout (Hawkins's 593 yards and 4.3 yard-per-carry average led the team that year), that looked unlikely.

---

3 Vanderbilt ended the season with the same plus-nine ratio that it had after the 5–0 start.

Running back Jared Hawkins carries the ball. (Jimmy Jones)

Perhaps that's why MSU, despite a 1–4 record, was just a two-point underdog. Sure enough, the 'Dores dropped their first game in Starkville after gaining a paltry 107 yards that afternoon. Nickson and Adams both threw big interceptions in the fourth quarter, with Nickson's setting the Bulldogs up at the VU 7 and eventually leading to a touchdown, and the one from Adams on Vandy's final drive to effectively end the game. Vandy left Starkville a 17–14 loser.

Johnson went with Adams as his starting quarterback the next week at Georgia, even though Nickson had led VU to an upset win the last time the 'Dores had gone between the hedges at Sanford Stadium. Adams threw a pair of scores to Graham, but also two interceptions. Vandy was outclassed by future pros like running back Knowshon Moreno (23 carries, 172 yards) and receiver A. J. Green (seven catches, 132 yards) and fell 24–14.

Surely, Vanderbilt fans thought, the team would get bowl-eligible with 3–3 Duke coming to town. The Commodores were 10-point favorites but fell behind 10–0 heading into the fourth quarter. Marve forced a fumble at the Vandy 2 that T. J. Greenstone recovered, and moments later, Adams hit Sean Walker with a 79-yard touchdown pass early in the fourth quarter.

But that would be it. Hahnfeldt missed a 43-yarder that could have tied the game with 7:16 left. Vandy turned the ball over on downs at its 19 and the defense miraculously forced a punt, giving VU the ball back with 1:58. Adams led Vandy to the Duke 39, and then on a second-and-10 play threw his second pick of the day when Chris Rwabukamba intercepted him at the Duke 1.

"The only way we scored was on a long pass, so it's back to the drawing board," Johnson said. We have some work to do and we've got a week off and we'll start working on that to get better."

The week off wouldn't be much help against powerful Florida, which would go 13–1 that year and beat Oklahoma for the national title. Reigning Heisman Trophy winner Tim Tebow accounted for four first-half touchdowns as the Gators led 35–0 at the break and had 330 yards of offense.

Johnson went back to Nickson, who hit Graham and Walker with second-half scoring passes, but it was far too late. The Gators won 42–14 and Vanderbilt was just now a game over .500.

Again, there were no obvious answers for an offense that had failed to gain more than 291 yards in any of its previous six games. So, Johnson turned to his defense for some answers.

Getting the monkey off the back

While Vanderbilt had not been good on offense the previous year—it averaged 326 yards and 21.7 points per contest—the drop-off to 2008 had shown the value of having a playmaker like Bennett. Maybe that was the inspiration for Johnson giving Moore an enhanced role on offense for the following Saturday night road trip to Kentucky. Moore registered his first two career catches on passes from Nickson (starting for the first time since the Starkville debacle) in the first quarter, those throws going for 25 and 18 yards. Both went for touchdowns, and Vandy led 14–0 over the Wildcats after a quarter.

The Wildcats bounced back on a 57-yard return of a blocked Hahnfeldt field goal, but Nickson hit Barden with a 1-yard scoring pass and then Hahnfeldt added a 39-yarder just before the half.

The way the defense played, the lead seemed fairly safe, but the 'Cats scored the third quarter's only 10 points, and the lead was just seven. Hawkins scored on a 4-yard run in the fourth, but UK quarterback Randall Cobb answered with a 10-yard run.

Midway through the fourth, Upson pinned the Wildcats back to their 23 with 4:59 left. Cobb took UK down to the Vandy 23 with 2:07 left, at which point Moore intercepted Cobb. The 'Cats had one time-out left, which they used after Hawkins ran for eight. On the other side of the time-out, Hawkins got three more, enabling Vandy to sit on the ball.

After twenty-six long years and four games of waiting, the Commodores were finally going bowling.

"We have been waiting a while to get here after starting the season 5–0. . . . It feels like a ton of bricks has been taken off our back after this game," Moore added.

Instead of capitalizing on the momentum of a 368-yard day, the offense spun back into the gutter. Vandy gave up 20 second-quarter points to Tennessee the next week, including a 45-yard interception touchdown return by Eric Berry. The only touchdown VU could muster came on Reshard Langford's 42-yard return of a pick, and the 'Dores fell 20–10 in Nashville to a Volunteer team that finished 4–7.

Vandy gained just 213 yards against the Vols, and just 249 at Wake Forest the next week. The quarterback situation had gotten bad enough that Johnson went to redshirt freshman Larry Smith late in the game, and the Alabaman hit Barden with a 6-yard pass to cut Wake's lead to 17–10 early in the fourth. But Smith was also picked deep in Vandy territory late in the game, and that led to the clinching Demon Deacon touchdown.

The season had ended in an ugly manner, with six losses in seven games. But it didn't matter in what sequence Vanderbilt had won or lost those contests, it only mattered that it had the requisite six to get to a bowl.

The Commodores wouldn't be traveling far to get there.

Music City Bowl-bound

On December 7, Vanderbilt accepted a bid to play in the Gaylord Hotels Music City Bowl at LP Field, which was just about three miles from campus. Las Vegas made the 9–4 Eagles a field-goal favorite for the New Year's Eve contest.

Smith started, and after a 17-yard completion to Walker and a 16-yard throw to Udom Umoh, Vandy had a first down at the BC 25 on its first drive. Johnson went back to Nickson and the drive stalled, but Hahnfeldt hit a 42-yard field goal. After the Eagles' second-straight three-and-out to start the game, Smith hit Walker on a bomb down the right sideline to get to the BC 14 on Vandy's first play of the next drive. Again, the drive ended with Hahnfeldt's field goal, this time from the 26.

Boston College hardly moved the ball during the first quarter, but picked up some momentum in the second when it took the ball from its 7 to the VU 48 before Hamilton picked quarterback Dominique Davis at the Vandy 15. By now, Vanderbilt was having its usual troubles moving the ball and had to punt. This time, Davis led BC on a 63-yard touchdown drive that ended with his 4-yard pass with 1:27 left before the break. After the point after, BC took a 7–6 lead at the half.

Vanderbilt got the ball to start the second half, and thanks to Nickson's 30-yard run, Vandy crossed midfield. Again, the drive stopped at the 42 and Upson came in to punt with the goal of pinning BC deep in its territory. Upson's boot, by design, may not have gotten 25 feet off the ground and bounced near Umoh and BC's Paul Anderson as the two ran downfield with their backs turned toward Upson.

Nobody in the stadium could tell exactly what happened; Anderson, at the 21 when the ball came near, immediately threw his arms out to the side as if to say "It didn't hit me," but Udom

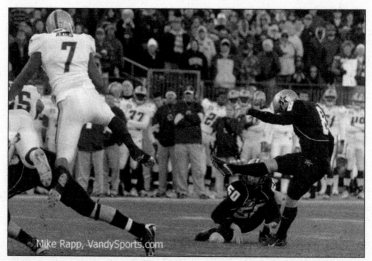

Bryant Hahnfeldt connects on a field goal in the 2008 Music City Bowl. (Mike Rapp)

kept racing toward the goal line, seemingly convinced that it had. No other Boston College player seemed to realize what was happening, and as the ball kept rolling toward the end zone, there were four Commodores around it.

When it went into the end zone, freshman Sean Richardson pounced on it. By this time, the partisan VU crowd started to realize that the ball may have hit Anderson, and the roar reached a crescendo. Two officials raced to the spot and both signaled "touchback," but each looked at the other with uncertainty.

The call would go to the replay official and after a few minutes of review, he ruled that the ball hit Anderson. Vanderbilt was awarded a touchdown, and now led 13–7.

"Funny thing is, I didn't even know that it hit him," Upson said. "I was behind three Boston College players running down the field."

The Vanderbilt offense once again sputtered, going three-and-out on its next four possessions. The Eagles got the ball back midway through the fourth quarter at their 11 and Davis quickly moved them to their 45. Davis spotted freshman receiver Colin Larmond open down the right sideline after Lewis, thinking he was running an out route, but on the move. It was an easy touchdown and the Eagles now led 14–13 with just 6:38 left.

Vanderbilt still didn't do much to move the ball, but the Eagles lent a helping hand. After Smith rushed five yards on VU's first snap, a face-mask penalty added 15 more. Smith tossed one incomplete to Wheeler on a third-and-2 from the BC 48, but a late-hit penalty on BC kept the drive alive. Smith hit George Smith with a 15-yard throw to the Eagle 25 and after Graham's rush for minus-3, it was once again up to Hahnfeldt to deliver with the biggest kick of his life. Holder Thomas Carroll put the ball down on the right edge of the left hash mark, and the Nashville native drove it through the uprights with enough room inside the left post to spare.

The teams traded punts and now it was up to the Vandy defense to deliver. Davis set his feet to throw to the right sideline and had plenty of time but waited too long to find his receiver and didn't get enough on the throw. Lewis stepped in front of it, made a leaping grab, and then tightroped the Commodore sideline to make sure he got both feet inbounds.

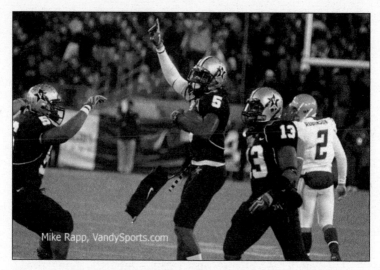

Myron Lewis (5) celebrates the game-clinching interception, with Chris Marve (13) watching behind him. (Mike Rapp)

The building exploded. There was just 1:36 left and since the Eagles were out of time-outs, all that was left was for Vanderbilt to snap the ball three times and hold on. When Smith took the final kneel-down at a few minutes before 6 p.m., the players rushed the field. The crowd, having waited too long to celebrate a moment like this, stuck around as fireworks filled the sky.

The cloud of 25-straight losing seasons, and of no bowl wins since 1955, would no longer hang over the program.

The aftermath

Vanderbilt, selected to finish last in the SEC East before the year started, had broken the streak in the oddest way. Moore, the team's best player, had gotten hurt in the first half and didn't return.[4]

---

4 Moore, a junior All-America player, announced after the game that he was heading to the NFL. His replacement, freshman Casey Hayward, had played well in his stead. Three years later, Hayward would be Green Bay's second-round pick.

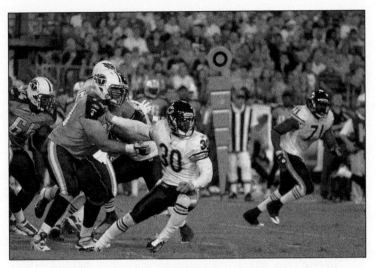

D.J. Moore (30) went on to a productive career with the Chicago Bears. (Jimmy Jones)

Smith led the team with 121 yards passing, even though he'd had just a half-game of experience coming in. VU had been outgained 331–200 that day, and Upson, the punter, had been selected as the game's Most Valuable Player.

"It may not be the prettiest victory in the world, but it is for us now," Johnson said afterward.

The season had gotten Vanderbilt on the map with more recruits. The VU staff felt as if the class of players it would sign just weeks later would be the best it had signed to date, and as players like left tackle Wesley Johnson; defensive end Walker May; defensive backs Javon Marshall and Trey Wilson; and running backs Zac Stacy, Warren Norman, and Wesley Tate proved, they were right in their gut feeling.

Johnson and company felt that it was even more important with the class of current high school juniors, and they were right again. The 2010 class, which included receivers Chris Boyd, Jordan Matthews, and Jonathan Krause; linebacker Chase Garnham; defensive backs Andre Hal, Karl Butler, Steven Clarke, and Kenny Ladler; defensive linemen Jared Morse, Vince Taylor, and Kyle Woestmann; offensive linemen Andre Bridges, Logan Stewart, and Chase White;

fullback Fitz Lassing; kicker Carey Spear; and quarterback Jordan Rodgers, would be one of the most important in school history.

The sad part is that Johnson and his assistants wouldn't be around to see most of the fruit of their labor. Many players returned for 2009, but it was becoming obvious that the offense, which averaged just 256 yards a game that year, needed a face-lift. When Vandy averaged just 16.3 points per game in a miserable 2–10 campaign, VU officials privately approached Johnson and asked him to shake up his offensive staff.

Johnson refused. On July 14, 2010, after months to ponder the situation, he abruptly retired and handed over the controls to offensive line coach Robbie Caldwell, who also went 2–10. Caldwell was dismissed after the 2010–2011 season, and VU would start over with the rebuild of its football program.

No one even remotely suspected it then, but thanks to those two recruiting classes, the program was on the verge of reaching heights not seen in almost three-quarters of a century.

2011 Football: Rising out of the ashes

"Who?"

That was the typical reaction when Vanderbilt athletics director David Williams hired Maryland offensive coordinator James Franklin to be the Commodores' coach. It would have been hard for Vanderbilt fans to have felt more let down than they were following the back-to-back 2–10 seasons that had necessitated this move, but that may have been the case on December 17, 2010, which was the day that Franklin met the media for the first time.

VU fans had gotten their hopes up that Gus Malzahn, fresh off a national title as Auburn's offensive coordinator, would be the new coach. Days earlier, it looked like a done deal. But something fell apart before things became official, and so it was Franklin who appeared in front of the cameras at a VU press conference that cold Friday.

The thirty-eight-year-old Pennsylvania native made headlines that day as Vanderbilt's first African-American coach. "It was obvious to me, right away, that this place could be successful," Franklin said as he stood at a podium wearing a dark suit and a black-and-gold-striped tie.

People laughed at Franklin's optimism, but they wouldn't be laughing a lot longer.

What's left in the cupboard?

Since 1960, Vanderbilt football had experienced five winning seasons. The 7–6 mark of 2008 had been the only winning season since 1982. As bad as those fifty years had been, the previous season had been one of the worst in that span. A road win over a 4–8 Ole Miss team was the only real highlight, and a 52–6 win over Eastern Michigan came against one of the worst teams in the FBS. VU was outscored by 14.3 points and outgained by 130 yards per game that season.

The trouncing of EMU in Week 5 was the last win for the short head coaching career of interim coach Robbie Caldwell. VU wouldn't come within 14 of an opponent the next seven games. That included a 34–13 drubbing in the season finale to a Wake Forest team on a nine-game losing streak. That disaster ended with not even five hundred fans in the stands at Dudley Field.

On the other hand, recent recruiting classes had helped raise the talent level. Many of those players would be sophomores and juniors in 2011. That included running back Warren Norman, who was the Southeastern Conference's Freshman of the Year in 2009. His backfield mate Zac Stacy, was a powerful runner who'd shown flashes of good things. Receiver Jordan Matthews looked good in spot duty at the end of 2010, and tight end Brandon Barden was becoming one of the league's best.

The defense had been poor the previous year, but there were some highlights. Linebacker Chris Marve had been one of the SEC's best linebackers for three years running. The real star was cornerback Casey Hayward, the ball-hawking defensive back who'd picked off six passes the previous fall.

Speaking of recruiting, Franklin made his mark right away. He landed a couple of well-regarded players from Florida in Josh Grady and Jerron Seymour, and one of the nation's better tight end prospects in Arizona's Dillon van der Wal. He got defensive lineman Barron Dixon (committed to Mississippi State) and Darien Bryant (Nebraska) to flip from more highly regarded programs.

Not all those players panned out, but some more lightly regarded players did. Franklin made a last-minute run at

Hendersonville's Joe Townsend, who was committed to Middle Tennessee State but had grown up a Vanderbilt fan. Townsend flipped on signing day, and while that wasn't huge news at the time, it would pay huge dividends later.

Franklin's exuberant personality also resonated with fans. He was the consummate salesman. He spoke of building traditions and multiple bowl games. Before long, even the most jaded VU fans were willing to give him a chance.

However, the same team that had won 4 of its last 24 games still had some major holes. Quarterback Larry Smith looked better in August practices, but he'd completed just 47.4 percent of his 247 passes and averaged barely more than five yards a throw in 2010. Backup Jordan Rodgers,[5] coming off shoulder surgery, didn't show the arm strength to challenge him. Norman looked like the team's best offensive threat, but there was a hidden injury from which he'd never really recover.

Defense was just as big an issue. People weren't going to throw at Hayward because teams had just abused whoever was lined up opposite of him the previous year. T. J. Greenstone, Colt Nichter, and Rob Lohr had proven they were legitimate SEC defensive tackles, but there didn't seem to be much else on the line outside of end Walker May, who just had six tackles for losses as a freshman. There were no real playmakers at linebacker outside of Marve, and even then, injuries had started to take a silent toll on him.

Special teams weren't exactly a strength, either, especially with Norman shelved. The Commodores' longest field goal the previous season came from 31 yards.

It would take a minor miracle to make this team competitive.

Steps in the right direction

The first test, a home game against Elon College on September 3, was a hurdle that Vanderbilt was expected to clear. Smith threw for

---

5   Rodgers is the brother of Green Bay's superstar quarterback, Aaron Rodgers.

two scores and ran for one more. Cornerback Trey Wilson, buried on the bench under the previous staff, had a 21-yard interception return for a score. Elon got within seven in the second half, but Smith's second touchdown toss, which went to emerging freshman receiver Chris Boyd, gave Vandy some space. Wes Tate added a 23-yard scoring run and Rodgers, in mop-up duty, hit Boyd for another score on his first Commodore pass.

In a lot of ways, the opener would be a blueprint for the rest of the season. There were things not to like; Vandy's 309 yards of offense against an FCS foe was troublesome. However, VU forced two turnovers that turned into scoring drives, committed just four penalties, and won the special teams battle decisively. The previous staff had been risk-averse, but three times on Saturday, Vanderbilt kept scoring drives alive with fourth-down conversions.

However, it was still Elon. As Franklin said in a rare moment of candor, "We beat a team we were supposed to beat."

Vanderbilt was a two-point favorite against Connecticut the next week. The Huskies had smacked the Commodores around by a 40–21 score in Storrs the previous season. As with Vandy's defeat of Elon, UConn's 35–3 win over Fordham the previous week gave little hint as to what kind of team the Huskies had.

After a slow start, Vanderbilt led 14–3 at the half, thanks to Boyd's 42-yard scoring reception from Smith and Seymour's 40-yard touchdown run. Early in the third quarter, the wheels started to come off. The Huskies picked Smith deep in VU territory and converted a field goal. UConn blocked a punt in the end zone and recovered for a touchdown. Smith fumbled, and Yawin Smallwood scooped it up and ran 66 yards for another score. After the Huskies converted a two-point conversion, the visitors led 21–14.

This is where, 95 percent of the time, Vanderbilt had traditionally packed it in. The phrase "same old Vanderbilt" had come to describe these moments perfectly. Franklin hated those words and when someone in the crowd shouted them, it set Franklin off. He charged up and down the sidelines, reminding his players again and again, "This is the 2011 Vanderbilt!"

They believed. UConn quarterback Johnny McEntee made the mistake of lofting a ball downfield in Hayward's direction.

Hayward jumped the route along the sideline to his right, cut back to the left, and followed a host of blockers into the end zone.

The game was tied at 21-all with 6:45 left. It may well have been the play that defined that season.

"I didn't think he was going to throw the ball to my side on the play, but when he did, there was a lot of space out there," Hayward said. "The defense made a lot of key blocks for me to get into the end zone."

The defense, which held the Huskies to 193 total yards that evening, got a stop. Stacy then rumbled 48 yards into UConn territory. Kicking had been an issue the previous season, but with 2:56 left, Spear knocked home a 31-yard field goal, and after the defense did its job again, VU had a 24–21 victory. It had now won consecutively for the first time since 2008.

Vegas was not a believer, anointing visiting Ole Miss a two-point favorite the following Saturday. For whatever reason, though, the 'Dores had the Rebels' number for years, going 4–2 against them and just 7–35 against the rest of the Southeastern Conference in that time. The Rebels had some issues coming into this one. Their top two tailbacks had been hurt and did not play in the Rebels' 42–24 win over Southern Illinois. Ole Miss was also rotating three quarterbacks, which is rarely a good thing.

Saturday's game figured to be close, and for nearly 25 minutes neither team managed a score. At that point, the dam burst. Smith scored untouched on a 19-yard option keeper to the right. On the next drive, May hit Ole Miss quarterback Zack Stoudt as he threw. Wilson grabbed it and streaked 52 yards down the left sideline untouched. After another Rebel punt, Seymour wiggled in from eight yards out as VU took a 21–0 lead at the break.

Lest the ghost of Vanderbilt past reappear, Vanderbilt came out strong in the second half. On Ole Miss's first possession with the ball deep in its territory, the Commodores showed blitz on a third-down play. The snap got away from Stoudt and a Rebel player kicked it through the end zone for a safety. Later in the quarter, Vandy caught Ole Miss in a run blitz and Stacy, heading over right tackle, scooted 77 yards into the end zone.

Ole Miss got a late touchdown on a 47-yard catch from Donte Moncreif with 2:15 to play, and blowing the shutout was really the only disappointment of the day. It actually felt more lopsided than the 30–7 score since VU outgained the Rebels by a 387–234 margin and won the turnover battle, 5–3. With Stacy (11 carries, 169 yards), the 'Dores also were starting to develop a star at running back, something they'd lacked for about two decades.

"The coaches had all the right calls, and we came out with a great effort. We forced a lot of turnovers and had a lot of tackles for loss, which led to getting the win," defensive end Tim Fugger said.

An emotional Franklin teared up during the postgame press conference. His team was 3–0 and he was the first VU coach to start his career with three wins since World War II.

"The feelings [I'm having] aren't because this is an SEC game. The feelings are because we've gotten better. It makes me feel so good to know how hard [our team] worked for the last nine months to have them have some success. They deserve it. . . . The fans deserve it," Franklin said.

Franklin had allowed his team to revel in its successful moments, but not for long. A look at the schedule ahead—consecutive games at South Carolina and Alabama, followed by a home game against Georgia—had the potential to dampen the mood quickly.

Reality check

There was no doubt that Vanderbilt was quite improved. There was also no doubt that the next three games were infinitely tougher than the past three. But the good news was that, since expectations were low coming in, just a respectable showing would be enough to keep excitement high. In that regard, Vanderbilt got mixed results the next two games.

At Carolina, the 'Dores grabbed an early 3–0 lead thanks to Spear's 33-yard field goal. The defense would play quite well that Saturday evening, picking Stephen Garcia four times and keeping the game close. The offense, though, did nothing against a Carolina defense littered with future NFL players like Melvin Ingram and Jadeveon Clowney.

Ingram had a fumble recovery for a score and Marcus Lattimore had a huge 52-yard touchdown reception just before the half that broke open a 7–3 game. Carolina added a touchdown run by Lattimore in the second half. Meanwhile, VU managed just 77 yards in a 21–3 loss.

The Commodores had begun to take some chances offensively, but that wasn't present at Carolina. Questioned about that later, Franklin's answer sounded defensive, but his statement was nonetheless true in some regards.

"[The play calling] was no more conservative than it's been any other week. . . . It's hard to call a game if you can't [pass-] protect and you can't run the ball," he said.

The Carolina game showed just how far Vanderbilt had to go to compete with the upper half of the SEC. The Commodores now faced Alabama, the toughest-possible opponent outside of an NFL team. Coach Nick Saban was in the midst of building one of the biggest dynasties in college football history; the Crimson 'Tide had won the national title two years prior, would win it that season, and for good measure, the year to follow also.

In that context, the 34–0 score that night wasn't a horrible outcome. 'Bama led just 14–0 at the half and it wasn't as if Saban eased off the gas pedal, keeping star quarterback A. J. McCarron in the game into the fourth quarter. The sophomore had one of the best nights of his career, hitting 23-of-30 passes for 237 yards and was uncannily on target from start to finish.

The Commodores had chances to score against an incredible 'Tide defense, but missed two field goals. The yardage figures—419 to 190 in 'Bama's favor—were lopsided, but since Alabama outgained teams 430–184 on average that year, it wasn't a bad performance.

In fact, some things started to click that night. Vanderbilt had shuffled its offensive line, moving Wesley Johnson from center to left tackle, sliding Ryan Seymour inside from left tackle to left guard, and inserting Logan Stewart at center. After being sacked six times the previous week, the line allowed none against 'Bama.

However, VU still couldn't mount a passing attack. Franklin yanked Smith early after he went 4-of-6 for 45 yards on the heels of the previous week's 12-of-16, 44-yard, one-interception game. Rodgers wasn't tremendous himself, hitting 11-of-18 throws for 104 yards and two picks, but it gave Franklin something to think about. Smith had been a highly regarded quarterback out of Prattville, Alabama, and although the personnel around him had been questionable, the results weren't there. A quarterback controversy had emerged.

In the second quarter against Georgia, Smith was 5-of-10 for 24 yards and two picks and had been outpassed by both punter Ryan Fowler (a 35-yard pass on a fake punt) and Stacy (a 43-yard scoring heave to Matthews). Franklin made the switch. Rodgers's passing numbers (4-of-19, 47 yards, one interception) were equally atrocious, but the junior kept making plays with his feet, running 11 times for 80 yards and converting multiple third downs to keep drives alive.

Vandy trailed 23–7 early in the third quarter until Andre Hal ran a kickoff back 96 yards for a score and gave his team a confidence boost. Georgia's Blair Walsh answered with another field goal in the third quarter, but the 'Dores kept rolling with every punch. Rodgers's real value that night was opening up the ground game, and Stacy benefitted from that, rushing 17 times for 97 yards against a stout UGA defense that had given up 70 yards rushing, period, in the previous three games.

When Seymour ran over from a yard in the third, Vandy trailed just 26–21. Georgia again seemed to put the game out of reach when Aaron Murray connected with Marlon Brown on a 75-yard scoring strike, but Stacy's 19-yard rushing touchdown with 9:15 left cut the margin back to five.

The Commodores never led that night, but nearly pulled a stunner at the end. Georgia's Drew Butler dropped back to punt deep in his own territory with 15 seconds left, and Udom Umoh blocked it. Butler's momentum spun him around in a circle as a host of Commodores charged for the loose football bouncing a couple of yards behind him among a couple of Vanderbilt players.

For a split second, Vanderbilt safety Kenny Ladler appeared to have a shot at the scoop-and-score. When he corralled the ball just inches from the ground, it was too difficult for him to keep running and maintain his balance as Butler tackled him. Ladler, knowing he had no chance, flipped the ball into a pile of players and Vandy's Steven Clarke picked it up but couldn't advance it more than a yard or two before a Georgia player brought him down by the ankles at the 20.

Seven seconds remained. Rodgers threw to a double-covered Boyd near the right sideline in the end zone. It ticked off his fingertips and fell harmlessly to the turf. A second remained for a final play , and a short pass to Barden ended with the senior tackled at the 16.

The evening was notable for two things. First, the Commodores had shown that, at least occasionally, they could compete with the conference's upper crust. Second, Franklin had instilled a fighting attitude into his squad—almost literally. It had not been a pretty game, with Georgia's Shawn Williams and Kwame Geathers and VU's Stewart all taking cheap shots at various points of the game. The SEC suspended all of them for the first half of each team's respective next games.

That led to a shouting match between Franklin and Georgia defensive coordinator Todd Grantham as the teams exited the field. Asked about it later, Franklin delivered a short response that served as an anthem for the team's foreseeable future:

"We're also going to fight and I want to make sure everybody understands that. We are not going to sit back and take stuff from anybody. Anybody. No one. Those days are long gone and they are never coming back. Ever."

The home stretch

Vandy was back to .500, but a bowl game was still a possibility. With Rodgers starting behind center, the offense exploded against Army in a way it rarely had over the past few years. The team's 558 yards were the most it had gained since the previous season's shellacking of Eastern Michigan, a span of 13 games. Rodgers still struggled with accuracy (10-of-27, 2 interceptions, 186 yards), but the Commodores would become a big-play team and Rodgers had one of those big plays, a 43-yard scoring strike to Boyd coming after the defense made a big play of its own when Fugger forced a fumble.

Army was overmatched athletically, but many a service academy has pulled an upset through a triple-option attack that teams aren't used to facing. The Black Knights were at a talent disadvantage when the teams played in 2009, but beat Vandy by a 16–13 count, anyway. Army rushed 51 times for 270 yards in this game, but the 'Dores recovered three fumbles. They also limited Army to 15 first downs, which meant that the Black Knights held the ball for just 25:45 that night.

Much of that was due to Stacy. The junior had really started to come into his own as a star, and when he galloped 55 yards for a score in the fourth quarter, he put the game away. In a 44–21 victory, Rodgers (18 carries, 96 yards) had also been efficient on the ground, and it was now clear that the offense was significantly better with him behind center.

Rodgers would credit the offensive line, which was now starting to find some cohesion and opening big holes. Franklin agreed.

"We're getting better [at running the ball]," Franklin said afterward. "We've been able to move our offensive line around and getting Logan [Stewart] back helped us in the second half. We're starting to get an identity."

The team clearly had more confidence. Two weeks ago, it had taken the same Georgia team that had beaten it 43–0 the previous year down to the wire. Arkansas, which had administered a similar 49–14 beat-down the previous season, was next. Coach Bobby Petrino's high-powered passing offense, which spread receivers all over the field and could score in a flash, figured to be a tough matchup. That Saturday afternoon, though, the Commodores were step for step with the Razorbacks the whole way.

It was a coming-out party for Matthews, who at that point had started to look like just a practice legend. He was big (6-foot-3, 205 pounds) and had good hands and deceptive speed, but for whatever reason, it hadn't translated to games. Since catching three balls for 58 yards in the opener, Matthews had recorded just five receptions for 59 yards in the six games since. Starting with the first quarter on that October 29 day, Matthews began a journey to becoming perhaps the best receiver that the Southeastern Conference had seen since Alabama's Don Hutson had played 80 years prior.

Matthews was the first man to find the end zone that day, catching a 21-yard scoring strike from Rodgers as he dashed across the field and made his way through traffic in the first quarter. The Razorbacks tied it on Brandon Mitchell's 4-yard scoring run, but two Rodgers touchdown runs of 19 and 3 yards, respectively, had Vandy up by a 21–14 count at the break.

Again, Franklin's habit of risk-taking paid off in the first half. Both of Rodgers's scores were set up by enormous gambles as the 'Dores converted a pair of fourth downs in the first half, both in unconventional fashion. With the ball resting on Vandy's 29-yard line in the first quarter, Rodgers handed it off to Stacy for two yards. The second came when VU had a fourth-and one from its 32 and while in punt formation, long-snapper Andrew East shot it directly to up-back Fitz Lassing, who gained 25 yards on the stunned Razorbacks.

Arkansas kicker Zach Hocker pulled the Razorbacks to within four with a third-quarter field goal, but Stacy got through a crease in the line and into the Arkansas secondary and dashed straight for the goal line 62 yards away. Vandy now led by 11. Hocker's 50-yard field goal cut the margin to eight at the end of the third quarter.

Defense had carried the Commodores through much of the season, but that day, it looked like the offense, which outgained Arkansas 462–388 that day, was going to lead VU to a win. The team was finally clicking on all cylinders; Rodgers threw for 240 yards and ran for 66, with Matthews catching 151 yards of those throws. Stacy finished the day with 128 yards on 19 carries, but made a killer mistake early in the fourth. On a second-and-goal play from the Razorback 3, he lost a fumble for the only time all season, and Arkansas linebacker Jerry Franklin picked it up and rumbled 94 yards for the score.

Instead of a potential 35–20 lead, the game was now tied after Arkansas scored on the two-point conversion. Hocker's 42-yard field goal with 6:53 left gave the Razorbacks the lead for the first time all afternoon.

Vanderbilt drove down the UA 10, setting up a chip-shot field goal for Spear to send the game to overtime. Instead, it went wide right, and the heartbroken Commodores had missed their shot for an upset of a top-10 team.

"That was a very, very tough loss," VU's Franklin said later. "When you play a really good team, you can't make mistakes. Turnovers, missed opportunities, penalties—you can't beat yourself. We're getting better every single week. You look at this team and how we're progressing—it's not even close. I believe in my kids, I believe in our process. We're light years [ahead] of when I came here and when I got on this campus.

"This is not the same old Vanderbilt. We're going to find ways to finish games like this."

Sometimes, a team can be hung over from a tough loss the next week, and perhaps that's what happened when VU traveled to Gainesville to face Florida. The Gators, who had not exceeded 230 yards of offense in any of their previous four games, jumped on Vandy for a 17–0 halftime lead. It could have been worse, as UF fumbled at the Vandy goal line and also missed a field goal.

Midway into the third, the Gators hit Rodgers as he threw, but he managed to get enough on the throw to find Matthews open in the end zone from 26 yards out. UF's Caleb Sturgis hit a 40-yard field goal, but Rodgers scored in the fourth on an 8-yard quarterback keeper on a third-and-goal play. Fowler's extra point brought Vandy to within six.

The Commodores now had a legitimate chance to pull an upset in The Swamp, but a series of bad fortune and crucial mistakes soon became their undoing. Vanderbilt drove past midfield and Rodgers found Matthews deep in Gator territory, where a defender shoved the sophomore wideout in the back, which everyone but the officials saw.[6] Instead of a first down to set up another scoring chance, VU had to punt.

---

6 As color analyst Andre Ware would exclaim on the TV broadcast, "How do you miss a call like that?"

Vanderbilt needed its defense to come through and get a stop, which it did until it did something unthinkable. Florida had the ball fourth-and- from its own 16 and coach Will Muschamp sent the offense out to go for it. Nobody expected the Gators to snap the ball and, likely, the only way the Gators would get a first down was if the Commodores jumped offsides.

Defensive tackle Rob Lohr had become a real playmaker for Vandy, but this time he made a huge mistake and jumped across the line. On a third-and-7 with 3:15 to play, safety Sean Richardson committed a critical pass interference penalty. Gator tailback Jeff Demps, who would help the United States win an Olympic silver medal in the 4×100-meter relays the next summer, sprinted 52 yards to put the Gators up by 12 after UF fumbled on a two-point conversion.

Rodgers led Vandy down the field again, and hit Boyd on a 10-yard scoring toss with 1:16 left. The lead was five, and if VU could recover the onside kick, it still had a chance. That didn't happen, and the Gators ran out the clock.

A lot had gone right. Rodgers had completed 19-of-28 passes for 297 yards, and just as importantly, no interceptions against the nation's seventh-ranked pass defense. Matthews proved the Arkansas game was no fluke, snagging nine of them for 170 yards. Now that the Commodores were competent on both sides of the ball, they were playing toe-to-toe with some great teams.

But one element of Same Ole Vandy kept hanging around, and that was the mistakes at the worst times. The Gators were the nation's most penalized team, and yet the Commodores were flagged twelve times for 106 yards while UF drew three flags for 17. One came when Stewart drew a 15-yard personal foul long after a play was dead, and right in front of an official.

Rodgers spoke to the lack of discipline afterward.

"It's definitely something we need to work on. Not reacting to what people say and playing within the whistles as hard as we can and nothing after the whistles. Those 15-yard penalties are huge," he said.

The Commodores went from being 13-point road underdogs versus UF to 14-point home favorites against 4–5 Kentucky the next weekend. Perhaps the 'Dores were sick of the mistakes and failing to make that key play in the final moments to win games, or maybe they were just a little more motivated than normal because it was Senior Day. In any case, they played their best game to date.

Vanderbilt put on an offensive and defensive clinic in the first half. It was 24–0 when the teams went to the locker rooms, and the Commodores had a massive 278–41 edge in total offense. Stacy had two first-half touchdown runs, Rodgers hit Boyd on a 14-yard touchdown pass, and Fowler hit a 32-yard field goal.

In the third quarter, Rodgers hit Matthews on a pass behind the line of scrimmage, and Matthews, as would become customary over the next few seasons, made something of nothing, bouncing off a few tacklers and sprinting for a 49-yard score. In the fourth quarter, Stacy made the play of the year, taking a handoff from Rodgers and rumbling around the left side of the line before he was met by a pile of UK defenders, and two more who leapt on top of him as he kept pushing the pile closer to the goal line.

The play nearly stopped inside the 10, but never did. At one point or another, eight Wildcat defenders had a shot at bringing him down, but none could. Stacy emerged from the pack on his feet with the ball in the end zone, and it put an exclamation point on a 38–8 rout that avenged last season's 38–20 defeat in Lexington.

Stacy carried 28 times for 135 yards and Matthews again had a banner game, hauling in six receptions for 131 more. The Commodores outgained the 'Cats by a 410–211 margin, and the team's 28 first downs were a season high. Vandy was now 5–5 and had a shot to get bowl-eligible against Tennessee in Knoxville the following Saturday night.

"We wanted to take out the frustration on everybody from all these losses, no matter who's next," senior offensive lineman Kyle Fischer said.

Vanderbilt hadn't beaten the Vols since 2005, when Jay Cutler and Earl Bennett led VU to an upset that season. The 'Dores looked like the better team coming in, but it's never easy to win in front of over 90,000 visiting fans, and a whole lot harder when a team's not sharp, as was the case that evening.

Something looked amiss with Rodgers from the start; the junior had been playing with confidence but looked so tentative that evening in Knoxville. If not for the play of linebacker Archibald Barnes, and perhaps the fact that the Vols (who finished 5–7 that year) weren't very good, the 'Dores may not have been in the game at the end. Barnes picked Tyler Bray in the second quarter and returned it to the UT 6, where Stacy scored on the next play. UT led 14–7 at the half and was about to score again in the third quarter, but Barnes made a break on another Bray throw, catching it in the end zone and running 100 yards untouched to tie the game at 14.

When Rodgers hit Boyd on a terrific 20-yard touchdown pass with 12:21 left in the game, it looked as if the Commodores might escape with a mild upset (Tennessee was a one-point favorite). The defense stopped a UT drive and the Vols had to settle for a 24-yard Michael Palardy field goal attempt, which Vanderbilt blocked.

However, Richardson ran into Palardy and that gave the Vols new life. On the next play, Bray connected with Da'Rick Rogers for six, and Palardy's PAT tied the game.

Still, Vandy had a chance to win. Rodgers drove the 'Dores into UT territory but was picked by Prentiss Wagner at the Vol 35 with 20 seconds left. The game went to overtime, where Rodgers was intercepted again on a screen pass intended for Wesley Tate. Tennessee's Eric Gordon picked it and ran 90 yards to the end zone.

Gordon's pick was more than a little controversial; officials on the field had ruled that his knee was down and a whistle blew while the head linesman waved his hands over his head to indicate the play was over. It was a bad break for Tennessee . . . or so everyone thought.

Tennessee coach Derek Dooley lobbied for a review of the play, at which point a member of the officiating crew told him it wasn't reviewable. That official was correct, but somehow, the play was reviewed anyway. Worse, the official who announced that the Vols had a game-winning touchdown claimed that the whistle hadn't blown.

It was one of the most glaring cases of revisionism in officiating history, but nonetheless, what was done was done. In fairness to Gordon, his knee never touched down and he was probably going to score even if VU players hadn't stopped playing at the whistle.

But the way it went down only added insult to injury. The Commodores, who had gotten dozens of apologies from the SEC office over the previous decades, had another before the night was done. As the SEC's coordinator of officials, Steve Shaw, announced on Twitter, "On the last play of the Vanderbilt-Tennessee game, in overtime, the Tennessee defender intercepted the pass, his knee did not touch the ground and he returned the interception for a touchdown," Shaw said.

"During the play, the head linesman incorrectly ruled that the Tennessee player's knee was down when he intercepted the pass by blowing his whistle and giving the dead ball signal.

"The play was reviewed as if there was no whistle on the field and as a result, overturned the incorrect ruling. By rule, if there is a whistle blown, the play is not reviewable."

At the end of that cool, dark fall evening, the 'Dores really had only themselves to blame. Rodgers was picked three times and also lost a fumble, with two picks coming inside the UT 30. Earlier in the evening, Boyd took a 72-yard pass to the Vol 1, but Josh Jelesky was whistled for a clip and the ball came back to the VU 13 as that drive stalled.

Rodgers summed it up well later.

"We started out slow. Penalties killed us, and turnovers. My play was unacceptable; I can't turn the ball over like that and give us a chance to win. That's about it," he said.

Salvaging a bowl

The loss in Knoxville stung badly. Franklin wound up in a shouting match with Vol fans who were harassing him as he left the field. The only real consolation was that the season wasn't done. The 5–6 Commodores had a final chance to go to a bowl with a win at Wake Forest.

The 'Dores were a one-point road favorite even though Wake, already bowl-eligible, had beaten Vandy by 13 or more points in its last three meetings ('07 and '09 before that). Wake was a team that didn't usually self-destruct, and as much as VU had improved over 2010, the team had proven time and time again that it was certainly still capable of that.

As good as the oddsmakers in Vegas usually are, they were dead wrong about the parity between those two teams that day. The Commodores would prove quickly that they were bigger, faster, and stronger—and on that Saturday afternoon, also apparently more motivated to play football.

Two Fowler field goals put Vandy up 6–0 in the first quarter, one set up as Fugger forced a fumble at the Wake 39. On a third-and-goal from the 10, Wake's Tanner Price threw a strike to Terence Davis and the point-after gave the Demon Deacons a 7–6 lead, but that wouldn't last long. Stacy scored on a 1-yard run the next time Vandy got the ball, eclipsing 1,000 yards rushing for the season on the drive.[7] After a Wake punt, Rodgers found Barden wide open along the left side, and the big tight end had two things he'd not had much that season: the ball, and a whole lot of open field.

Barden, originally staying in to block, slipped outside the hash marks and caught it at the Vandy 34. He crossed midfield at ease and as a Wake defender went low to tackle him, Barden hurdled him at the Wake 42. He now had Boyd running interference two yards ahead as he slipped through one Deacon defender, who reached out to grab him. Another defender had a shot from behind, but Barden stiff-armed him at the 15 and it was over. Rodgers had a 73-yard pass to add to his stats and the Commodores led, 20–7.

Barden must have inspired his teammates with that play, because it seemed to launch one highlight-reel moment after another from there. The 'Dores had trouble closing halves to that point, and Wake had driven into Vandy territory with under two minutes to play before the half. May sacked Price for a 9-yard loss on a third-and-10 and forced a punt with 1:38 left.

The Commodores drove to the Wake 20 with under a minute left and on a third-and-10, the ball went to Stacy. The junior found daylight to his right thanks to blocking from Fischer, Jelesky, and Barden. He lowered his shoulder and collided with a pair of Wake

---

7   Vanderbilt had not had a player go over 1,000 yards rushing since Jermaine Johnson's 1,072 yards in 1995.

defenders at the six. Those defenders got the worse end of the deal. Stacy kept his balance, stayed in bounds, and made it to the end zone. Vanderbilt led 27–7 at the break, and the way the team was playing, it didn't seem as if it would be denied that day.

In the third quarter, Smith, in as a receiver, took a lateral from Rodgers and hurled a beautiful 45-yard scoring strike that hit Matthews in the numbers inside the 5. All that was really left now was to see if Stacy could break the school's single-season rushing record. On a second-and-11 play from the Wake 40, the junior took a toss sweep going to his right, and thanks to Fischer, Jelesky, and Lassing, found space down the sideline. A Wake defender had a shot at the 2, but Stacy put his shoulder down and knocked him to the ground while staying on his feet. He stepped across the goal line with both the record and the game's last score.

With a 41–7 win, Vanderbilt would now be heading to just its second bowl since 1982—an amazing feat, as nobody had expected Franklin to go to the postseason while rebuilding a program in his first year.

Marked men

Franklin's name was popping up for coaching vacancies across the country. On December 2, Williams announced an extension and a raise for Franklin as the 'Dores awaited their bowl destination.

Two days later, Vanderbilt learned it would go to Memphis to play Cincinnati in the Liberty Bowl on New Year's Eve. The Bearcats were no pushover, as they'd ended the regular season with a 9–3 record and a share of the Big East title.

Stacy started the scoring with a 7-yard run to stake the Commodores to a 7–0 first-quarter lead, but UC reserve tailback George Winn scooted 69 yards for a tying score in the second quarter. Once again, VU gave up a back-breaking score just before halftime as Bearcat quarterback Nick Collaros, playing for the first time since breaking his right ankle on November 12, threw an 8-yard scoring strike to Anthony McClung as Cincinnati took a 14–7 lead into halftime.

Kyle Fischer (72) and Josh Jelesky (69) celebrate Zac Stacy's touchdown versus Cincinnati in the 2011 Liberty Bowl. (Mike Rapp)

Vandy battled back with Seymour's 5-yard touchdown run in the third quarter to tie, but an early fourth-quarter field goal by UC's Tony Miliano pushed Cincinnati back in front. Rodgers had not played well, hitting just 4-of-14 passes for 26 yards, and Franklin pulled him for Smith. The senior hit Boyd on a bubble screen that Boyd turned into a 68-yard touchdown pass and Vandy led again. It didn't last long. Ralph David Abernathy raced 90 yards with the ensuing kickoff 12 seconds later to give UC a 24–21 lead.

That seemed to kill Vandy's momentum. The next two drives were three-and-outs, but Barnes made a huge play on special teams when he blocked Miliano's 39-yard field goal with 3:58 left. Vandy marched into Bearcat territory, but then Smith's pass intended for Matthews was picked by Nick Temple and returned to the VU 31. Isaiah Pead, the game's MVP (28 carries for 149 yards and three catches for 15 more) scored the clinching touchdown on a 12-yard run with 1:52 left.[8] Fowler kicked a 35-yard field goal with 24 seconds left, but when the onside kick failed, UC had a 31–24 win.

---

8 It wasn't the last time Stacy and Pead played on the same field. The UC star was picked by the St. Louis Rams in the second round of the 2012 NFL Draft. Stacy, picked in the fifth round of the '13 draft, then beat Pead out for the starting tailback job.

Reflections

It was a heartbreaking way to end a season, but it didn't much dampen the mood around what had been accomplished.

"As I told some of our fans on the way over here, this game does not define us," Franklin said. "No disrespect to the past or previous situations, we talked after the game in the locker room about the Wake Forest game last year and what it was like and how much things have changed in twelve months. I feel for these [seniors] because they aren't going to be part of the future, but what they have done is laid a great foundation for our future."

A bunch of those seniors had left their marks that year, particularly on the defensive side. Hayward had become a second-team All-America selection and with two picks in the Liberty Bowl, he tied Leonard Coleman's all-time school record with 15 interceptions before Green Bay took him in the second round months later.

Safety Sean Richardson also went on to play for the Packers. Fugger, a second-team all-league pick had a breakout year at the end, and he'd be drafted by the Colts a few months later. Defensive tackle T. J. Greenstone, a lightly regarded recruit, had become a solid contributor in the middle of the Vandy line.

Injuries had reduced Marve to something less than the superstar he once was, but the league's coaches still tabbed him a second-team All-SEC pick. He may have also been the team's best leader that season.

The UC game had shown that the offense still had its limitations, but it was still young. The underutilized Barden would graduate, and the loss of Fischer, who'd become a difference maker on the offensive line, also hurt. Smith was also done, but Rodgers was clearly the better option now.

The coaches deserved a lot of credit. Franklin had brought a passion and enthusiasm perhaps unrivaled by any Vanderbilt coach in history. The offense, which had been in shambles, exceeded anyone's expectations that year and saw Stacy and Matthews become stars. The team's play calling had been so vanilla in previous years. Offensive coordinator John Donovan, though, was willing to take some risks, and the risk-reward payoff was off the charts in Vandy's favor.

The offensive line, under the guidance of Herb Hand, the lone holdover from the previous staff, had taken tremendous strides in the season's second half. The biggest success was the move of Jelesky, who had been a defensive tackle his entire career, to guard. The junior ended up as a starter and threw a bunch of key blocks in the season's second half.

As good a job as the offensive staff did, it may have been one-upped by the defense.

The hiring of defensive coordinator Bob Shoop was enormous. Fans had ridiculed Franklin's selection of William & Mary's defensive coordinator for the same spot—for crying out loud, didn't Franklin realize that this was the SEC?—but the Yale grad was brilliant. He loved to blitz and disguise coverages and between getting pressure on quarterbacks and having defensive backs who could make plays, it ended the season ranked 18th nationally in total defense.

The defensive line had been awful for about 15 years running, but Sean Spencer's "Wild Dogs" were well conditioned and Spencer's constant rotating in and out of players kept the team fresh at the end of games. There were no superstars, but the fact that he could be two, sometimes three deep at the various positions, helped him to get a lot out of his guys.

Linebackers coach Brent Pry didn't have a lot of players, but developed Barnes and Chase Garnham from little-regarded reserves into legitimate SEC players.

The biggest negative was that the 'Dores finished at 6–7 that year, but the team was better than the record reflected. Vanderbilt outscored opponents 347–281. That was an average of nearly five points more per game than its opponents. It was the first time Vanderbilt had outscored an opponent for the year; even the Music City Bowl champs of 2008 had been edged by almost a half-point a game.

The real culprit was two things, starting with a schedule that had featured Georgia (10–4), South Carolina (11–2), Alabama (12–1), and Arkansas (11–2). Furthermore, Vandy just couldn't catch a break:

after winning the early-season nail-biter over UConn, VU then went 0–5 in games decided by seven points or less.

Critics looked at the program and said the 'Dores would never keep Franklin for long, and wrote off the bowl game as a fluke. But if you were really paying attention, this looked like a program on its way up. Next year proved that to be the case.

2012 Football: Ranking with the best

The 2011 season had given Vanderbilt confidence. Before 2012's first game, Franklin commented that his bunch had become almost too confident, but given what the team had accomplished and its returning players, it was hard to fault the players from feeling the way they did.

On offense, the Commodores had a trio of playmakers in receivers Jordan Matthews and Chris Boyd and tailback Zac Stacy like they hadn't had in God-only-knows-how-many years. They had a developing star in junior left tackle Wesley Johnson, and returned starting guards Ryan Seymour and Josh Jelesky as well as starting tackle Andrew Bridges. The question was whether quarterback Jordan Rodgers was ready to play at a higher level; his 50 percent completion mark and 7 yards a throw from 2011 needed to improve.

There were some questions on defense, too. All-American selection Casey Hayward, one of the best players in school history and the team's defensive catalyst, had graduated. VU returned Chase Garnham and Archibald Barnes at linebacker, but was otherwise thin at that position. However, cornerback Trey Wilson and safety Javon Marshall returned as starters and junior Kenny Ladler looked like a blossoming star at the other safety spot. There was depth on the defensive line. Plus, the 'Dores had coordinator Bob Shoop, who was beginning to look like one of the Southeastern Conference's premier defensive minds.

To anyone paying attention, the Commodores looked like a team ready to put it all together . . . and yet the Commodores failed to receive a single vote in either the AP's or coaches' preseason polls.

Slow out of the gate

Ninth-ranked South Carolina visited Nashville for the opener. The Gamecocks, six-point favorites, were ranked ninth in the AP's preseason poll. ESPN found the matchup attractive enough that it had moved the game to the Thursday evening of August 2012, making it the college football season's opener. Periodic rainstorms made for a hot, humid night.

South Carolina's Marcus Lattimore, a Heisman candidate the previous year until he blew out his knee, started the scoring by bouncing off tacklers in the VU secondary on his way to a 29-yard touchdown run. Adam Yates added a 20-yard field goal and Carolina led 10–0 until Matthews got behind the Gamecock defense and won a 78-yard footrace to the end zone. Carey Spear added the extra point and later, a 25-yard field goal. The game was tied at the half.

Vandy held a 13–10 lead heading into the fourth quarter thanks to Spear's 44-yard field goal. USC went back in front after a nine-play, 66-yard drive capped by Lattimore's 1-yard scoring run in the fourth quarter.

With the clock under two minutes and the Commodores facing fourth down in their own territory, Matthews (eight catches, 147 yards) broke open briefly against Carolina safety D.J. Swearinger and Rodgers delivered on time. Swearinger grabbed Matthews's arm before the ball arrived, and though it appeared obvious to everyone—Swearinger even confessed to it later—that pass interference had been committed, there was no flag, and Carolina ran out the clock for a 17–13 victory.

"You did know that the SEC just came out with very clear rules about talking about the officials and what happens after games?" Franklin responded when asked about the call. "Trying to get me fined?"

Once again, Vanderbilt had gone toe-to-toe with a ranked foe and come up just short. The game was about as evenly matched as you could ask for; VU had 276 yards to Carolina's 272. The difference was Carolina quarterback Connor Shaw (14 carries, 92 yards), who converted one first down after another with his feet. Carolina had 17 first downs to VU's 11, and won the time of possession battle, 31:36 to 28:24.

Vanderbilt next went to Northwestern as a three-point favorite. Rodgers hit Matthews for a 22-yard scoring strike on the game's first drive and it looked like the Northwestern secondary, which was torched often in the previous week's 42–41 win at Syracuse, would get burned often again that night.

It didn't happen that way. VU went to the fourth quarter clinging to a 10–6 lead. Venric Mark's 7-yard scoring run with 9:28 left put the Wildcats ahead for the first time all evening. Spear tied the game with a field goal with just over four minutes remaining, but Northwestern's Jeff Budzien answered with one of his own.

As Vanderbilt tried to mount a late comeback, a rainstorm fell over Evanston. With under two minutes left, Rodgers fumbled away Vandy's chances and quarterback Kain Coulter iced the 23–13 win with a 29-yard touchdown run.

Once again, VU was left to play the "what-if game." What if Rodgers hadn't fumbled the ball away at the end, or in a first-half possession when the 'Dores led 10–3 with the ball deep in Wildcat territory? What if a catch that Northwestern's Rashad Lawrence was ruled to have made on a third-and-15 play from the NU 42 hadn't been ruled a catch? The Big Ten's television crew didn't think it should have stood, and neither did much of anyone else, but it did, and the Wildcats had a first down at the VU 22 on the drive that led to Budzein's last field goal.

Instead, it was just another close loss.

"We didn't make the big plays that we've made in the past on defense. Offensively, we weren't running the offense. . . . Special teams, I thought we did a good job of containing their returner, but we didn't do a good job making any plays. That's kind of where we're at," Franklin said that evening.

Vanderbilt needed a confidence booster, and it had the perfect opponent the next week in FCS foe Presbyterian.

Franklin was not happy with Rodgers, who had now played poorly in three of VU's last five games dating back to the previous season. He gave the start to junior quarterback Austyn Carta-Samuels, who'd sat out the previous year after starting two seasons at Wyoming.

It didn't really seem to matter who the Commodores started at quarterback that week. Stacy ripped off the longest run in school history, racing 86 yards for a score on VU's first offensive snap. He got the ball on the first two touches of Vandy's next drive and added 50 more to his total. The drive stalled, but Spear added a 23-yard field goal. Barnes forced a fumble that Barron Dixon recovered at the PC 30, and Wes Tate added a 6-yard touchdown run on fourth down to end that drive. Later in the quarter, Spear hit a 28-yard field goal.

Presbyterian drove down inside the VU 5 and threatened to score before halftime, but Wilson, about three yards deep in the end zone, stepped in front of Tamyn Garrick's throw and took it the distance. Vandy led 27–0 at the half and had outgained PC 297–127, with Stacy rushing for 140 of those yards.

Steven Scheu, Tate, Warren Norman, and freshman Brian Kimbrow all added second-half touchdowns. Spear booted a 42-yard field goal in the fourth quarter, and when the dust had settled, VU had a 58–0 rout.

Stacy probably could have shattered some school records that day, but was limited to just eight carries, which he turned into 174 yards. Kimbrow, the state's top-rated recruit the prior year, rushed 14 times for 137 yards. Carta-Samuels showed that he could be a capable backup, completing 13-of-20 throws for 195 yards, one score, and no picks. Vandy didn't turn the ball over and outgained Presbyterian by a 605–149 margin. It was the first shutout that VU had recorded since a 45–0 blanking of Western Carolina in the opening game of the 2009 season.

The next week against Georgia, the shoe was on the other foot.

Bulldog quarterback Aaron Murray was on his game, completing his first 12 passes. UGA also had a pair of NFL-caliber tailbacks in Todd Gurley and Keith Marshall, and each scored a first-quarter touchdown. Murray threw a second-quarter touchdown pass and added a rushing score. Vandy managed a Spear field goal before the half, but another touchdown throw by Murray, combined with scoring runs by both star backs in the third quarter, took away any drama on how it would end.

The 48–3 shellacking was Vandy's worst defeat since a 48–0 loss to Tennessee in 2003. VU gave up 567 yards and gained just 337. VU was never really in the game at any point. It committed eight first-quarter penalties, one of which was a bogus roughing-the-punter call on freshman Caleb Azubike that led to Marshall's first-quarter score.

"I think the difference in the game was played up front, especially with their offensive line. They did a really good job of running the ball with power and forced us to load the box, which opened up the passing game on the outside. I didn't feel like we played with the confidence we normally play with on the outside," Franklin said.

It was the first time in a while that Vandy had truly played poorly from start to finish. It was the ideal time for a week off, which Vanderbilt got.

Following the bye week, the Commodores traveled to Missouri for their first game against the Tigers since Missouri joined the SEC the previous fall. The team that hadn't caught many breaks the previous two seasons finally caught one that Saturday night in Columbia.

Missouri quarterback James Franklin was the kind of quarterback who gave Vanderbilt fits, a guy who could beat Vandy with his legs or his arm. Franklin led the Tigers on two early drives deep into VU territory. The Commodores looked powerless to stop the UM offense until it got inside the red zone, at which point the VU defense stiffened and held the Tigers to a pair of Andrew Baggett field goals.

But at the end of that second drive, Franklin hurt his knee and wouldn't return. Freshman backup Corbin Berkstresser did not have anything close to the experience of Franklin, who'd thrown for 2,865 yards and run for 981 the previous year, and Missouri didn't threaten for much of the night.

Missouri snapped a punt through the zone, cutting the lead to 6–2. The Vandy offense didn't gain a first down until nearly 24 minutes into the game, but the defense held Missouri off the scoreboard until Stacy added a 5-yard scoring run with 3:37 left in the half.

The 'Dores took a three-point lead to the locker room. Baggett answered with a 22-yard field goal, but Stacy's 14-yard run put the 'Dores up seven again after Fowler's point-after.

Then, disaster struck. On a third-and-22 from Missouri's 15, Berkstresser threw a pass intended for another Tiger receiver, but the ball slipped out of Berkstresser's hand as he threw. The Commodore defense reacted to where the ball was supposed to be thrown, but instead, Missouri's Bud Sasser saw it land in his hands. Eighty-five yards later, Missouri was a point away from tying the game.

"It was one of those plays where you see the quarterback aiming for a different target and the pass went over No. 2 and he ended up hitting No. 1," safety Javon Marshall said.

But the Tigers mishandled the extra-point snap, and Vandy's lead stood at a point. Spear tacked on a 21-yard field goal with 7:20 left. Those two plays turned out to be huge.

Berkstresser drove Missouri to the VU 24 in the game's final minutes, but on first down, Karl Butler and Kenny Ladler stopped Kendial Lawrence for a loss of one on a rushing attempt. Missouri coach Gary Pinkel ordered passing plays on the next three downs. Shoop called a blitz on each play, and Walker May got pressure on the final two. All three throws fell incomplete, and when Stacy gained 14 yards on a third-and-9 play from the VU 26 with under two minutes left, the Commodores escaped with a 19–15 win.

"Obviously when you can go on the road and win in the SEC, it's very important," Vandy's Franklin said. "I think what's important for us is that our team found a way to win a tough one. Adversity hit us there when they scored late in the game on third-and-22."

There was no letup in the schedule, as the 'Dores came home to play fourth-ranked Florida the next week. UF had two major things going for it: better overall athleticism on defense and special teams, and the kind of mobile quarterback in Jeff Driskel that gave Vandy fits.

Rodgers, playing in front of a sold-out crowd at Dudley Field, hit Matthews with a 10-yard scoring pass to give Vandy an early 7–0 lead after Spear's PAT. Driskel answered by racing 37 yards untouched for a score, and coach Will Muschamp's roll of the dice came up successful when Trey Burton ran for the two-point conversion. Florida's Caleb Sturgis added a 23-yard field goal, and the Gators led 11–7 at the break.

Driskel opened the second-half scoring with a 13-yard run, and the lead remained 18–7 into the fourth. Rodgers, harried all night by UF's outstanding front seven, fumbled in the first play of the fourth quarter and Sturgis connected from 29 to push the lead back to 14. The 'Dores, though, never allowed UF out of reach, and when Stacy scored on a 1-yard run, Vandy was back to within seven.

But the Gators always had an answer. Andre Debose returned the ensuing kickoff 60 yards to the VU 37, and Sturgis kicked a 26-yarder to make it 24–14. Again, Spear answered from 22, but on UF's next offensive snap, Driskel sprinted 70 yards to the end zone, untouched once again. He finished the evening with 11 carries for 177 yards and three scores.

"The quarterback was way faster than we expected," Vandy cornerback Andre Hal said. "I didn't think he was that fast. They're a pretty good team and they have speed everywhere."

The stat sheet showed that the game had been competitive, as UF won the total offense battle by a 403–363 margin, but once again it was mistakes, and mistakes at especially inopportune times, that proved to be lethal.

Rodgers's fumble was VU's only turnover, but the defense failed to force one. A questionable holding penalty on Matthews wiped out what would have been a 57-yard scoring run from Stacy. Stacy also dropped a touchdown pass that hit him in the hands. Vandy's special teams had been good so far, but in addition to Debose's back-breaking kickoff return, UF's Solomon Patton picked up 54 yards on a fake punt.

"Our kids played really hard. We had a game plan, but you can't make those types of mistakes against the No. 5 team in the country on your own field," Franklin said. "We had opportunities in the passing game. We had too many dropped balls in critical situations. . . . Defensively, we can't give up big plays. . . . We did not adjust well to the quarterback running game. . . . On special teams, I didn't think we played well all night long."

Vanderbilt fell to 2–4, and most SEC fans were now convinced that the 'Dores' bowl season of 2011 had been a fluke. Playing good teams week after week, though, can make good teams look mediocre. The four teams that had beaten Vandy—Georgia (5th), South Carolina (8th), Florida (9th), and Northwestern (17th)— would all finish in the AP's Top 25 at season's end.

Going back to the previous season, that was now nine straight games in which the Commodores had a shot to win in the final three minutes, and yet they failed to do so. It should be noted that most of those opponents were better than Vanderbilt, but at the same time it's almost statistically impossible to lose that many games that narrowly.

Taking everything into context, there were still the makings of a good team here. What Vanderbilt needed was a few breaks, and it was about to get some in the schedule ahead.

A winning streak!

Two seasons earlier, Auburn had been the national champion under coach Gene Chizik. But without quarterback Cam Newton, the Tigers were nowhere near the same team, and they limped into town at 1–5. The oddsmakers had VU as a seven-point favorite.

VU came out of the gates nicely, marching 75 yards in 16 plays and capitalizing when Tate scored from seven yards out from the wildcat formation. But Vandy's creativity, which had been so successful in Franklin's year and a half as a coach, soon backfired. Tate tried a pitch to Stacy out of the wildcat that failed, and Auburn recovered at the VU 37, where it would settle for a Cody Parkey field goal. Later, Vandy unsuccessfully tried to convert a fourth-and-1 at the AU 48 and when the team subsequently turned the ball over on downs, Auburn mounted a scoring drive that ended on Tre Mason's 1-yard run. After a Spear field goal on the half's last play, the game was tied at 10.

Vandy forced a punt to start the second half, and then drove 85 yards in seven plays before Stacy scored on a 2-yard run. Vanderbilt was about to coast to victory by grinding it out with Stacy, who'd rush for 169 yards on 27 carries and break the school's career rushing mark that day. But the normally sure-handed Stacy fumbled at the Auburn 32 with 2:24 left.

It was now up to the defense, which held Auburn to 212 yards for the game, to win this one. Just as it had done at Missouri, it did its job again. When Clint Moseley's throw to Sammie Coates on a fourth-and-13 play at the Vandy 44 sailed out of bounds with 52 seconds left, the Commodores knelt on the ball and celebrated their second SEC win.

It was so unlike many Vandy games of the past. Once again, the Commodores hadn't caught any breaks—they had fumbled three times and lost all three, and Auburn hadn't turned the ball over all day. In its own way, that was a big positive; though Auburn was destined for a 3–9 season, the Commodores had beaten a name team and had done it without gimmicks.

Franklin made that point well in the postgame press conference.

"Great win for Vanderbilt," he said. "We had an SEC opponent come into our stadium, [and we got a win]. I think you make progress when you don't play your best football and still beat an SEC opponent."

There would not be much drama against lowly Massachusetts the next week. Thanks to an 0-7 mark that included a number of blowouts, the Minutemen were 33-point underdogs in Nashville. VU was underwhelming for the first 25 minutes, but Rodgers threw for a score late in the first half and then ran for another as VU led 21–0 at the break.

Midway through the third quarter, the Commodores delivered a succession of quick punches before the Minutemen could blink. With 6:34 left in the third, Rodgers hit Boyd with a 14-yard score. On UMass's next possession, Wilson got another pick-6 when he dashed 17 yards thanks to Mike Wegzyn's errant toss. After a UMass punt, Kimbrow flashed his track-star-like speed when he went 74 yards untouched for a score. After another defensive stop, Jonathan Krause fielded a low, line-drive punt and turned it into a 40–0 VU lead.

It was a remarkable flurry; within that span, the only time that VU touched the ball and didn't score came when Krause lost two yards on a punt return that set up Kimbrow's dash.

The only disappointment came when UMass's A. J. Doyle connected with Deion Walker for a touchdown pass with 6:05 remaining. Vanderbilt had let off the gas long ago, and it ultimately went in the books as a 49–7 win. The Commodores also won the turnover battle, 4–1, which pleased Franklin, as that had been a recent point of emphasis.

"We focused on it all week, as far as creating turnovers and stripping the ball and going after the ball like the play Trey made. It paid off, because we were able to do that tonight," Lohr said.

Vanderbilt was now 4–4, and the next week's game at Kentucky looked like a breather, though Vegas had favored VU by just seven.

Vanderbilt had not shut out an SEC opponent since 1968, but it broke the streak that afternoon in Lexington behind a defense that held the Wildcats to 260 yards in a 40–0 win. Five different players scored touchdowns, all those coming in Vandy's first six possessions, and Spear added a pair of field goals.

"I feel like we are hitting our stride at the right time," Ladler said as the 5–4 Commodores got over .500 for the first time all season.

A road trip to Ole Miss was next. Losing badly to Vanderbilt the previous season had gotten Houston Nutt fired, and now, the Rebels were under the guidance of offensive mastermind Hugh Freeze. Trailing 23–6 early in the third quarter thanks to the hot hand of Ole Miss quarterback Bo Wallace, who'd throw for 403 yards and not commit a turnover, things looked bleak until Rodgers hit Matthews across the middle with a 52-yard touchdown bomb with 9:52 remaining in the third. Roughly six and a half minutes later, Wesley Tate scored on a two-yard run to cut the gap to three.

The Rebels had a chance to perhaps put it away late in the fourth when Wallace marched Ole Miss down the field for a first-and-goal at the Vandy 6. Wallace lost three yards on two runs and then his third-down pass to Randall Mackey fell incomplete, and so the Rebels settled for a 26-yard Bryson Rose field goal and a six-point lead.

With 2:43 left, Rodgers and Vandy got the ball back. Facing a fourth-and-2 at the VU 46, the Rebels were in Rodgers's face quickly, but somehow, he scrambled for nearly three yards. On a third-and-6 at the Rebel 47, he hit Kris Kentera for a 21-yard gain. On the next snap, the Rebels left Boyd unguarded along the left sideline and when Rodgers saw him, the Commodores had perhaps their easiest score of the season. Spear added the point-after, and the 'Dores had a 27 point-after 26 lead with 53 seconds left.

Wallace quickly got Ole Miss to its 49, but three plays later, the defense had held and the Commodores had a rarity: a comeback win on the road in the SEC.

Vanderbilt fans, who'd felt snakebitten for so many years, could finally feel the program starting to turn the corner. VU would now be going to back-to-back bowls for the first time in school history, but their attention was now squarely focused on the bully just down the block.

A Big Orange blowout

The previous season's heartbreak in Knoxville had been difficult to swallow. Vanderbilt was the better team and should have won probably both in that season as well as in 2008. It just seemed that Vanderbilt was destined to lose to the Vols no matter what—well, almost no matter what. There had been the 2005 season, when Jay Cutler and Earl Bennett connected on a late touchdown pass and Jared Fagan had sealed the game with an interception in the end zone on the game's last play.

But other than that, it had just been one futile attempt after another. The 2005 victory had been Vandy's first since 1982 and before that, the 1975 season had been the only time the Commodores had knocked off the Vols in their annual rivalry since 1964. Vandy had the better team on paper, but certainly, history explains why the Commodores were just field-goal favorites on their own field.

Perhaps the history also explained the first half. Stacy dashed 72 yards on the game's first play, but the drive stalled at the 1½, and Vandy had to settle for a Spear field goal. After another one of those, plus an 11-yard touchdown catch by Boyd in the back of the end zone that was all over ESPN that night, the Commodores clung to a 13-10 lead at the break.

But Vanderbilt was making Tennessee quarterback Tyler Bray look awful. Vol coach Derek Dooley went to backup Justin Worley in the first half, and Hal had picked him off to set up Boyd's score.[9] With nothing working, Dooley went back to Bray, and the Vols went three-and-out to open the half. Matthews took a jet sweep and sliced through the Vol defense untouched for a 47-yard touchdown and a 20–10 lead.

Hal intercepted Bray and ran the ball to the UT 4, where Tate hit Kentera with a jump pass out of the wildcat for a 17-point lead. Stacy added a 10-yard scoring run with 1:53 left in the third, and the rout was on. By the time Matthews took a short pass and dashed 72 yards to the end zone with just under 10 minutes left, the outcome had been decided.

Tennessee's Cordarrelle Patterson scored on an 81-yard punt return to account for the 41–18 final, but it could have easily been worse. The Commodores thought they'd brought Patterson down on the punt return, but as they slung him to the turf, he landed on a defender and his leg never touched the ground. Earlier in the game, there were plenty of mistakes too. A teammate's unnecessary block in the back cost Boyd a touchdown. Stacy had Rodgers wide open for what should have been a score on a throwback pass, but was short in his aim. Rodgers was robbed of another TD pass when an open Kentera bobbled a pass in the end zone and it was intercepted.

The box score spoke to the kind of one-sided game it was. Though Tennessee came in averaging 37.9 points per game, VU outgained the Vols, 442–303, and won the turnover battle, 3–1. Bray was just 11-of-29 for 103 yards and two scores. Tennessee receivers Patterson and Justin Hunter were getting hyped as potential NFL

---

9 Hal's two picks that day earned him the SEC's Defensive Player of the Week.

Chris Boyd hauls in a first-half touchdown pass against Tennessee in 2012.
(Mike Rapp)

first-rounders, but Matthews (seven catches for 115 yards and one rush for 47) was clearly the best receiver on the field that evening.

To top it off, the Commodores had more of their fans in the stands than did the Vols. The notion of even mentioning that for a rivalry game like this would normally be laughable, but given UT's track record for success over the past eighty years compared to Vandy's, coupled with the fact that Tennessee has several times as many alums in state (and even in Nashville) as does Vanderbilt, it was understandable. To boot, VU students, who'd started to show up a bit more for games, were on break.

When it was done, just about all of those in black and gold stuck around to celebrate the outcome. After taking his players into the locker room, Franklin ordered them back out to celebrate with the fans. Players ran from one side of the stands to the other to greet fans, who just kept cheering.

"I think it's a testament to them staying with us through the tough times. We've had a lot of tough times. It has been since '82 since we beat Tennessee here. They've been waiting a long time for that. So we wanted to celebrate with them and honor them," Rodgers said.

Jordan Matthews celebrates after Vanderbilt's 2012 rout of Tennessee at Dudley Field. (Mike Rapp)

The icing on the cake was this: Vanderbilt had clinched a winning season and insured that the Vols would finish with a losing record. It was also Vandy's largest margin of victory in the series since a 26–0 win in 1954. One game later, Dooley, who had made some inflammatory remarks after the win in Knoxville the previous season, would be out of a job.

"This is what we all envisioned when we came here, that we could put [on] something special here at Vanderbilt right here in Nashville," Franklin said.

For all those who had waited so long for a moment like this one in the rivalry, it was special indeed.

Unfinished business

By now, the spirits surrounding the program were at least as high as they'd been since the 1982 season, which was the last time Vandy had beaten the Vols at Dudley Field. Between that and the pounding Vanderbilt had put on Wake Forest the previous year, the Commodores were sky-high as they hit the road for a game in Winston-Salem. As had been the case the previous season, the game was tight for much of the first half before the Commodores began to assert themselves in the second quarter.

It started when Tate scored his second touchdown of the day on a 15-yard touchdown run. On VU's next two drives, Rodgers and Matthews hooked up for a score on a 64-yard bomb, and then Stacy ended the half's scoring with a 4-yard run.

Andrew Williamson opened the second-half scoring by blocking a punt, which walk-on Casey Hughes recovered in the end zone. Krause scored on an 83-yard punt return, and Stacy broke his own school record with a 90-yard touchdown sprint. Long before the 55–21 score, it was over.

It was a game that made history in a number of ways. It gave VU its first six-game winning streak since 1955, and the eight-win season was the first since '82. Stacy became the first Vandy back to go over 1,000 yards rushing in back-to-back years, and Matthews was now the school's all-time leader in receiving yards for a season.

With all the excitement around the program, it was a major letdown when the Gator Bowl snubbed Vanderbilt in favor of Mississippi State, leaving Vanderbilt to once again play a bowl game in its home state. As with 2008, that would be three miles down the street at L.P. Field, where North Carolina State would be the opponent.

Vanderbilt put distance between itself and the Wolfpack early. Boyd made another one-handed, highlight-reel grab in the end zone that was so good, officials didn't think he could make the catch until they saw the video replay and overturned it. After Stacy's 6-yard scoring run early in the second quarter, the lead was 14.

The Wolfpack answered with a touchdown, which Tate answered with one of his own, at which point State's Tony Palmer ran the ensuing kickoff back for a score. But Matthews made another one of his fantastic plays by taking a screen pass 18 yards and making some nifty moves to get to the end zone. Vandy made the lead 31–14 after Spear's 30-yarder in the third.

By virtue of playing in front all day, Wolfpack quarterback Mike Glennon, who would be starting for the NFL's Tampa Bay Buccaneers by that time next season, had to throw it on most downs. Glennon threw for 383 yards, but Vanderbilt got the best end of that deal, as the Commodores' coverage was exceptional. Glennon often had time, but he got picked at various points in the day by Ladler, Wilson, and senior safety Eric Samuels. Ladler also pounced on a fumble, as did Azubike.

By the time Glennon finally threw for a score, just 2:04 remained, and with Vanderbilt leading 38–24, it was over. The Commodores weren't impressive offensively, with just 225 total yards, but Vanderbilt sat on the ball for most of the second half, often running Stacy and Tate out of the wildcat. Stacy (25 carries, 107 yards) was the game's MVP.

It was a great day for Commodore fans. Of the 55,801 in attendance, probably 80 percent were cheering for VU. Matthews finished his season with 94 catches and 1,323 yards, and Stacy's 1,141 rushing yards were second in school history only to his total of the previous season. The team's 30-point average for the season was the first time VU had done that since 1948.

Matthews made a few third-team All-America squads and was VU's first player to make the coaches' All-SEC team since 2008. Stacy made the coaches' second team, as did punter Richard Kent. Hal and Spear were selected to the AP's second team all-conference team, also. The Commodores also ended the season with the longest winning streak of any SEC team.

There would be other milestones. Days later, when the final polls were released, the Commodores finished 20th in the *USA Today*/ Coaches' Poll and 23rd in the Associated Press's version. Vanderbilt had not finished in the AP's ranking since the 1948 club went 8–2–1 and finished 12th.

Some personnel loses, particularly Stacy, would be tough to replace. Some speculated that Vandy might be replacing its coach, also. However, Franklin let the world know as soon as the game was over, that he and the team would be back to give things another run at a high level.

"It's not over. These guys will be a part of the Vanderbilt family for the rest of their life. And I cannot wait until they come back next year and find out all the exciting things they're doing. . . . This is a great foundation," he said.

Franklin was right about most of that, but before the kickoff of the next season, a shocking turn of events would have him facing far greater challenges than he'd ever anticipated.

2013 Football: The sequel

Vanderbilt's football roster was as stocked as it had been in decades heading into 2013. Seven starters returned on each side of the ball, as did kicker Carey Spear and long-snapper Andrew East. In its media guide, Vanderbilt touted Spear, wide receiver Jordan Matthews, cornerback Andre Hal, and left tackle Wesley Johnson as All-America candidates. It listed eight more players—defensive end Caleb Azubike, receiver Chris Boyd, linebacker Chase Garnham, receiver/return specialist Jonathan Krause, safeties Kenny Ladler and Javon Marshall and defensive ends Walker May and Kyle Woestmann—as potential All-Southeastern Conference selections. With back-to-back bowl appearances and a top-20 ranking in the Coaches' Poll the previous year, the college football world was now taking the Commodores a bit more seriously.

In late-June, though, a bombshell dropped. Defensive backs Brandon Banks and Cory Batey, wide receiver Jaborian "Tip" McKenzie, and tight end Brandon Vandenburg were kicked out of school amid a sex crime investigation by the Metro Nashville Police Department.[1] In mid-August, Boyd was charged with involvement in a cover-up and was suspended from the team but allowed to stay in school.

---

1 As of press date for this book, the case had not gone to trial.

The incident dominated the Nashville news for much of the next four months and made national headlines. It became an increasing distraction as rumors circulated that more players and coaches were involved.[2]

In addition to the black eye that it dealt the program, it also hurt VU on the field. Batey, Banks, and McKenzie were slated to be second-teamers. Tight end was Vanderbilt's weakest position, and the Commodores thought that Vandenburg, a JUCO transfer with excellent grades, would start immediately and later play in the NFL. It was unclear how long Boyd would be gone, but the absence of another potential future NFL player was huge, especially when the drop-off, from the rising junior to the rest of the receivers on the roster, was enormous.

Franklin had always had challenges at Vanderbilt, but with the events of the summer hanging like a storm cloud over the program for virtually the entire season, it would be his toughest year yet.

Another slow start

Vanderbilt opened its season on a hot, humid Thursday night on ESPN as Ole Miss came to town. The Rebels, under second-year coach Hugh Freeze, were a program on the rise. Several of the nation's top recruits would make their debuts that evening. It was an evenly matched game, but perhaps due to the fact that Boyd was still missing, the visitors were field-goal favorites.

VU started the evening in terrible fashion, thanks to rough debuts from a couple of new starters. Austyn Carta-Samuels was picked at the VU 31, which led to an Ole Miss field goal. Punter Taylor Hudson shanked a 16-yard punt that gave Ole Miss the ball at the Vandy 42, and that possession led to a touchdown.

But the Commodores finally caught fire in the second quarter as a 3-yard run by Tate, a 55-yard dash by Matthews off a short throw from Carta-Samuels, and another 3-yard run by

---

2 None of this has been proven.

Jerron Seymour accounted for three quick scores. It might have been the best quarter a Franklin team had at Vandy, and the 'Dores led 21–10 at the half.

The Commodore defense had begun to dominate, as Rebel quarterback Bo Wallace spent much of the first half on his back. Freeze made a critical adjustment by putting one of those star recruits, big Laquan Treadwell, in the slot, where VU covered him with a linebacker. He simply had his freshman run near the first-down marker and turn around, where time and time again Wallace delivered. Freeze also got Wallace the ball on the read option, which had given Vandy fits for three years running. By late in the fourth quarter, the Rebels had a 32–28 lead.

Around the two-minute mark, VU had the ball on a fourth-and-18 play. Matthews had left the game earlier to get intravenous fluids in the third quarter and then had departed again after being belted by safety Cody Prewitt, but he returned to hook up with Carta-Samuels for a miraculous 42-yard catch and run to keep VU's hopes alive. Just as had happened the year before, a stunned Rebel team left a man open on the left sideline on the next play, and when Steven Scheu hauled in the Carta-Samuels pass, he could have practically walked the 34 yards into the end zone. With 1:30 to play, Vandy led by three.

Ole Miss got the ball back, and what happened next stunned everyone. On a second-down play, Freeze got the ball to tailback Jeff Scott heading toward the left sideline. It was designed to be a quick gainer to get him out of bounds and perhaps pick up a first down if it was there. Just as Scott was about to step out of the field of play, he looked to his right, where it looked as if the Red Sea had parted. Scott was the fastest player on the field, and once he saw daylight, no one was beating him to the end zone.

Seventy-five yards later, just 23 seconds after Scheu's score, the Rebels led again. Matthews nearly made another amazing play on Vandy's next drive, but instead, he tipped the ball into Prewitt's hands for a game-winning interception.

"We stole one tonight," Freeze said later.

Austin Peay was the perfect bounce-back opponent the next week. Vandy was still without Boyd, but the Governors were

47.5-point underdogs coming to Nashville. Vandy started slowly again, leading just 3–0 after a quarter, but posted five second-quarter touchdowns to take a 38–0 lead at the break. Carta-Samuels ran for one and threw for another, and sat out the second half after throwing for 223 yards, which included 111 to Matthews. VU took its foot off the gas pedal after halftime and coasted to a 38–3 win.

Vanderbilt went to Columbia to try to exact revenge for the previous year's heartbreak against South Carolina. The team had targeted this as a big week; it had gotten over the Ole Miss debacle and was scheduled to get Boyd back. The junior sat in a Nashville courtroom on Friday morning and was expected to be cleared of felony charges based on what he'd told the coaches about his involvement in the incident.

By the nature of the way VU handled the case, turning it over to Metro Nashville Police from the outset, it really did not know many of the details. Boyd pled guilty to a reduced misdemeanor charge and the court accepted that, but in a strange twist, the D.A. read the details of Boyd's involvement, which were far worse than he'd led the coaches to believe.

Instead of boarding a plane to Columbia, Boyd stayed home. Teammates were stunned; no one had seen this coming.

Perhaps hung over from this, the Commodores were awful for the first quarter and a half. The Gamecocks scored touchdowns on their first four possessions and only when Steven Clarke picked Dylan Thompson and returned the ball to the Carolina 1, where Seymour scored from there, did Vandy show any life. Spear hit a 54-yard field goal just before the break, but the stat sheet, which showed Carolina gaining 381 yards and 21 first downs to Vandy's 94 and 4, told the story more than did the scoreboard.

Trailing 35–10 less than a minute inside the fourth quarter, Vandy mounted a comeback. Carta-Samuels scored on a 1-yard run, and when Carolina fumbled the kickoff, Tate caught a 19-yard screen pass and ran it in. A pass to Scheu gave VU a two-point conversion, and within a 13-second span, Vandy was back in the game.

When Vanderbilt recovered a muffed punt and marched to the Carolina 5 midway through the fourth, things got quite interesting.

But Carta-Samuels was picked in the end zone and Carolina essentially ran out the clock.

"I don't think we executed and played with passion like we have in the past in the first half. I think we got dominated on the offensive and defensive line in the first half. I thought we showed up in the second half and played with passion and emotion," Franklin said.

The following Tuesday, Boyd was dismissed from the football team permanently. Vanderbilt had another easy game at Massachusetts the next weekend, but again, the Commodores, 30-point favorites, didn't play well, leading just 10–7 with 13:44 left in the game until Matthews made a tremendous open-field run on an 11-yard touchdown pass. Seymour's touchdown run with 4:41 left clinched a 24-7 victory.

Franklin tried to spin it positively later, but it wasn't a good day. Vandy gained just 406 yards against a team that was giving up well over 500 a game and would go on to a 1–11 record.

"Prettiest win I've seen because we got the 'W,'" he said. "That's all that matters."

Vanderbilt had another layup with lowly Alabama-Birmingham at home the next week. For a change, the 'Dores started quickly and led 24–6 at the break. Tate's 8-yard scoring run late in the third, coupled with Carta-Samuels' touchdown throws to Matthews and Fitz Lassing, put it out of reach as VU won, 52–24.

The next Saturday's matchup with Missouri was an interesting one. The Tigers, thanks to a slew of injuries everywhere, had gone just 5–7 in their SEC debut season the previous year. Missouri had arranged its schedule to get all four out-of-conference opponents first, and it wasn't a huge shock to see the Tigers take care of Murray State, Toledo, Indiana, and Arkansas State in succession. But other than Murray State, Missouri hadn't really run away from anyone and it made it tough to assess how good the Tigers were at that point.

Vandy found out quickly that the Tigers were plenty good. It was like the Carolina game all over again; before Vandy could breathe, it was more or less out of the game. Missouri led 20–0 just 12:10 in and 30–7 at the half, rolling up almost 300 yards by the break.

Vandy pulled within 16 twice, but it seemed that Tiger quarterback James Franklin and an endless collection of gazelles that the Tigers lined up at receiver could just score at will. The final was 51–28, and it seemed worse than that.

"I apologize to the fans and the people who came to the game. That's not what you came to see," Vandy's Franklin said later.

At 3–3, the Commodores were actually a game better at midseason than they'd been the previous year. But with the exception of that Georgia game (which turned out to be an outlier), the 'Dores hadn't gotten manhandled by some of the league's better teams the way they had now.

The season's second-half schedule looked a lot tougher than the second half of last year's. Just finishing over .500 again would be a small challenge, and another 9–4 season now seemed to be almost an impossibility.

A second wind

The first half of the season had so many elements of adversity. There was the Ole Miss game, which Vanderbilt had won until it didn't. There was the fact that Missouri turned out to be a lot tougher than people had thought; the Tigers would play in the SEC title game. The rape case, though, really seemed to cast a pall over everything. Not having the dismissed players was bad enough, but Franklin got asked about it every week, and a few players had their names dragged into the case through unfortunate circumstance rather than any culpability. At one point, a blog started a rumor that Franklin himself had a hand in an alleged cover-up, though the same writer offered no evidence to support the claim.

The season seemed like a never-ending nightmare. When Matthews had scored an amazing touchdown against UMass a few weeks previous, a bizarre scene ensued; almost nobody came to congratulate him. It just seemed that all the joy of playing was gone, and even Franklin, who generally ran around as if his underwear had been lined with Tabasco sauce, seemed sapped by it all. On top of it all, it seemed as if several Commodores were playing hurt, but it was always hard to know for sure, as Franklin never gave out updates on injuries.

What Vanderbilt needed was a break, and it finally got a bit of one with Georgia coming to town. The Bulldogs looked like a top-five team earlier in the season, but that was before injuries cost the Bulldogs' star tailbacks Todd Gurley and Keith Marshall. UGA was also banged up at receiver.

Still, Georgia had tons of talent, with four- and five-star recruits starting across the field more often than not. It also helped that the 'Dores had an off-week. Perhaps that's why the same team that destroyed VU by a 48–3 score the previous season was just a seven-point favorite that Saturday afternoon.

It looked like another day of bad breaks for Vandy early, though. Carta-Samuels was hurt in the second quarter and so Patton Robinette was forced in for his first meaningful action. Robinettte had neither Carta-Samuels's experience nor his arm, and things looked bleak when Vandy trailed 27–14 midway through the third quarter.

But freshman Torren McGaster recovered a fumbled punt late in the third, and Robinette scored on a 2-yard run. Spear hit a 40-yard field goal to get Vandy within three, but with 4:44 remaining in the game, time was starting to run out.

Ironically, the 'Dores got the break on a Georgia punt that they hadn't two years before. UGA punter Collin Barber dropped a snap and though he fell on it, Vandy took over at the 13. On the next play, Seymour rumbled in for the touchdown, and Vandy led for the first time in the half.

Georgia had a chance to come back, but linebacker Jake Sealand forced a fumble that Hal returned 10 yards to the Bulldog 33. Vandy failed to run out the clock, but when it punted, Georgia took over at its 28 with just 14 seconds left. Marshall picked Aaron Murray at the Vandy 25, and VU had scored a 31–27 upset.

It was a big win not only to stay in the hunt for a bowl game, but also because it was the first time the 'Dores had beaten a ranked opponent since Franklin had been the coach. To boot, they had done it with an inexperienced freshman quarterback leading the comeback. Yes, Georgia had injuries, but it still had All-America quarterback Aaron Murray, who had gone just 16-of-28 for 114 yards and failed to throw a touchdown. Vanderbilt had also out-gained the Bulldogs, 337–221.

"We persevered. We persevered all year long. We persevered as a campus. We've persevered as a community. I'm happy for our kids and our program," Franklin said.

It was the first time all year that Vanderbilt fans had legitimate reason to smile, but next week nearly erased all of the joy. The Commodores went to Texas A&M, where reigning Heisman winner Johnny Manziel was hurt, but didn't play like it. Manziel had three touchdown passes in the first quarter alone, and when Trey Williams added an early second quarter rushing score, it was 28–0.

Vandy finished the second quarter by scoring 17 straight points, and for a bit, it looked like the 'Dores might make it a game, since the A&M defense was one of the worst in the country. But VU struggled to protect Robinette and the freshman struggled to get much on his throws. A&M's Howard Matthews picked off a pass and raced 26 yards, and the Aggies were back up by 18 just seven seconds into the second half.

The bottom fell out from there. The Aggies coasted to a 56–24 win behind a fantastic 25-of-35, 305-yard, four-touchdown game from Manziel, who was done before the fourth quarter arrived.

It almost certainly would have been worse had the Vandy defense not forced five turnovers. This team had some obvious holes; A&M was giving up nearly six yards a carry, but VU averaged just 2.2 yards on 44 tries that day. Vanderbilt had been good in special teams the previous couple of years, but was struggling to punt and getting nothing in the return game. Matthews had broken the SEC's all-time receiving yards record that day, but with Krause being banged up and VU having no real option after him, plus the fact that Robinette did not have Carta-Samuels's arm, it was difficult to get him the ball.

It was a great time for another off-week, which was coming.

Bowl-eligible, again!

As optimistic as everyone had been about the prospects for the 2013 season, it was obvious that this team wasn't nearly as good as the previous season's. However, there was one parallel with the

2012 season, and that was that the schedule once again eased up considerably down the stretch.

Next up was Florida, which had major injury issues of its own. The Gators were down to using inexperienced Tyler Murphy at quarterback and had few offensive weapons otherwise. What UF did have was a talented defense, but it was getting taxed through the offense's inability to do much of anything. So maybe Vandy had a chance.

On the other hand, VU had fallen twenty-two straight times in the series and had not won in Gainesville since 1945. That, coupled with Vandy's issues, made the Commodores 12-point underdogs.

It was never really close. Robinette led Vandy down the field on the game's first drive, and Spear hit a 31-yard field goal. Then Murphy started giving the game away. Hal picked him at the Gator 30 and brought it back to the 10, where Seymour scored on the next snap. Ladler had an interception and ran it deep into UF territory, and Robinette scooted to the end zone on a 5-yard run.

It was 17–0 barely 20 minutes into the game. The Gators had a chance to edge closer late before halftime with a first and goal at the Vandy 1, but the defense held Florida to a field goal.

The second half started the way the first left off, with Andrew Williamson returning a pick inside the 5, where Seymour scored again. The Gators threatened briefly with 7:40 left in the game, catching a huge break when Vandy's Paris Head batted down a pass in the end zone. The ball kicked off Head's foot into the arms of Gator Ahmad Fullwood for a touchdown and the lead was 31–17.

With 5:18 left, UF started another drive at its 15 and moved to the Vandy 41, but the defense stiffened. On a third-and-10, Marshall sacked Murphy and on fourth-and-23, Azubike brought him down for a loss of 26. Spear hit an insurance field goal with 45 seconds left, and the 'Dores had a 34–17 victory.

"It was crazy. We had fun today. We were playing together like the old Vanderbilt team," Hal said.

Vandy was now a win away from clinching a bowl, and Kentucky, which came to Nashville as an 11.5-point underdog, provided an excellent opportunity.

Very little came easy for this team, though, and UK delivered a bit of a surprise when the 'Cats marched down the field and scored a touchdown on the game's first drive. However, freshman defensive lineman Adam Butler, who was emerging as a real force, blocked the point-after, and Clarke returned it the length of the field for a two-point score. Kimbrow had a 21-yard touchdown run late in the first quarter, but neither team was able to move the ball, and the 'Dores maintained just a 9–6 lead into the fourth quarter when Spear hit field goals from 26 and 38.

With under a minute left, Franklin did something slightly controversial. With a nine-point lead and fourth-and-4 at the UK 13 and 52 seconds to play, it was unlikely (but not impossible) that the Commodores would blow the lead. Instead of having Spear kick a 30-yard field goal, Franklin had Robinette fake a run and throw a jump pass to Kentera, who scored on the play. It made for a 22–6 win instead of 15–6, but the full significance of the play would be realized the next week against Tennessee in Knoxville.

By now, it was clear that Vanderbilt was building its team around two things: riding Matthews (14 touches, 172 yards) and a defense (four interceptions, 262 yards allowed) as far as it could.

It would be just enough to get where Franklin wanted to go.

Starting a streak of their own

Victories over Tennessee had been extremely rare for the past 87 years. As legend has it, the Vols brought General Bob Neyland to Knoxville because they were tired of losing to Dan McGugin and Vanderbilt. At the point of Neyland's hire as UT's head coach in 1926, Vanderbilt held a commanding 18–2–3 edge in the series, and most of those had not been close.

Neyland lost his first rivalry game by a 20–3 count, but Vandy wouldn't defeat the Vols again until 1935. From 1927 on, the teams would play every year except for 1943 and 1944, and Vanderbilt had managed just 10 wins and 3 ties. Not once in that span did the Commodores manage to win consecutive games, and just once ('74 and '75) did Vandy even string a tie and a win together in back-to-back games. Franklin never talked about anything other than "going 1–0" in the next game, but you can bet his players knew they had a chance to make history.

Unfortunately, Vanderbilt played one of its worst games of the season that chilly evening in Knoxville. Vandy certainly got the best of its rivals in the first half, outgaining the Vols 165–84, and it helped that Carta-Samuels was playing for the first time since the first half of the Georgia game.

However, Vandy repeatedly failed to cash in on opportunities. Matthews had a rare fumble at the Vol 5 that cost VU points. Kimbrow fumbled a possession away at the VU 41. The game was tied at 7 and when the Vols' Michael Palardy hit a 32-yard field goal, Tennessee led for the first time all day. Vanderbilt freshman Darrius Sims, who was becoming a real threat as a kickoff returner, raced 71 yards to the Vol 27 on the ensuing kickoff, but Robinette lost a fumble at the Vol 16.

The Commodore defense had been fantastic. Among other things, Butler had blocked a first-half field goal to prevent the Vols from going ahead. However, when all four senior starters in the secondary would be lost to injuries by the time the night was over, and Franklin had to replace them with four freshmen and sophomores, Vandy's chances took a big hit.

However, those replacements stepped up in a huge way. One of them, Paris Head, had a first-half interception of quarterback Josh Dobbs and early in the fourth, picked off Palardy on a fake field goal.

It still wasn't enough. On a night where the wind swirled inside the stadium, Spear had a rare miss of a 41-yard field goal with 7:15 left. The Vols strung together a couple of first downs, and Palardy pinned VU back to its 8 with just 4:16 left. As poorly as the offense had played, a comeback looked unlikely.

Franklin had called the game conservatively all evening, but at this point he knew Vandy had to start throwing downfield. Matthews took a short throw from Carta-Samuels for eight on the first play. On a third-and-6, he connected with Krause for 18. Two plays later, another toss to Krause went for 17 and a personal foul on the Vols moved the ball to the UT 23. Matthews took another short throw and appeared to have a first down, though a controversial spot had him a yard shy of the first down at the

Vol 34. On a third-and-1, a rush to Tate went for no gain and Vandy burned a time-out with 48 seconds left.

The play call was a sneak to Carta-Samuels, and as he dove forward, he appeared to easily have the first down. Officials did not agree, spotting the ball inches short of the first-down marker. The crowd of 97,223 started celebrating a Vol win, but ironically for Vanderbilt, which had lost a game in a strange manner due to instant replay the last time it played in Neyland Stadium, replays overturned the officials' spot and awarded VU a first down.

The Vol crowd grumbled, but it was clearly the right call. On the next snap, Carta-Samuels hit a well-covered Matthews for 25 to the Vol 8. A Carta-Samuels rush got the 'Dores three yards closer with 21 seconds left. But Carta-Samuels obviously didn't have his normal mobility, and Franklin, who had rotated quarterbacks all night, went back to Robinette.

Maybe Franklin also knew that Robinette had a little extra motivation, for the freshman had played his high school ball 20 miles down the road at Maryville High. Here was Vanderbilt play-by-play announcer Joe Fisher's call of what happened next.

"Robinette takes the snap. He's gonna keep—fake the jump pass! He'll run to the right! He'll run to the end zone! Touchdown, Commodores! Patton Robinette faked the jump, got the corner, and got the end zone!"

Robinette's garbage-time touchdown pass against the Wildcats the previous week seemed insignificant at the time, but could have been one of the more important plays in Vandy history in the way that it set up Tennessee the following week. The pump fake was enough to get the Vol linebackers and defensive linemen to freeze, and enough to make the defensive backs stationed in the middle of the end zone worry about the pass. Robinette had good speed to begin with, but the trickery was enough to make sure he crossed the plane of the goal line standing before a Vol could lay a finger on him.

"We kind of expect that in the design of the play. After the jump pass against Kentucky, we felt like they would key on that one, so we faked it a little bit and ran it in. I had great blocks with those guys and Jordan Matthews outside, so it worked out well for us," Robinette said.

Vandy led 14–10 and just 16 seconds remained. The Vols got to the Vandy 48, when Dobbs had time for one last Hail Mary. Vandy put Matthews into the game in case the 'Dores needed to win a jump ball. Dobbs's pass fell short in the end zone and the throng of Vanderbilt fans in Knoxville erupted in jubilation.

They'd done it. Vandy had done what for the past few decades seemed impossible, beating its hated rival twice in a row with something way short of its best effort.

"We started the game out on certain sides of the ball trying our hardest to lose the game," Franklin said. "But the thing that I think is so special about this team is this team knows how to win. Over the last three years, we've created a culture that the players expect to win and they find ways to win. Sometimes it's not always pretty."

The win was doubly sweet. It clinched Vandy's first back-to-back winning seasons since 1974–75 and for the second straight season, made Tennessee ineligible for a bowl.

Vegas made Vanderbilt a 14.5-point favorite for the 'Dores game with Wake Forest next weekend, and given the way VU had worn out the Deacons, that wasn't a surprise. On the other hand, maybe it was too much to expect; the 'Dores hadn't been blowing anyone out and were coming off an emotional win.

When Vanderbilt gave Wake Forest a touchdown on Carta-Samuels's third-quarter pick—giving away a touchdown about every other game was becoming a bad habit for this team—the 'Dores trailed 21–17 midway through the third. Spear's 25-yard field goal with 6:58 to play pulled Vandy closer, but it couldn't get over the hump.

With VU facing a fourth-and-11 at the Wake 48 with under two minutes left, Carta-Samuels threw it up along the Vanderbilt sideline, hoping Matthews could once again bail Vandy out. One Wake defender was holding him as he turned back for the ball and another was right behind him. Matthews leapt and snagged it with both hands and held on as he fell backward.

"Schematically, we shouldn't have thrown the ball there. That's who [Matthews] is, though," Franklin said about the grab.

The play went for 25 yards and now, Vandy just wanted to hang onto the ball and let the reliable Spear win the game. It got the ball to the middle of the field, and the senior kicker connected on a 38-yarder with 39 seconds left.

Wake moved the ball to the Vandy 44 on a pair of pass completions, but May sacked Tanner Price for a loss of nine on a first-and-10. After two more incompletions, the Commodores hung on for a 23–21 win.

Nobody had expected eight wins at midseason, but that's what Vanderbilt now had. It would be a week before VU found out who it needed to knock off to get back to nine.

"We are not bowl snobs. Wherever they tell us to go, we will be happy to go there," Franklin said.

Bowling is a habit

Franklin wasn't exactly telling the truth. After the Gator Bowl passed on Vandy for Georgia and then the Liberty Bowl passed up the Commodores to take Mississippi State, the third-year head coach privately fumed. The 'Dores, despite eight wins, were the SEC's last bowl-eligible team left standing and were left with the BBVA Compass Bowl.

Fans were furious. Birmingham's Legion Field was located in the middle of a slum. There was barbed wire around the outside of the stadium, and as VandySports.com photographer Mike Rapp joked upon arriving at the game, "Is that to keep fans in or out?" Once one got inside Legion Field, it almost seemed like a legitimate question; it looked as if the place hadn't been touched in 30 years.

On the bright side, VU also drew a good Houston team. The 8–4 Cougars certainly made for a more attractive opponent than what Vandy would have drawn in Memphis.[3] Whatever disappointments the fans and players felt, they got over them quickly. About 35,000 Vanderbilt fans alone showed up and were loud from the beginning.

Carta-Samuels had been playing with an injured knee and had opted for surgery, leaving Robinette as the quarterback. On a first-quarter play from midfield, the freshman fired a quick pass to Matthews near the line of scrimmage and the senior did his thing,

---

3 MSU crushed Rice, 44–7, in that game.

Jordan Matthews races to the end zone for VU's first touchdown of the 2013 Compass Bowl in Birmingham. (Mike Rapp)

following a block from Krause and scoring the game's first points. Garnham, an Alabama native, forced a fumble that Williamson recovered, and then Robinette scored on an 8-yard run on Vandy's ensuing possession. Spear's field goal put Vandy up by 17 with 10:27 left in the second quarter, and then Matthews got behind the Houston secondary for another 50-yard scoring pass the next time Vandy had the ball.

At halftime, the 'Dores had a 24–0 lead and had dominated the game, allowing just 22 Houston yards in the first half. But Vandy's third quarter was a complete nightmare. Robinette lost a fumble at the Vandy 6 and Houston scored on the next play. A 62-yard run and a 58-yard pass on Houston's next two possessions set up a touchdown and a field goal, respectively.

Those were real stunners, as the Commodores defense hadn't given up a lot of long gainers in Franklin's tenure. As the third quarter wound down, Houston quarterback John O'Korn hit

Deonte Greenberry for a 67-yard score. That put Houston at over 300 yards in the third quarter alone, and suddenly, the game was tied.

That was real trouble for Vandy, because Robinette was clearly having trouble delivering the ball downfield. He'd complete only 6 of 19 throws that day for 154 yards and two interceptions, with five of those balls going to Matthews for 143 yards. The last pick came early in the fourth, setting Houston up in good field position at its 41.

But the defense held, and Vanderbilt got the ball back on its 18. The 'Dores had not run the ball well all season, but picked a good time to start. On a third-and-2 from its 26, Robinette picked up almost exactly what he needed to move the chains. Two plays later, the slippery Seymour took a hand off, cut left and then back to the middle, and rumbled down to the Houston 34. Kimbrow spelled him and got 13 on the next snap. On the following snap, Kimbrow ran left and saw all kinds of room. Twenty-one yards later, Vandy led by seven again.

Two snaps later, safety Jahmel McIntosh intercepted O'Korn at the Houston 42 and ran it back to the 17. Spear hit a 35-yard field goal to put the 'Dores up 10 with 6:17 left. Houston's DeMarcus Ayers ran the kickoff back to the Vandy 38, where Spear ran him out of bounds, but a three-and-out gave VU the ball back at its 40. Vandy punted and pinned Houston back to its 16, where Hal picked O'Korn at the Houston 31 and returned it to the 2.

When Seymour scored on a second-and-goal play from the 2 and Spear hit the PAT, it was all but over. The 41–24 score held, and the Commodores had won their second straight bowl game for the first time in school history. Matthews was selected the game's MVP.

"The thing that's probably the most exciting to me is, there's a culture of winning at Vanderbilt. These guys know how to win. A lot of different ways they do it, ugly, pretty—people can describe it how they want," Franklin said.

Rarely had Franklin spoken truer words as Vanderbilt's coach. It would be nearly his last dose of honesty in Nashville.

The end of an era

That day in Birmingham had been a landmark moment in Vanderbilt football history. Vanderbilt didn't look like a Top 25 team until perhaps the bowl game, but at 9–4 wound up at 24th in the AP's rankings and 23rd in the USA Coaches' poll. The run didn't appear to be ending soon, as Franklin had assembled a Top 25 recruiting class the previous year—most of those players redshirted—and was putting another one together. After the rape scandal had started to fade from the news, Franklin probably could have run for mayor of Nashville.

Athletics Director David Williams, the man who found and hired Franklin, considered the coach one of his good friends. Vanderbilt had never much committed to football before, but with Williams in Franklin's corner, Vanderbilt was finally starting to do things behind the scenes to ensure the program would stay competitive, such as completing the $31 million indoor practice facility that Franklin had wanted.[4]

Franklin was one of the more PR-savvy coaches in SEC history, and it would have been difficult to imagine a scenario under which he could lose all that goodwill within days. But the problem with Franklin was that he had mastered the art of saying whatever best suited him in a given situation, and now, it was about to bite him.

When Bill O'Brien left Penn State for the Houston Texans, Franklin soon moved to the top of the list of candidates, along with Miami's Al Golden. In a way, going to Penn State made sense. Franklin was from Pennsylvania and had resources there he could never get at Vanderbilt—among other things, an enormous stadium and a huge fan base. Those had been two things that Franklin had been dissatisfied with during his Vandy tenure.

But Penn State was also a complete mess. The Jerry Sandusky rape scandal had resulted in PSU getting hit with major probation as well as the ouster of its president and athletics director. It had an

---

4 The indoor practice facility had been started after Franklin's first year, and completed in October 2013.

interim president and a new athletics director whose competency had been questioned. Many who had presided over the botched Sandusky affair were still on the board.

In spite of that, rumors had started to spread in Birmingham that Franklin coveted the PSU job. Franklin ducked the media, hiding out at a vacation home in Pensacola, Florida, all week before heading to Pasadena, California, to help ESPN with its coverage of the BCS National Championship Game between Florida State and Auburn. All along, Vanderbilt officials refused to let the media speak to him. Despite keeping most of the media at arm's length, Franklin had privately told a few members of the national media that he was indeed heading to Penn State. The only hitch was that he had to wait for formal approval from the PSU board the next Saturday.

When news that Franklin was leaving started to leak, Franklin denied that he had made up his mind. His players, of course, had also wanted to know whether he might be leaving. When he eventually left, several players were upset, though as Butler would say, it was the way it happened rather than the fact that it happened.

"Now, if [Franklin] repeatedly told us, 'If they give me X amount of money, I'll leave,' or, 'If they don't give me this amount of money, I'll stay,' [we'd understand]," Butler said. "[Be] straight-forward with your own players, you know. Be true to your players. But he repeatedly told us he wasn't leaving and then all of a sudden, he up-and-left."

Franklin officially broke the news in a players-only meeting at McGugin Center that Saturday, a week after the bowl game. There was no press conference, as VU's departing head coach sprinted in and out of the building in an effort to avoid fans and media. Franklin offered each player a chance for a quick hug and a good-bye, which some took while others did not.

Obviously, the fact that Franklin had not been honest with Williams, despite their friendship, upset a lot of fans and people inside Vanderbilt. To make matters worse, there were plenty of fall-outs from Franklin's departure. Franklin had apparently known for days what he was going to do, and while he allegedly got a jump-start on his new job, Vanderbilt was unable to get a head start on replacing him.

The time lapse also poisoned VU's recruiting, as signing day was less than a month away. Recruits hate uncertainty, and many had already begun to ponder shopping around. Even though it was an NCAA-mandated "dead period," during which coaches couldn't initiate contact with recruits, two of Franklin's Vanderbilt recruits changed their commitments to Penn State by the end of the weekend.

Eventually, about two-thirds of the recruiting class that Franklin had assembled at Vanderbilt de-committed and three additional Vanderbilt-committed recruits wound up at Penn State. Many recruiting analysts said the gutting of the VU class was virtually unprecedented. Ultimately, Vanderbilt scrambled until it officially hired Stanford assistant Derek Mason to replace Franklin a week after Franklin's official departure.

In spite of that, history shows that Franklin was the perfect coach for Vanderbilt at the time. Nobody in their wildest dreams would have suspected that the Commodores would go 24–15 and finish in the Top 25 twice in just three years. In spite of the ending, there's no doubt that Franklin left Vanderbilt in a better place; even if Mason takes the program to bigger things, Franklin will always be remembered as the father of the great turnaround that for decades seemed would never happen.

James Franklin celebrates with his players after Vanderbilt defeats North Carolina State in the 2012 Music City Bowl. (Mike Rapp)

PART II:
MEN'S BASKETBALL

2003–04 Basketball: A sweet ending

After Vanderbilt hired coach Kevin Stallings in 1999, his first four seasons weren't what the school envisioned.

Athletics Director Todd Turner nabbed one of the nation's top up-and-coming basketball coaches from Illinois State, two years after Stallings had made the NCAA Tournament in back-to-back seasons. The success had not translated. In four years in Nashville, Stallings had not yet been to the NCAAs. Heading into 2003–04, he was coming off an 11–18 season that included a 3–13 mark in the Southeastern Conference. The last time a VU team had performed that poorly was 1977–78, when Wayne Dobbs's team went 10–17. Four years in, Stallings's overall record was 62–59 and just 21–43 in the Southeastern Conference.

Making matters worse, the team had lost 10 of its final 11 games to end the 2002–03 season. In one, a 106–44 loss at Kentucky, the team appeared to quit. Stallings raised eyebrows when he had publicly questioned whether he was the guy to reach his players, something others had already questioned amid the transfer of key players.

Vanderbilt has long shown a patience with coaches that few other major institutions have. But everyone, including Stallings, knew that time was running out. With three senior starters and a pair of highly regarded rising sophomores, 2003–04 needed to be a special year. As Vanderbilt took the floor in its opener three miles from campus at Belmont's new Curb Event Center on November 21, this would either be the beginning of something better, or the end of Stallings's Vandy career.

A strong start

The last thing Vanderbilt needed to do was to open a season by losing to a school that had recently moved up from the NAIA. Midway through the second half, it looked like a possibility. The Commodores held a 47–40 lead, but behind senior forward Matt Freije's 24 points, Vandy went on an 18–2 run and got a 74–59 win.

Indiana came to Vanderbilt three nights later. The Hoosiers had been national runners-up just two years earlier and had beaten VU by 17 in Bloomington the previous season. But this wasn't the same kind of IU team and Vandy jumped on it early, leading 31–21 at the half. Freije had 32 points and hit all 18 of his foul shots, and defensive ace Jason Holwerda limited Bracey Wright to 18 points after he'd gotten 31 the prior year. The Commodores coasted to a 73–60 win in front of 12,478 enthused fans at Memorial Gym.

That night, you could start to see that Stallings had some pieces to really improve over the disastrous 2002–03 campaign. Freije, the preseason SEC Player of the Year, was adept at scoring from both the inside and outside. VU had a pair of competent guards in senior Russell Lakey and sophomore Mario Moore; Lakey was reserved and content to dish the ball to teammates and let them make plays, while the boisterous Moore liked the limelight and wasn't afraid to shoot anywhere, any time. Holwerda wasn't much of a shooter, but was an explosive finisher around the rim as well as a terrific defender. Forwards Scott Hundley and Corey Smith were versatile players who were also outstanding defensively. Freshman shooting guard Dan Cage provided distance shooting, and sophomore guard Adam Payton offered some athleticism off the bench in an emergency. In the front court, athletic Julian Terrell and Ted Skuchas were respectable complementary players, and Dawid Przybyszewski was the team's best shooter.

Matt Freije (35) and Jason Holwerda jostle for position in the lane.
(Mike Rapp)

Freije was the team's only star, but if everyone else played up to his potential and there was selflessness and cohesion, there was some potential. The big question was whether Stallings could get the 'Dores to compete at a high level from start to finish. The team's trip to Spain for an exhibition tour had made the team tighter, and now it was showing on the floor.

When VU routed Tennessee-Martin and came back from a nine-point deficit to beat IUPUI by 18, those were steps in the right direction. When Moore and Holwerda played sick, and Terrell played with foul trouble, and yet VU still managed to beat a 4–0 Michigan team by an 83–63 margin next, that raised some eyebrows.[1]

Consecutive home blowouts of Tennessee State, Tennessee Tech, Wofford, and Appalachian State followed. On January 3, VU took its first out-of-town road trip of the season to Texas Christian, which resulted in a 95–60 Vandy rout.

---

1 Michigan won the NIT that season.

Conference play was four days away. Three weeks earlier, the Commodores had cracked the AP Top 25 and now had moved all the way to 20th. However, other than the game with Lehigh, Vandy had not faced a team that would make the NCAA Tournament and even then, Lehigh made it only to the tournament's opening game in which it lost to fellow 16-seed Florida A&M. The 16-game SEC schedule would feature eight games against teams that would head to the NCAA Tournament, and five more against NIT-bound teams. That would reveal how good VU really was.

No easy ones

Auburn was not one of the teams that would make either post-season tournament, but the Tigers proved to be a tough challenge in the conference opener, anyway. Vanderbilt blew a 14-point half-time lead and trailed 53–48 with 5:32 left. The defense clamped down and Auburn did not score again. Vandy had cut the lead to one when Lakey hit a huge three pointer from the top of the key and then got a big steal on the other end. Lakey hit two big foul shots moments later, and VU's 12th win in a row established a school record to start a season.

Vanderbilt went to Rupp Arena with the hopes of avenging last year's blowout to Kentucky, and the 'Dores were within 2 with 5:51 left. UK went on an 18–8 run to end the game though, and the Wildcats had a 75–63 win. A second loss followed when Tennessee beat the 'Dores in Knoxville by a 76–66 count.

The Commodores had to get Freije, who was 12-for-41 from the field in three league games, going again. Stallings said he "kind of spent the day" with Freije two days prior to the coming Florida game in an effort to get him jump-started. His star got 15 first-half points and got to the line 10 times that night, hitting nine of those tries. Vandy got up 29–20 early and the sellout crowd of 14,168 fans was rocking Memorial Gym like it hadn't in years. Still, the Gators went on a run before the break and went to the locker room up 32–31.

Mario Moore guards Kentucky's Cliff Hawkins in Vandy's epic home win over Kentucky in 2004. (Mike Rapp)

Whereas Freije owned the first half, Moore, with 18 points after the break on just six shots, owned the second. Smith had his best all-around career game to that stage of his career with 14 points, seven boards, six assists, and three steals in 28 minutes. VU shot 53 percent from the field, 67 percent from three point range, and 75 percent from the line, and the Gators, who'd been ranked No. 1 just a couple weeks earlier, fell 86–72.

Vandy had a week off before heading to Arkansas, where the Razorbacks, which would be an SEC-worst 4–12 that winter, got one of those four victories in Fayetteville on January 24, thanks to the 'Dores's chilly 37.7 percent shooting. Vandy now needed a win against pesky South Carolina in Nashville to get back to .500 in the league.

Late January was the time of the year when the 'Dores had started to fizzle in recent seasons. The previous season's squad was also 3–4 at this juncture of the season. It was a tense evening from the beginning, and the 'Dores lost Smith when he and Carolina's Renaldo Balkman were both ejected for fighting in the first half.[2]

2 Smith's ejection may have been mildly unfair; Balkman had been looking for a fight all night and threw the first punch.

There were 18 lead changes in the game and Freije (26 points, 11 rebounds) made sure Vandy was in it until the end. In the final seconds, Carolina's Josh Gonner missed a layup, but Kerbrell Brown tipped in the miss with 1.9 seconds left, and the Gamecocks left Nashville with a 57–55 win.

It was a frustrating time for the Commodores. Foul shooting had recently gone south for Vandy, which had been one of college basketball's leaders there earlier in the season. The team looked as if it had lost confidence and maybe even some focus, as nobody boxed Brown out on the last play.

With Smith suspended for the next contest, the last thing probably needed was another game with Kentucky, which had beaten Vanderbilt four games in a row and 22 of the previous 23 meetings. The Wildcats were ranked fifth in the country, but when Vanderbilt hit its first six 3s, including three from Przybyszewsi, Vandy led 23–12 and the Memorial Gym crowd roared. The 'Cats clawed back with a 16–2 run to go up two before a Commodore spurt gave VU a 40–35 lead at halftime.

Stallings threatened his starters by saying they'd all be benched if Kentucky had a second-half run, so after UK scored the half's first eight points, the coach followed through. It didn't immediately work, and UK now led 53–43 with 13:07 left. Vandy chipped away and got within one on Lakey's layup, but UK went back up 58–52 before Cage hit a pair of free throws and Przybyszewski added a field goal.

Kentucky's Cliff Hawkins hit a jump shot with 3:10 left, but those would be the 'Cats' last points. Freije hit a layup at 2:51 to get within two, and then Cage hit a three pointer from the left side that put Vandy up one. A Freije foul shot pushed the margin to two.

In the final minute, Lakey stripped Hawkins of the ball in the open court and was fouled. He missed the front end of a one-and-one, but Freije tapped the miss to Hundley, who got fouled and then hit a pair of free throws to ice the game with 14 seconds left. Vandy had a 66–60 win and was now back to within a game of .500 in the SEC.

"I could not be happier and more proud of our team," Stallings said. "We're staring bad news down the face in the second half.

We get down 10 and get out-scored by a bundle to start the second half. I was really impressed with how our players responded and came back, and, as we've been talking about for some time, made winning plays."

"They are staying composed even when they're behind," UK coach Tubby Smith said of the Commodores. "That's why they're one of the top teams in the country."

Florida exacted revenge in Gainesville as the 'Dores lost that one at the foul line; Florida hit 89.7 percent of its 39 free throws, while Vandy managed to hit just 55 percent of its 20 in an 81–71 Gator victory.

The 'Dores managed much better in their next game, hitting 19 of 20 charity tosses against Georgia in Nashville. It helped that UGA's leading scorer, Rashad Wright, was sidelined that night with a sprained ankle, forcing coach Dennis Felton to play several walk-ons. Stallings employed a zone for much of the evening, and the Bulldogs shot just 28.3 percent in VU's 61–39 win. It was the fewest points the Commodores had allowed in a game since 1993.

But Vandy had to go to Carolina, which had beaten the 'Dores six of the last seven times, and it didn't go well once again. The Gamecocks raced to a 16-point first-half lead and led by double-digits almost the entire time from there.

Vanderbilt was now 0–5 on the road in the SEC, and needed to stop the skid at Alabama's Coleman Coliseum, where VU had dropped 12 of the last 14 games it had played there. Freije was unstoppable out of the gate, outscoring 'Bama by himself in the first 10 minutes as the 'Dores led 28–9.

At halftime, the lead was 42–24, but the 'Dores suddenly lost their touch. When 'Bama's Chuck Davis rammed home a dunk with 4:43 left, the game was tied at 60. But the game became a foul-shooting contest down the stretch, and thanks to a 14-of-18 performance there plus 32 from Freije, VU left Tuscaloosa a 70–67 victor.

The Commodores returned to Nashville with a chance to get back to .500 in league play against LSU. Vandy started slowly, hitting just 29 percent of its first-half shots and trailed by six at the break. The second period was a different story, with VU hitting 64 percent after the break. Przybyszewski and Freije each hit 3-point shots to tie the game early in the half, and Holwerda threw down two of the better dunks that Memorial Gym had ever seen in a 12–4 VU run midway through the second half. Freije had 23 and Przybyszewski had 21 (on just nine shots) as Vanderbilt routed the Tigers by a 74–54 count.

"We had one of our best practices of the year yesterday. I was not surprised we played well. I was surprised it took us 20 minutes to get there," Stallings said.

The schedule didn't ease up; Ole Miss was one of the league's worst teams (it would finish 5–11 that year), but Vanderbilt had lost eight straight games at the Tad Smith Coliseum dating back to the 1988–89 season. The 'Dores blew a 12-point halftime lead, and then blew open a tight game with a late 18–2 run and clinched it by hitting 11-of-12 foul shots down the stretch. Freije (20 points) became the program's all-time leading scorer, and Przybyszewski scored 16 for his sixth-straight game in double-figure scoring in a 77–65 victory.

Vandy came home to face eventual league champion Mississippi State. Freije had 26, but MSU killed the 'Dores on the offensive glass late in the game and walked out a 72–69 winner.

Another close home game followed when Tennessee led the 'Dores nearly the entire evening until Vandy clawed back late. At the two-minute mark, Freije hit a three-pointer to give VU its first lead since the game's first minute. A fantastic spin move in the lane by Lakey pushed it to three with 57 seconds left. Vandy held on to win 61–58, thanks to 31 from Freije, who'd taken a physical beating from the Vols all night while playing in his last home game along with fellow seniors Lakey, Hundley, and Martin Schnedlitz.

"There's not a better way I can imagine leaving Memorial Gym, us four seniors, than beating UT, and not only beating them, but beating them the way we did," Freije said.

The 'Dores had a chance to finish two above .500 in the SEC, but as was normally the case, things didn't go Vandy's way at Georgia's Stegeman Coliseum. The Bulldogs were a torrid 10-of-16 from long distance, and VU managed just 6-of-16 from the free-throw line. Freije had one of the worst games of his season, hitting 3-of-11 for eight points in a 71–61 loss.

At 19–8 overall and 8–8 in a strong SEC, the 'Dores were probably going back to the NCAA Tournament, but nobody wanted to take any chances. A big showing in the SEC Tournament, which started five days later, could prove to be important.

Vanderbilt came out like it wanted it, clobbering Ole Miss, 70–50, behind 17 from Przybyszewski and eight assists from Lakey, who supervised an efficient offense that shot 51.1 percent and had just 11 turnovers. Vanderbilt was almost assuredly in the NCAA Tournament field, but a rematch versus MSU gave it a chance to improve its seed.

It was classic tournament basketball. Vandy trailed 34–28 at the half and then 41–30 in the second half, but the 'Dores hit back with a quick succession of punches, starting with Smith's three-point shot with 16:18 left and Terrell's layup. Lakey stole the in-bounds pass, and Moore got a layup off that trip. In the blink of an eye, it was a four-point game, and though MSU would hold a six- or seven-point lead for much of the rest of the night, the Commodores always hung around.

It would not be a great offensive night for Vandy, which hit 37.1 percent of its shots as Freije connected just five times on 14 tries. Rebounding was still an issue, as MSU collected offensive rebounds at a 41.6 percent rate, but that was better than the 50 percent VU had allowed in the earlier defeat. After getting just nine offensive boards in the earlier game, the 'Dores collected 22 of their 44 misses that night. And, the defense couldn't have been much better than it had been that night, with State hitting just 36.8 percent of its shots. Terrell played his best game of the season with 11 points and did a tremendous job on SEC Player of the Year Lawrence Roberts, who was only 4-of-12 from the field that night.

Vandy trailed by two with 58.6 seconds left, when Moore hit a three pointer from the left side. Roberts hit a pair of free throws with 48 seconds left to put State back up. The Bulldogs went to a 2–3 zone, and Freije found an opening inside and was fouled. The senior hit the second of two foul shots to tie the game with 33.8 seconds left.

With the shot clock off, MSU controlled its fate. Vandy went man-to-man with Lakey and Holwerda, hounding the State guards and pushing them outside the three point arc. VU hedged on Roberts's screen and point guard Timmy Bowers found himself double-teamed near the sideline with the clock hitting four seconds. He lobbed a pass between the circles to Roberts, which Holwerda nearly stole. Instead, Roberts collected it and fired a desperation 25-footer that hit the back rim, sending the game to overtime.

A driving Lakey fed Freije for a layup with 2:02 left that put Vandy up three. Clinging to a one-point lead with under a minute remaining, Lakey turned the ball over near midcourt, and as MSU raced for the go-ahead bucket, Moore sprinted down the floor and intercepted a bounce pass. MSU fouled the sophomore, and with 36.9 seconds left, he hit one foul shot. State threw the ball away on its next trip, and when Smith hit two free throws with 20.2 left, Vandy had a 74–70 win that probably cost the Bulldogs, who finished the season 25–3, a one seed in the NCAA Tournament.

"They played well and hit big shots. Mario Moore and Russell Lakey controlled the tempo of the game, and Julian Terrell was a force inside. Vanderbilt's play on the defensive boards was a huge difference in this game," Mississippi State coach Rick Stansbury said.

In the tournament's quarterfinals, Vandy played a Florida team that had an extra day's rest. The 'Dores trailed 40–38 at halftime, but the tired legs showed up in the second half as one jump shot fell short after another. Vandy was outshot 62.7 percent to 36.8, and the Gators ran away with a 91–68 win.

Vandy, though, had done more than enough to earn its first NCAA Tournament bid in seven years. It headed back to Nashville anticipating the release of the bracket the next evening.

An extended dance

The Commodores drew a six seed, and immediately became a popular upset pick from some commentators, including the *Boston Globe*'s Bob Ryan, who said that Vanderbilt "had too many white guys" to beat 11th-seeded Western Michigan. At 26–4 with a 45 RPI, the Broncos, winners of both the Mid-American regular season and tournament titles, would be a tough draw. It's rare that a six seed is an underdog, but Las Vegas made WMU a two-point favorite for a Friday afternoon game in Orlando.

Vanderbilt played into the critics' hands early, as it was sloppy with the ball and had defensive lapses that helped WMU star Mike Williams to 16 points at the half. Western led 34–31 at the break.

"He was on fire," Smith said later. "We tried different guys on him, and he still found a way to score."

Stalling was hot with his team, telling Freije at halftime that he "couldn't guard anybody." With 16 minutes left, Smith, who had guarded Williams, picked up his fourth foul. Freije was now charged with guarding the Bronco star.

"I just tried my hardest to keep him in front of me and limit his touches, and try to contest every shot he took," Freije said later.

Williams went 3-for-10 in the second half. The rest of the VU defense did its job, too, as WMU, a 38 percent shooting team from three point range that year, hit just 2-of-19 behind the arc. The Commodores fought back to take the lead when Cage hit a three pointer with 10:59 left, but couldn't extend it.

With the game on the line, Moore took over. He buried a three point shot to put the 'Dores up 58–53 with 4:34 left and later, connected on a pair of leaners for a 10-point lead. The Nashville native went 7-of-7 from the field in the second half, and the 71–58 final made it look easier than it had been. It was VU's first NCAA Tournament victory since 1993.

Moore fired back at the team's critics, who'd called Vandy "soft" afterward.

"I think it's funny. If they make those assumptions, they really don't know how hard we worked in the summer and how hard we worked all year," he said.

Again, Vanderbilt would be underdogs in Sunday afternoon's game against North Carolina State, the three seed in the Phoenix Region. Vandy led by three at the break and by as much as eight in the second half, but N.C. State's Ilian Evtimov was a one-man wrecking crew who took over and put State ahead. He hit 10-of-13 shots for 28 points that day, and the Wolfpack held what looked like a comfortable 67–56 lead with under 3 ½ minutes to play.

Slowly, though, everything started to unravel for N.C. State.

With 3:26 left, Marcus Melvin fouled Freije on a missed three point attempt and the senior hit the free throws. State star Julius Hodge answered with a follow-up of his own miss, but he fouled out hacking Freije on a three pointer. Again, Vandy's star hit each foul shot.

The Wolfpack's Engin Atsur broke free for a back-door layup to stretch the lead back to nine at 2:27, but the 'Dores inbounded quickly as Lakey raced up the floor, turned, and stopped between the circles and scooped an underhanded pass to Freije, who didn't even hesitate for a split second to fire from about 26 feet. The ball hit the front of the rim, and then the backboard, and then the front of the rim again before dropping through. The lead was six with 2:17 to play.

Vandy was now feeling it. The 'Dores went into a rare full-court press that called for trapping the ball handler when warranted. That rattled the Wolfpack. Hundley left his man to jump a bounce pass and knocked it loose, dropping to his knees and flipping the ball to a charging Smith, who was winning a footrace to the hoop. Melvin slapped his right arm from behind, and then inadvertently bumped him to the floor.

Everyone knew it was a foul, but when the trailing official surprisingly whistled it as intentional, most everyone was stunned. Smith hit both shots with 1:51 left. On the next possession, Moore went left off a high screen from Freije, and with a taller defender in his face hit a 23-footer with 1:43 left.

Atsur missed a three pointer and Lakey rebounded, Holwerda found Freije open in the left corner, and when the senior got around a defender with a dribble after a pump fake, he nailed an 18-footer. With 53.7 seconds left, Vandy now led by 1. Hundley fouled Evtimov on the low block, and the sophomore calmly nailed both ends of a one-and-one with 33.6 seconds left to give the Wolfpack a 73–72 lead.

Moore ran the point on Vandy's next trip. He trotted to the left sideline and then circled back to the top of the key, where Smith approached him from the right as if he'd either get a pass or set a screen. But Smith instead cut 90 degrees toward the hoop. Holwerda had shuffled toward the right corner, leaving his defender with his back exposed to the hoop. Meanwhile,

Przybyszewski was vacating the low block on the left side of the floor and taking his defender to the sideline.

Smith sprinted down the right side just outside the foul lane and his defender quickly realized what was happening. Moore had just inches to deliver a bounce pass. If Vanderbilt ran the same play 1,000 more times, it wouldn't have executed it better than it did just then. Smith caught the ball, set his feet, and launched a layup just as Przybyszewki's defender realized what was happening and turned around. Smith was hacked in the face and on the chest, but banked it in anyway with 21.1 seconds left.

Smith turned and pumped his fist toward the T.D. Ameritrade crowd. N.C. State huddled in disbelief. Smith collected himself and hit the free throw, and Vandy led by two.

As the Wolfpack got into their half-court set, it was as if the 'Dores knew everything State was trying to do. Nothing was developing. Atsur had the ball between the circles with eight seconds left and saw Lakey closing in, Smith and Hundley flanking him to the left and right. Atsur drove right and Smith cut him off. He backtracked and went right where Hundley stone walled him. With two seconds left, he had no choice but to launch a 28-footer. Hundley seemed to get a finger on it and it fell feet short as time expired.

The arena and the VU bench erupted. Vanderbilt players raced around the floor as Hodge, perhaps feeling responsible for triggering the run, sobbed uncontrollably on the bench. Freije, now tearing up for a different reason, had scored 31 points, a school record for an NCAA Tournament game. The Commodores had not missed a shot, whether that had been a three-pointer or a free throw—there were 11 of the latter—in the last 4:48.

Vandy, which had been dead last among the SEC's 12 teams the previous year, had made its first Sweet 16 since 1993.

Huskies prove too tough

Vanderbilt would draw second-seeded Connecticut in Phoenix next. Everyone knew the run was realistically over; the Huskies had six players—Emeka Okafor, Ben Gordon, Charlie Villanueva, Hilton Armstrong, Marcus Williams, and Josh Boone—who would eventually play in the NBA, while the only one VU had was Freije.

UConn led by 22 in the first half, and though Vandy cut it to just seven with 12:08 left, a viewer had the distinct feeling that the Huskies were just toying with Vanderbilt. Sure enough, UConn went on a 21–7 run to end the game by a 73–53 score.

But there was no shame in it ending there. The Huskies then beat Alabama by 16, Duke by 1, and Georgia Tech by 9, as coach Jim Calhoun won his second of three national titles. As for Vandy, the 'Dores finished 23–10 and ranked 25th in the final Coaches' Poll. It was the first time VU had been ranked in that poll since February 3.

No doubt, that season had saved Stallings's job, and it proved him to be one of the better Xs and Os coaches in the business.

There would be a couple of steps back in the years ahead, but it was the start of a greater trajectory for the program in the decade to come.

Coach Kevin Stallings shares a laugh at a press conference during the 2003–04 season. (Mike Rapp)

2006–07 Basketball:
Almost elite

Coach Kevin Stallings had brought Vanderbilt basketball back to relevancy with the magical end to the 2003–04 season. It seemed that better things were ahead. Stallings had signed a highly regarded class of DeMarre Carroll, Shan Foster, Alex Gordon, Alan Metcalfe, and Davis Nwankwo, all of whom entered Vanderbilt the

Dan Cage's ability to capably man the power forward spot despite his size limitations was a huge key to VU's success in the 2006–07 season. (Mike Rapp)

next season. Virginia's Derrick Byars, who had nearly come to Vandy out of high school, transferred that off-season and was eligible for 2005–06. The 2005 signing class of George Drake and Kyle Madsden was a bust, but adding Jermaine Beal and LSU transfer Ross Neltner in 2006 proved huge.

Everyone understood that 2004–05 was going to be a transition year, and so the 20–14 record that included eight Southeastern Conference wins and two more in the NIT wasn't a disappointment. But with those recruiting classes, combined with seniors Mario Moore and Julian Terrell, it was one of the more talented rosters that Stallings would ever coach. An NCAA bid was a minimal expectation.

The squad started 9–1, but there were early signs of trouble. Moore was suspended early in the season (it was later revealed that he failed a drug test), and when Stallings went out of his way to make an example of his senior, the two clashed behind the scenes all season. Stallings's abrasive manner also rubbed others the wrong way. There was little joy in the team's 17–13 season, which ended in a first-round NIT loss at Notre Dame.

Afterward, Carroll, who'd later play in the NBA, transferred to Missouri, and Nwankwo, whose heart had literally stopped and caused him to collapse during a March 6, 2006, practice, was also done with hoops per doctor's orders. If Stallings were to get back to the NCAAs, he'd have to do with a roster decidedly less talented than the previous season's.

After seven years and just one NCAA Tournament during Stallings's career, not to mention a 44–68 SEC record, the excuses were getting old and Stallings knew it. It would be time to put up, or get out, that spring.

Teetering on the edge of collapse

As the calendar year 2006 wound down, it looked as if Stallings would not survive the season. Vandy was waxed at home, 86–70, by Georgetown in the season opener, and a 10-point loss to a Wake Forest team that would go 15–16 followed. After a 9-point defeat of lowly Elon, the Commodores needed some late-game heroics by the freshman Beal to survive the Toledo game at home.

Three games later, VU got an unexpected win over No. 25 Georgia Tech, but an upset loss in overtime to Appalachian State in Puerto Rico dropped Vandy to 8–4. The Commodores picked up two wins over subpar Alabama A&M and Rice squads just before conference play started. When the 'Dores lost 68–65 to an Auburn team that would go 17–15 and wouldn't make a postseason tournament, it seemed fair for fans to start speculating about a new coach.

In the midst of a bad year, there's one thing that always energizes Vanderbilt fans, and that's a visit from Tennessee. Stallings's mediocrity was magnified by the fact that his rival to the east, Vol coach Bruce Pearl, had taken a team that went 14–17 (and lost its two leading scorers) to a 22–8 mark and a No. 2 seed in the NCAA Tournament during the prior season, his first in Knoxville.

Pearl had the 16th-ranked Vols rolling along at 13–2 coming into that January 10 evening at Memorial Gym. When UT's Duke Crews threw down a two-handed dunk with 4.7 seconds left, the Commodores, who once led by double digits, now trailed by a point.

The 'Dores had one last chance. Byars, who had a world of talent but not the aggressive streak to go with it, had started to take charge that night. Neltner got him the ball and Byars dribbled down the right side of the lane for what looked like it would be a wide-open dunk. But UT's Ramar Smith floated over at the last minute and Byars flung the ball at the goal as the seconds ticked down.

The ball missed everything but the backboard. Had the clock run out then, it would have seemed like a fitting ending. Instead, the fractions of a second ahead would prove predictive of where the season was heading.

A second chance

Stallings has always said that in defending last-second shots, the most dangerous guy on the floor is the one in position to grab an offensive rebound. The Vols failed to defend the weak side

Shan Foster tips in a missed shot at the buzzer, giving Vanderbilt a home win against Tennessee. (Mike Rapp)

where Foster grabbed the basketball as it careened off the glass. Before his feet hit the floor, he threw it back toward the backboard, where it banked and rolled around the rim. It hung on the front rim for a split second and looked as if it might fall out, but instead, fell into the net as the buzzer sounded. Foster and teammates sprinted deliriously around the floor in celebrating a win that gave the program some new life.

"We have a little bit of a grudge against those guys," said Cage, who'd scored 15. "They swept us last year, but more than anything, it's a morale boost for us. . . . To beat a legit team like UT definitely gives us confidence."

Cage could not have been more correct, though it would still take a bit to get there. Vanderbilt went to Georgia, and fell 85–73 at the Stegeman Coliseum, which was not unusual, as the 'Dores had lost five of their last six there. As soon as the team returned to Nashville, the rest of the season began.

Shan Foster ended his career as Vanderbilt's all-time leading scorer. (Mike Rapp)

Rebirth

There were other reasons to think that the 'Dores might be headed for a turnaround, and they started with Cage. Vanderbilt was not a tall team anyway, and VU was dealt what looked like a serious blow when Metcalfe, the team's starting center, went down with a broken foot against Wake on November 21. Out of desperation, Stallings had moved Cage to the 4 spot. Cage was 6-foot-4 and wasn't particularly athletic, which could lead to some defensive problems. It also didn't help that Neltner, at 6-foot-7, was now the team's starting center by default.

However, Cage could shoot the lights out, and VU was now a nightmare to defend. Byars and Foster were also exceptional outside shooters and the trio all combined to shoot better than 44 percent from three point range that year. Gordon, though primarily a pass-first point guard, came within an eyelash of shooting

Shan Foster, Alan Metcalfe, and Ross Neltner celebrate a big win at Memorial Gym with their fellow students in the crowd. (Mike Rapp)

40 percent from behind the arc that season also. Even Neltner could step out and drain the occasional three pointer when needed.

The interplay between the five on offense would soon create more problems than having an undersized power forward would create on defense. Tenth-ranked Alabama learned the hard way when the 'Dores, led by Foster (27 points), Byars (15), Neltner (14), Cage, and Gordon (12 each), blistered the nets as the team shot 15-of-28 from three point range that evening, coasting to a 94–73 win at Memorial Gym.

As big a disappointment as the previous year had been, it had included a surprising upset of Kentucky in Lexington; the teams met annually there but that had not happened since 1974. That, and the two recent wins over ranked teams, gave the Commodores the confidence to do it again. VU trailed by a point with three minutes left, but Foster hit an 18-footer and then a steal and a feed to Byars for a fast-break layup.

When Cage hit a three pointer with 1:13 left, the lead was six and the game was effectively over. Byars (23 points) and Foster (16) had led the way to a 72–67 win.

Back-to-back road wins over ranked teams have been virtually nonexistent in VU hoops history, but after a 64–53 win at Louisiana State, the 'Dores had done it again. Vanderbilt led by 17 with 10 minutes to play, and when LSU closed to within six with 2:56 remaining, Foster, a native of nearby Kenner, Louisiana, answered with a layup and then a three pointer. Byars (18 points, 10 rebounds) again led the way.

Suddenly, Vanderbilt was 14–6 and 4–2 in the SEC and knocking on the door of the Top 25 itself. The schedule eased up when NIT-bound Ole Miss visited Memorial, but it wasn't easy.

Vandy blew a 15-point halftime lead and watched as the Rebels took a one-point advantage midway through the half. Neltner hit a pair of free throws with 2:22 left and then a put-back of Gordon's blocked layup, and when the 'Dores hit their free throws down the stretch, they had their first four-game league winning streak since 1996–97. The national ranking followed on Monday when the AP writers placed Vanderbilt 24th. That streak ended when the 'Dores went to top-ranked Florida and fell, 74–64. It wasn't a bad showing; VU led by 11 at halftime, but that evaporated when the Gators scored the first 13 to start the second half.

The 'Dores avenged the loss at Georgia when Byars (20 points) and Cage (19) led Vandy to a 66–61 win, but Vandy followed that with its worst loss of the season in an 84–57 thumping at Tennessee in a contest that was never close. Again, Vanderbilt rebounded with a 10-point win in Nashville over lowly South Carolina, thanks to 11-of-24 shooting from three point range. Byars, now making a serious case for the league's Player of the Year, erupted with a career-high 32 points and missed just four shots.

The double-digit road losses had knocked Vandy out of the polls, but the polls didn't really matter in some ways. The 'Dores had a goal of getting back to the NCAA Tournament for the first time since 2004, and the tournament's selection committee didn't give two hoots about the rankings. It looked at a team's total résumé, and though Vanderbilt had some great wins in January, it still might have some atoning to do for the poor November and December. The Commodores were about to do that, and then some.

Answering the bell

In the age where most great college players go to the NBA after their freshman seasons, it had become extremely difficult to build a dynasty in college basketball. However, Florida coach Billy Donovan was in the midst of doing it. Led by sophomores Joakim Noah, Al Horford, Corey Brewer, and Tauren Green, the Gators, recovering from losing the bulk of the previous season's team, weren't even ranked until the season's third week in 2005–06. Donovan's squad got hot and won the SEC Tournament, and as a three seed in the NCAAs, waltzed through its six NCAA Tournament games—only Georgetown, which UF defeated 57–53 in the Sweet 16, came within 13 points of the Gators—en route to Florida's first NCAA hoops title.

The 24–3 Gators were ranked No. 1 as they visited Memorial Gym on February 17, and were about a month and a half from repeating their title when they'd knock off Ohio State, 84–75, in the 2007 title tilt. They were also riding a 17-game winning streak that included an 11–0 start to SEC play. But in a game that would easily make the short list of best games that a Vanderbilt team had played in its hoops history, the Commodores showed that they could also play at an elite level.

As they had in Gainesville, Vanderbilt raced out to an early lead and was up 35–27 at the break. Stallings later recounted a couple of players mentioning how the 'Dores had blown that big halftime lead so quickly in the first game between the teams, and when Vandy jumped up 13 early in the second half, Commodore fans felt a lot better.

The Gators, though, were too good to stay far down for long. With under 13 minutes left, Donovan's team cut the lead to six. Skuchas answered with a thunderous dunk and after getting fouled by Noah, added a free throw.

The lead was now nine and UF got no closer than eight the rest of the day. Byars and Foster, who had 24 each, were at their absolute best, raining outside jumpers and also getting fast-break points in the open floor. Byars also had eight assists, teaming with Gordon, who had five himself, to supervise an offense that really clicked that day. Neltner (15 points, six rebounds) hit both his three-pointers and played one of the best games of his career. Cage had only five that day, but more importantly, held his own against Horford and Noah defensively.

By the time Vanderbilt had coasted to an 83–70 victory, many in the sellout crowd of 14,316 were likely hoarse. It had been a complete game from almost start to finish. Of the 11 losses that the Gators suffered during those two national championship seasons, only South Carolina, which had beaten UF by 14 the previous year, would hand them a worse defeat.

"This is one for the ages, right here," said Byars, who also had five steals on a day where UF uncharacteristically turned the ball over 22 times. "Twenty years from now, I'll be able to tell my little kids this. I've played in some big games before, but man, sometimes, you're just right there and can't get over the hump. But this one right here, it's just really special."

VU climbed to 17th in the polls the next week before a road trip to Starkville. Perhaps VU was due for a letdown, as it trailed

Mississippi State by 18 at the break before losing by the exact same score by which Vandy had just beaten Florida.

After returning home, Vanderbilt, which trailed by nine at halftime and had played from behind the entire day against Kentucky, was down by two with 29 seconds left when UK's Ramel Bradley fouled Byars on a shot. The senior hit the first free throw and missed the second, but Cage tapped it back to Byars, who hit an eight-footer to give VU a 66–65 lead. Kentucky's Sheray Thomas then lost the ball at midcourt and when Foster seized it, the Wildcats fouled him. He hit one of the two shots, setting up Kentucky's final possession with nine seconds left.

Bradley, guarded by Byars, drove the length of the floor and got to the middle of the lane, where he was met by two more defenders. Bradley threw up an unanswered prayer and as the ball squirted loose on the floor, time expired. VU had a rare regular-season sweep of Kentucky and now, a four-game winning streak in the series also.

An NCAA Tournament bid was now almost a virtual certainty, but for good measure, Foster got 33 and Byars scored 8 of his 18 in overtime as the 19th-ranked 'Dores recovered from blowing a 17-point second-half lead to get a 99–90 win over South Carolina in Columbia.

Vanderbilt now had an opportunity to improve its seeding, but for whatever reason, Senior Day has generally turned into a nightmare for Vanderbilt under Stallings, and an 82–67 loss to Arkansas followed. The Commodores had a shot to avenge that loss in the first round of the SEC Tournament in Atlanta, but Gary Ervin hit a shot with 11 seconds left to give the Razorbacks a 72–71 win.

That ended the regular season on a sour note, but some redemption was around the corner.

Dancing, in style

Once again, the sixth-seeded Commodores were pegged as a possible upset victim by fans and commentators across the country as they prepared for their first-round game against George Washington, which had just won the Atlantic 10 Tournament. ESPN's Doug Gottlieb referred to the Commodores as being "fraudulent as a six seed," though others, like ESPN's Jay Bilas and Hubert Davis, said the 'Dores had what it took to make the Sweet 16.

If you dug deeper into the first-round matchup, though, some things became clearer. While Vanderbilt may have been seeded a bit high due to those early season losses, plus the two straight defeats by Arkansas, GW—which ended that season ranked 94th in stats guru Ken Pomeroy's rankings—may have been a bigger stretch at an 11. The Colonials' only good win that season came over fifth-seeded Southern Cal, which would make the Sweet 16.

The other big thing was this: GW played a 1-3-1 almost exclusively. That was a defense that Vanderbilt had shredded in recent years. In addition, the Commodores, with what was essentially a four-guard lineup, always had someone in position to find a gap in that alignment and get an open look. Sure enough, Vandy hit 10 of its first 12 tries from three-point range in its NCAA Tournament opener.

The shooting cooled off, with the 'Dores hitting just two of their last 19 behind the arc, but it didn't matter. By halftime, the game was practically over, with VU leading 45–20. Stallings cleared the bench, with 10 players playing double-digit minutes. Foster (18 points) led the way in a 77–44 romp, the worst beat down a 6-seed had served to an 11-seed since the NCAA had expanded the field to 64 teams in 1985.

"From the first five minutes in the game, it was just a matter of trying to survive," conceded GW coach Karl Hobbs. "We fell behind quickly, and that pretty much put us on our heels."

On a Saturday night, Vanderbilt now had to knock off third-seeded Washington State to stay alive. It would turn out to be one of the better games of the entire tournament, a matchup of Vanderbilt's terrific offense against one of the country's best defensive teams, coached by one of the nation's best young leaders in Tony Bennett.

Defense won out in the first half, with the Cougars taking a 33–25 lead at the break. Vanderbilt struggled to get into offensive rhythm for much of the game, but when Byars hit a three-point shot with 16:15 left, the 'Dores started to find some offensive momentum. The problem was that the Cougars were scoring, too, but suddenly VU busted out when Gordon hit a three-pointer with 11:24 left, followed by two more three-pointers by Byars on Vandy's next two trips. WSU had gone cold, and when Byars hit another three-pointer at 7:53, Vanderbilt led by four.

But the Cougars crawled back and it became a back-and-forth game down the stretch. With Vanderbilt trailing by two, Foster hit a three-pointer at 1:11, but then Washington State's Kyle Weaver tied the game with a free throw with 46 seconds left. Byars had a shot at a go-ahead layup with 25 seconds left, but Ivory Clark blocked it from behind. When WSU's Daven Harmeling missed an outside shot with four seconds left, Vandy survived to head to overtime.

It was going to be tough, though, as Byars, Foster, and Skuchas all had four fouls. Still, Byars hit a three pointer at the 2:22 mark to put Vandy up by three, and after WSU answered with a two, Byars hit a field goal of his own with 58 seconds left. Again, State answered with a Derrick Low shot outside the paint with 40 seconds left.

Commodore fans watched in horror as State's Taylor Rochestie stole Alex Gordon's in-bounds pass with six seconds left and raced the other way for a layup that seemed would win the game . . . until Byars again saved the day, running the length of the floor and coming from behind to swat the shot out of bounds. The ball went off a State player and Vandy's Foster took a three-pointer at the buzzer, but it didn't fall and the game went to a second overtime.

Skuchas opened double overtime with a pair of free throws, and after Low countered with a jumper, he answered with a layup. At 2:30, Foster stole a pass and rammed it home to put the lead at four. Moments later, Foster picked up another steal and Gordon added a free throw to push the margin to five with 50 seconds remaining.

Harmeling hit another trey to cut it to two and Gordon missed a pair of free throws. State had a shot to win with a three-pointer, but Rochestie misfired with 15 seconds left. Cage rebounded and fed Foster, who iced it with a layup with three seconds left.

With 27 points and one huge season-saving play, the nation saw why the Memphis native had been named the SEC's Player of the Year.

"Considering the stage, this was the best game I've played," Byars said.

With a 78–74 win, VU was now headed to the Sweet 16 for the second time in four seasons.

"That was one of the best college basketball games I've ever been involved in," Stallings said. "And as happy as I am for our team, my heart goes out to Tony Bennett and the Washington State players, because neither team deserved to lose that game."

The shoe would be on the other foot soon.

Robbed

Vanderbilt might not have been one of the best eight teams in the country from start to finish, but it might have been at that moment. The Commodores would get a rematch with Georgetown in New Jersey for a chance to prove it.

The Hoyas scored the game's first four points, but then, VU went on an 18–2 run on a pair of treys and a two-point shot by Cage. The lead bulged to 13 and then VU settled for a 32–24 advantage at the break.

Georgetown stormed back in the second half and took a 39–38 lead on a DaJuan Summers layup. From that point on, neither team ever led by more than four again.

With 4:45 left, that was Vandy's lead when Foster hit a three-pointer, but the Hoyas' Jesse Sapp answered with one of his own 33 seconds later. Georgetown surged ahead by two on Sapp's layup with 2:03 left, and Neltner hit a foul shot to cut it to one before Jonathan Wallace hit a field goal with 1:03 left to put the Hoyas up three. Byars countered with a pair of free throws with 48.8 left to cut the lead back to one.

Vandy caught a break when Patrick Ewing Jr. missed a shot and the Hoyas fouled Cage on the rebound with 17.9 seconds left.

The senior calmly stepped to the line and hit both shots, and VU again led by a point.

The Hoyas called time-out. Sapp got the ball to Jeff Green to the right of the foul line and the Georgetown star started to move, and then fumbled the ball. He appeared to switch pivot feet as two Commodores guarded him just before he put the ball on the floor.

Had the whistle blown then for a travel, only a miracle could have kept Vanderbilt from advancing to the Elite Eight. One never came. Green spun around and banked in about an eight-foot shot and the Hoyas led again.

With just 2.5 seconds left, Vandy got the ball to Gordon, whose desperation shot just inside midcourt was tipped by Sapp and fell well short.

Seniors Byars (17 points, 5 assists) and Cage (17, 4 assists, 7 rebounds) had been great also. But it wasn't quite enough, and the stunned Commodores could only stand and stare while Georgetown celebrated.

Georgetown's Jeff Green, guarded by Shan Foster (left) and Ross Neltner (right), appeared to travel on this play. But officials never blew the whistle and moments later, Green hit the shot that eliminated Vanderbilt from the 2007 NCAA Tournament. (Mike Rapp)

Good enough

That play was the talk of the college basketball world. Everyone knew Green had walked. Stallings declined comment on the play and instructed his players to do the same.

To add insult to injury, North Carolina, Georgetown's next opponent, was vulnerable on Sunday. The Tar Heels missed 22 of their last 23 shots, blowing a 10-point lead in the last six minutes of regulation and then losing 96–84 in overtime.

Had the whistle blown two days before . . . well, who knows? Perhaps the Commodores could have gotten their first Final Four berth.

Instead, Vanderbilt's season was over at 22–12. The Commodores would finish 19th in the final Coaches' Poll. Recruiting was going well. Vanderbilt may not have had its second Elite Eight appearance in school history, but the program had been brought back from the brink of disaster. Losing those seniors would be tough, but sustained success was on the horizon.

2011–12 Basketball: Three days to a title

The 2007–08 season marked the beginning of a transition for Vanderbilt basketball. Coach Kevin Stallings had a nice foundation returning in Jermaine Beal, Alex Gordon, Shan Foster, and Ross Neltner, and when he added polished Australian big man A.J. Ogilvy, things clicked right away. Thanks to a 16–0 start, VU finished 26–7 and got a four seed in the NCAAs. Primarily due to shoddy defense, the team went home after its first game with an embarrassing 83–62 loss to 13th-seeded Siena in the last game for Gordon, Foster, and Neltner.

Thanks to recent success, Vanderbilt had become an attractive place to play basketball. In 2007, Vanderbilt landed Festus Ezeli, a Californian who had never played a game of high school basketball before bursting on the AAU scene late that spring. Literally every program in America wanted him, but the Commodores were one of the few schools that had a scholarship left. Ezeli, who planned to redshirt and study to become a doctor, picked VU.

In the 2008 class, Stallings inked four 4-star prospects[1] in Lance Goulbourne, Jeff Taylor, Steve Tchiengang, and Brad Tinsley to form one of the country's top recruiting classes. The real coup came in 2009, when Gallatin's John Jenkins, who led the country in scoring at over 40 points per game at Station Camp

---

1 All recruiting ratings are according to Rivals.com.

High School, became the only five-star player in the era of online recruiting service to sign with Vandy.

The young 2008–09 team struggled but finished a respectable 19–12. Big things were expected the following season, and the team earned a four seed thanks to a 24–8 overall mark and a 12–4 record in the Southeastern Conference. Again, the Commodores fell as a four seed when Murray State's Danero Thomas hit a 15-footer at the buzzer for a 66–65 upset.

With Ogilvy gone, but just about everyone else back, 2010–11 set up as a potentially historic year. The Commodores, though, underachieved with a 23–11 mark that included just a 9–7 record in the league. Once again, the 'Dores fell in the first round to 12th-seeded Richmond when Kevin Anderson hit a floater in the lane with 18.7 seconds left.

Many thought that Taylor and Ezeli might head for the NBA and forego their junior seasons. Jenkins, who was allegedly privately feuding with Stallings, was thinking of passing on his last two seasons. But by the time fall rolled around, all three decided to return.

Thus, the Commodores found themselves in the unfamiliar position of being ranked seventh in both the major preseason polls after adding a pair of highly regarded guards in Kedren Johnson and Dai-Jon Parker. But those three tournament losses branded the Commodores as a team that had trouble living up to their potential. This was a bunch that needed to prove something before it left campus.

Disaster out of the gate

Before the season even started, the NCAA suspended Ezeli six games for accepting a meal and a hotel room from a Vanderbilt alumnus. Without him, VU opened its season behind 24 points and 11 rebounds from Taylor in a 78–64 win over Oregon, but turned the ball over 21 times in a stunning 13-point home loss to Cleveland State. A home win over NIT-bound Bucknell followed, and then there was a pair of close wins over N.C. State and Oregon State in the TicketCity Legends Classic in New Jersey.

VU handled Monmouth, coached by former Commodore assistant King Rice, easily in its last game before getting Ezeli eligible. But the big man had a creaky knee and wasn't ready to play yet. A mouthy Xavier squad came to Memorial Gym and knocked off the 'Dores by 12 in overtime. Next, VU fell in overtime at Louisville in a game that the 'Dores led by nine with 8:18 left.

Things got worse. Backup center Josh Henderson, who was averaging nine minutes a game with Ezeli still hobbled, broke his foot and would be done for the year. Vandy got Ezeli back and in his season debut, he scored 15 in a 4-point road win over NCAA Tournament–bound Davidson. But when the Commodores returned home, they suffered another defeat in a 61–55 game to an Indiana State squad that eventually went just 18–16.

The 'Dores were now 6–4. Was a season that seemed to hold so much promise going to bring disappointment again?

Taking care of business

The Commodores drilled a pair of subpar teams in Longwood and Lafayette at home before going to Marquette. Coach Buzz Williams had assembled a fine team that would make the Sweet 16 that year, and the Golden Eagles were ranked 13th at the time. That December 29 night in Milwaukee showed how good the Commodores could be when everything clicked.

VU put the game away from the start, leading 35–8 with 7:24 left in the half as MU missed 18 of its first 20 shots. At the break, VU led 44–22 and was able to coast in the second half to a 74–57 victory. The offense clicked for much of the night; VU had assists on 17 of 23 buckets and hit 45.5 percent from three-point range as Taylor (19 points), Jenkins (14), Goulbourne (14), and Tinsley (11) led the way in scoring, while Goulbourne and Taylor played great defense against Marquette's standout backcourt.

It was so surreal at one point it prompted an unusual reaction from Stallings.

"I was sure that I was like in a mirage or something, just seeing things. I tried to stop looking," he said.

The 'Dores had a bit of a letdown against a Miami (Ohio) team that would go 9–21, but managed a 69–62 win. The start of the SEC season, just around the corner, would turn out to be something less than challenging as Auburn, South Carolina, and Georgia, the three teams up first, would be the league's bottom three teams at year's end. Of course, with this bunch, you never quite knew what could happen, but at the same time, several other Commodores had suffered from a variety of lesser injuries—concussions and sprained ankles, to be exact—and now, VU was getting healthier.

The "good" Commodores showed up in the conference opener at Memorial, shellacking Auburn by a 65–35 count with Jenkins (17) and Taylor (16) leading the way. Vandy led 22–12 at halftime at Carolina and built the lead to 24 behind a 13-for-22 performance from three-point range, coasting to a 67–57 victory even as Carolina scored the game's last 14 points. Back home against Georgia, the team got its seventh straight win in a game that Stallings termed "not a thing of beauty," as VU won 77–66 through 18 from Jenkins and 16 from Taylor.

The schedule got much tougher from there.

Getting to the meat

Vanderbilt now played Alabama in Tuscaloosa, and even though the Crimson Tide made the NCAAs that season, Vanderbilt had all the answers. Trailing 17–11 early, VU ended the first half on a 15–2 run and then scored 15 of the second half's first 20 points. VU successfully switched between man-to-man and zone and held 'Bama to 32.9 percent shooting, while Jenkins's 20 helped VU to a 69–59 victory.

But in what was becoming a troubling pattern, the 'Dores lost for the sixth time in their last 14 home games when an NIT-bound

Mississippi State team came to Memorial and left with a 78–77 overtime victory. Vandy led by 11 at halftime, but MSU went on a 19–2 run in the first 4:36 of the second period to take the lead. It extended it to 10 at one point, and Vandy led only briefly (and by one) in overtime. The 'Dores had three cracks at a game-winning shot, but the last one (from Jenkins) clanked off the front rim.

"We had a letdown. That's all there is to it. We didn't have the same mindset we had in the first half. We let the game go," Goulbourne said.

Those were troubling words for a team that had five seniors logging 154 minutes that day. However, "good Vandy" showed up again three nights later at Memorial when the Commodores administered a 65–47 spanking of Tennessee, with Taylor going for 23 points and playing his usual fantastic defense. The offense hadn't been sharp, but as Stallings would say, "It's all about how we play," referring to the fact that the 'Dores held UT to 35.3 percent shooting behind good perimeter defense from Jenkins, who to that point in his career hadn't exactly been known for his capabilities in that area.

In a rare out-of-conference tilt at this time of the season, Middle Tennessee State came to Memorial, and the Blue Raiders, whose physical back court led the team to a 27–7 season that ended three games into the NIT, were a handful. The Blue Raiders led 72–70 with 4:56 left, but Jenkins (26 points) had a layup and a free throw to push Vandy ahead. MTSU answered with a 3, and then Jenkins hit a layup. Tinsley and Goulbourne each hit a pair of free throws in the final 30 seconds, and Vandy escaped with an 84–77 win.

But once again, even a mediocre Arkansas club—it wouldn't even make the NIT—proved too much for Vandy in Fayetteville, winning by an 82–74 count. Subsequently, Taylor had one of his career-best games, scoring 25 at Florida, but 17 turnovers and 41.5 percent shooting did the 'Dores in during a 73–65 loss.

In the next matchup, Vandy trailed NIT-bound LSU four minutes into the second half, but Taylor hit back-to-back three-point shots midway through the second half, and Ezeli, who'd started to play well as he got healthier, had 21 as Vandy won, 76–61. That set up the showdown of the year at Memorial between Vanderbilt and top-ranked Kentucky, which had but one loss in a buzzer beater at Indiana in its 26 games to date.

For the first time in history, ESPN had its GameDay broadcast in Nashville. The sell-out crowd of 14,316, which as usual consisted of a couple thousand blue-clad visiting fans, was treated to a great one. It was such an event that several fans, including some who paid as much for $260 for tickets that turned out to be counterfeit, didn't get in that day.

Vandy trailed by 13 at halftime, at which point VU's senior class kicked into gear. Tinsley's three-pointer with 4:10 left put Vandy up 63–61, but UK answered with an 8–0 run and the Commodores couldn't get over the hump from there, with freshman superstar Anthony Davis making things difficult in the paint for the 'Dores, who missed their last nine shots.

"This was two teams slugging it out, it really was," UK coach John Calipari said. "[Vanderbilt] wasn't going away and we weren't going away. We made some shots, they missed some shots, we won

Festus Ezeli (3) and Jeff Taylor (44) battle with Kentucky's Anthony Davis in a 2012 game at Memorial Gym. (Mike Rapp)

the game. Hats off to Vanderbilt fans. It was a great environment. It is why we do what we do, both players and coaches."

Losing a game that way can often result in an emotional let-down, but Vandy gave perhaps its best effort since the Marquette game in a 102–76 demolition of Ole Miss in Oxford less than a week after the UK game. Vanderbilt shot a blazing 70.8 percent in the first half, aided by a 10-of-12 showing behind the arc. VU led by just 22–21 early, but as Ole Miss missed its next 12 shots, Vandy held a 53–28 edge, with Taylor tallying 23 before the break.

"It was ridiculous," Taylor said. "Everyone got on a roll. When we get on a roll, we're hard to defend."

That was almost an understatement. It was a special night for Taylor, who finished with 28 points and nine boards, and hit 5-of-6 from three-point range. Jenkins was also remarkable, scoring 26 points on only five shots from the field. Jenkins had 28 three days later in Athens in a 61–52 win against Georgia.

Though Jenkins had 21 points on 10 shots from the field and Ezeli had 14 points on four shots, the rest of the team (including Taylor, who had a season-low four points on eight attempts) strug-gled in a win at South Carolina. But one thing was different about this VU team, from that of previous years: it could defend.[2] The 'Dores held both Georgia and Carolina well under 40 percent in shooting, and Stallings, who never doled out an insincere compli-ment, was effusive in praise that day.

"The story of the game was John's defense, particularly on [South Carolina's Bruce] Ellington. It was superb . . . We had nine blocked shots—that's a lot for any team," he said.

It was the season's 20th win, tying Roy Skinner for the most 20-win seasons in Vanderbilt history.

In the next game, after leading by one at the half, Vanderbilt gave Kentucky a run for its money in Lexington, trailing by just one with 4:22 left. But Davis had a career-high 28 points, hitting 10-of-11 shots from the field. The 18-footer that the phenomenal

---

2 Stats guru Ken Pomeroy ranked Vanderbilt 32nd in Adjusted Defensive Effic-iency that season. The previous three seasons, VU ranked 72nd, 70th, and 129th.

freshman hit with 1:08 left proved to be the dagger as the Wildcats secured their 51st-straight home win by an 83–74 margin.

Three days later, on Senior Day, which had been a real minefield for VU in recent years, Vanderbilt played one of its season-best games in scoring a 77–67 win over Florida. Jenkins wasn't a senior, but it would be his last home game as he declared for the NBA Draft later that spring. Again, he was efficient in collecting 22 points on 10 shots. Vandy nearly blew a late lead as UF guards Erving Walker and Bradley Beal kept getting to the hoop again and again, and so Stallings, a staunch man-to-man disciple, switched to a 2-3 zone.

It worked. The Gators kept missing perimeter jumpers while Vandy built its lead at the foul line, where it would go 19-of-26 that Saturday. Meanwhile, Taylor shut down UF's other guard, Kenny Boynton, who needed 10 shots to manage 11 points—6.3 less than his average.

With a chance to clinch second place in the SEC in Knoxville, and perhaps even work its way back into the Top 25, Vanderbilt blew it against an inferior Tennessee squad that had been picked 11th of the SEC's 12 teams in the coaches' preseason poll. The Vols picked up a huge 68–61 win that tied them with Vanderbilt at 10–6 in the league and gave them, and not the 'Dores, the No. 2 seed for the next week's SEC Tournament.

On the bright side, the 'Dores at least had a first-day bye, and that turned out to be important.

Making history

The SEC Tournament started in 1933 and was played every year through 1952, excepting 1935. During that span, VU had one main moment of glory, snapping Kentucky's seven-year winning streak in the event with a stunning 61–57 win.[3] The SEC

---

3 In ESPN's 2009 edition of its *College Basketball Encyclopedia*, it selected a "win for the ages" for each program. That was Vandy's.

held no tournament from 1953 to 1978, and since its resumption in 1979, Vandy's 37.3 winning percentage (20–33) was the worst among the league's 12 teams. Only South Carolina had failed to win a conference tournament title in that span, but nevertheless the Gamecocks had been to the championship game twice; that was twice more than VU.

Playing in New Orleans on a Friday night, Vanderbilt started slowly, trailing Georgia 25–24 at the break, until its defense showed up and saved the day. VU had just eight turnovers to UGA's 17 and outshot the Bulldogs, 43.9 percent to 31.9. Thanks in part to Taylor, Vanderbilt held Georgia's high-scoring guard tandem of Gerald Robinson and Kentavious Caldwell-Pope to three and two points, respectively, on 14 combined shots. A 12–2 run early in the second half gave the Commodores some separation and they'd coast to a 63–41 victory.

On Saturday, conquering Ole Miss wouldn't be as easy as it had been in Oxford, especially when Ole Miss slowed the tempo. Clinging to a 25–23 lead at the break, Vandy trailed by one at 16:12, but the 'Dores got hot, hitting half of their 12 three-pointers after the break behind 23 total points from Jenkins and had a 36–29 edge on the glass.

"On a night when we didn't shoot the ball well, our defense and rebounding won the game for us. That's a good thing, because we have had two nights in a row where we have not shot it particularly well, but our defense has been able to help us win," Stallings said.

Vanderbilt was in its first title game in 61 years, and just as the last time it had played in that game, Kentucky was the opponent. The 'Cats were 31–1 for the season, but Vanderbilt had played them as well as anyone. Taylor matched up well with Michael Kidd-Gilchrist on the wing, and Ezeli was one of the few players in college hoops who could oppose Davis and not get embarrassed. With so many shooters, the Commodores had the kind of players who could spread Kentucky out and get some good looks.[4]

---

4 How good was UK that year? In addition to winning the national title in the coming weeks, the 'Cats finished second in Adjusted Offensive Efficiency and eighth defensively in Pomeroy's rankings.

It felt like a Kentucky home game, with most of the crowd of 18,114 at New Orleans Arena wearing blue. Just as it had in the first half in Lexington, VU played UK toe-to-toe, and the teams were tied at 37 when they went to the lockers. When Darius Miller dunked with 8:04 left, Kentucky led 59–54. Davis added a pair of free throws at 5:23, and UK's lead was seven.

Miller's two-point shot, however, was the last field goal the 'Cats hit that day. VU clawed back within five on two Jenkins foul shots and then Taylor's layup at 4:06 inched VU within three. A Johnson free throw got VU within a bucket and then Ezeli's tip-in at 1:55 tied the game.

Vandy was now playing toe-to-toe with perhaps the best college basketball team of the last decade, and didn't look intimidated. Johnson, now in a time-share with Tinsley for minutes at the point, drove from the left wing, went to the hoop, hit a reverse layup, got fouled, and hit the shot. Davis hit a free throw, but Ezeli rebounded a Johnson miss and hit a pair of free throws.

When Marquis Teague missed a three-pointer with 31 seconds left and Taylor rebounded, all Vandy needed to do now was take care of business. Jenkins hit a pair of free throws with 25 seconds left to put Vandy up by six. UK's Jones hit a free throw, but when Jenkins hit two more with 14 seconds remaining, he gave Vandy a 71–64 lead that accounted for the final.

For all the fanfare that accompanied the senior class, this had previously never been a team that delivered the expected accomplishments in return. But now, this bunch had made history. Stallings, feeling the weight of all the pressure to achieve something combined with the feat of beating a Kentucky juggernaut,[5] sat alone on the bench sobbing uncontrollably, his head buried in a towel.

"I couldn't be happier for my players because this season has had its ups and downs and we have been the target of much criticism, and to my players' credit, they never let that get to them, they never let it create a seam in our squad or let it create any division in anything we did," Stallings said.

---

5 Of the nine players to play for UK that day, six made the NBA.

"They stayed with us all as coaches, they stayed with each other as teammates. This is the result of that sticking together."

Vanderbilt ended the game on a 16–2 run. Kentucky missed its last 14 shots as Stallings went to a zone down the stretch. Taylor's 18 led the way, with Jenkins and Ezeli just behind with 17 each. Jenkins was named the tournament's MVP and Goulbourne joined him on the all-tournament team.

Vandy's three-day run in New Orleans had made for one of the most memorable weekends in Commodore sports history. But time was now running out on the seniors, who knew that items of unfinished business remained.

Parting shots

The seniors had been reminded many times of how they'd failed to win a game in college basketball's premier event. However, the buzz generated from the Kentucky win put the players in an unfamiliar position. Instead of the nation jumping on the bandwagon of whomever the 'Dores played first, many were now picking the fifth-seeded Commodores to get to the Final Four. Once again, though, Vandy drew a tough first-round opponent in Ivy League champ Harvard.

The Commodores didn't allow for a ton of drama that afternoon in Albuquerque, New Mexico. They led by 10 at halftime and then by 18 in the second half. Harvard made a late run to cut the lead to five with 1:51 left, but Jenkins hit all six of his foul shots down the stretch as part of a 27-point day. Tinsley was terrific, hitting 5-of-6 from the field and scoring 16. The shorter Crimson struggled to score against the bigger VU front line consisting of Goulbourne, Tchiengang, Rod Odom, and especially Ezeli, whose 11 boards and four blocks were big.

Vanderbilt now drew fourth-seeded Wisconsin, which came in at 26–9. Playing Bo Ryan's club was like getting a root canal; the Badgers weren't overly athletic, but between their plodding pace, physical defense, and a tendency for their defenders to flop every time an offensive player got in the neighborhood, it could try the patience of coaches and players alike.

The game was close the whole way; the Badgers led by one at halftime and then the margin bulged to nine with 6:43 left. Vandy mounted a comeback and took a one-point lead when Ezeli hit a layup at 2:19, but the Badgers' Jordan Taylor, closely guarded a few feet behind the three-point line, nailed a bomb with 1:42 remaining.

That was the last field goal for either team. Jenkins missed a three-pointer with 1:22 left and then Ezeli, who got the offensive rebound, misfired on the front end of a one-and-one. With VU still trailing by two, Jenkins got a great look at a three-point shot and misfired with four seconds left. Ezeli appeared to be in great position for an offensive board, but was held by a UW defender and officials didn't see it.

Wisconsin's Ryan Evans grabbed the ball and hit one of two free throws with 1.9 seconds left. Goulbourne tried a baseball pass to get VU a half-court look, but it was tipped and never made it to midcourt. The Badgers prevailed 60–57, and the career of five special seniors, plus that of Jenkins, was over.

The legacy

It was one of the most successful, yet most disappointing, four-year periods of basketball history at Vanderbilt. By the standards most teams are judged—NCAA Tournament wins—nobody had expected that this bunch would deliver just one. Nor did anyone figure, with Kentucky down for most of their tenure, that the 'Dores would fail to get closer than two games to winning an SEC East title.

It could be said that the 'Dores ran into some tough luck in the NCAAs. Perhaps Wisconsin, which finished seventh in both Pomeroy's and Jeff Sagarin's final ratings, deserved better than a four seed in 2012. Richmond (40th in Pomeroy, 31st in Sagarin) and to a lesser extent, Murray State (45, 53) may have had a case for better seedings. Of course, an argument exists that both the 2009–10 (40, 33) and 2010–11 (41, 36) VU squads were treated generously by the selection committee in their seedings.

As for the final squad, it was puzzling how a team that had future NBA players in Ezeli, Jenkins, and Taylor could lose to Indiana State and Cleveland State at home and tie with Tennessee in the regular season, and yet beat one of college basketball's legendary squads in what was essentially a road environment. It was one of those seasons where Stallings and the Commodores would probably love to have to do over again, which Pomeroy's final rating (he had VU 12th) screams quite loudly about the talent on that team.

Whether or not it met expectations, the four-year run was historic for VU. At 91–43, it was the best stretch for the Commodores since Roy Skinner led the 'Dores to national prominence in the 1960s. No group of seniors had ever gone to the NCAAs three times.[6] The trophy case may have been emptier than anyone liked, but there was no denying that Commodore hoops became more nationally relevant than it had in a long while.

---

6 That's not an apples-to-apples comparison, though, since Skinner's teams between 1964 and 1968 would have gone each year under the current tournament structure.

PART III:
WOMEN'S BASKETBALL

The remarkable run of Melanie Balcomb

Consistency, thy name is Melanie Balcomb.

Since her arrival in 2002, coach Balcomb has been on the sidelines for twelve seasons of Vanderbilt women's basketball, and each year the Commodores have made the NCAA Tournament. Granted, Balcomb had a nice head start based on what her predecessor Jim Foster did. When Foster left for Ohio State after the 2001–02 season, he'd been to three-straight NCAA Tournaments and two-straight Elite Eights.

Still, Balcomb's track record is impressive in its own right. Only five other teams—DePaul, Duke, Notre Dame, Stanford, and Tennessee—have made every tournament since she's been Vandy's coach. Here's a retrospective of Balcomb's career in Nashville as she heads into the 2014–15 season.

A powerhouse among powerhouses

It's not often that a coach leaves after consecutive Elite Eights, and Foster's huge 2001–02 postseason was no fluke. The Commodores had been the No. 1 seed in the Midwest Region, but ran into arch-rival Tennessee in the regional final, where they fell 68–63. That illustrated the big problem for Foster. No matter how good his team was, it was almost always usurped by the legend 180 miles to the east. That, of course, was legendary University of Tennessee coach Pat Summitt, who had won six national titles and would win two more before retiring after the 2012 season.

Summitt, though, was far from the only difficulty that Vanderbilt faced. The Southeastern Conference had twelve teams at the time, and eight of them—that list also included Arkansas, Florida, Georgia, LSU, Mississippi State, and South Carolina—had made the NCAA Tournament that March. Auburn and Ole Miss did not make the postseason those years, but each had been national powers as well.

Summitt was also just one of many legendary coaches within the league. Georgia's Andy Landers had won seven SEC titles and had made the NCAAs nineteen times.[1] Auburn's Joe Ciampi had been a three-time national coach of the year. At LSU, Sue Gunter had started to take the Tigers deep into the NCAA Tournament most years. Gary Blair had turned Arkansas from an afterthought to an annual NCAA Tournament team.

But rather than those being reasons that Balcomb wouldn't take the job with the Commodores, they instead became reasons for Balcomb to leave what was a stable job at Xavier.

"I took the job at Vanderbilt probably for two reasons. I thought the SEC was the best conference with the best coaches and I wanted to compete at the highest level. I've always believed that to be the best, you have to coach against the best, play against the best, and I was excited to go somewhere that I felt, if you did well in our conference, that you could win a national championship. The competitiveness—to compete against Pat [Summitt] and Andy [Landers], Joe Ciampi, Gary Blair—I wanted to go somewhere that we could win a national championship," Balcomb recalls.

Those other schools had more leeway to get in players than Balcomb would with VU's stricter academic standards, but Balcomb also saw that as a reason to run to Nashville rather than away from it.

"The second reason would be the university itself. I grew up around Princeton University and coached at a lot of private

---

1 Landers would make the next eleven NCAA Tournaments before that streak was snapped in 2013–14.

schools, and I really liked coaching kids that wanted academics first. I really wanted a school that was integrity first. I wanted it to fit my values as a university, which it did," she said.

That national championship hasn't happened, but as for the rest, Balcomb's intuition was correct. In those first dozen seasons

Coach Melanie Balcolmb has put together an impressive string of consecutive NCAA Tournament appearances. (AP Photo/James Crisp)

at VU, she's 256–107 overall (70.5 percent) and more impressively, 118–67 in the SEC (63.8 percent). With top-notch recruiting classes continuing to arrive, it certainly appears there will be plenty more success on the horizon.

Picking up where Foster left off

With All-America veterans like Chantelle Anderson (who'd be the second overall pick in the WNBA Draft after that season) and dynamic point guard Ashley McElhiney, Balcomb was set up for a good run in her first VU season. The 'Dores went 22–10 and 9–5 in the SEC before bowing out in the NCAA Tournament's second round in an 86–85 overtime loss to Boston College.

Anderson and McElhiney graduated, but there was still plenty of talent remaining for 2003–04. Her second team went 26–8 and won the first of Balcomb's three conference tournament titles before once again getting its heart broken in the NCAA Tournament's Sweet 16.

"I felt like that was probably the best team I ever coached because it takes two years before the kids understand the system and buy into the system. And, I had a senior class of Ashley Earley and Jenni Benningfield that really had great leaders. And then I had an influx of great [recruits] in Dee Davis and Carla Thomas; they were sophomores then. They knew the system. I felt like we had a great shot. We ended up getting beat by Stanford on a buzzer shot, and to me that was the toughest year in looking back," she recalls.

"I think that's the year we should have gone on. We would have played Tennessee in the [Elite Eight], ironically enough, but that was probably the most heartbreaking loss I've had as far as postseason here. We were very good. We were just a really good basketball team from top to bottom."

The Commodores took another half step forward the next season, going 24–8, but more importantly, 10–4 in the SEC, which was good enough for second place in the regular season. But the postseason draw was unkind, and the 'Dores lost a Sweet 16 game to national runner-up, Michigan State. The next year, the eighth-seeded Commodores went 21–11, but were then ousted by Final Four participant North Carolina in the second round.

That would be something that the Commodores would run into constantly in the years to come.

"We always ran into that [high-seeded] team," she recalls.

Still, Balcomb had won six NCAA Tournament games in four years. She had developed players like Benningfield, Abi Ramsey, and Ashley Earley into stars.

That was a good start, but the question remained, what could she do when she no longer had Foster's former recruits at her disposal?

Leaving her own stamp

The good news is that Balcomb had recruited exceptionally well. Four years after her arrival, in the 2006–07 season, the whole roster was composed of her players.

"Jim had left eight scholarships in that first class, so I signed six kids and saved two," she remembers. "One of my kids was Caroline Williams and she was the seventh I brought in as a walk-on, but she ended up being the best three-point shooter to ever play at Vanderbilt! So I brought seven kids in actually. That first recruiting class was ranked No. 1 in the country. The two best players were Dee Davis and Carla Thomas."

That set 2006–07 up to be a special season. The team won ten SEC games, tying the school record for league wins in a season,[2] and went 28–6 overall. Vandy got a two seed in the NCAAs, where for the third time in five seasons it lost its last game by three points or less. This one came to No. 7 Bowling Green, which would fall in its next game to Arizona State.

But more good things were on the horizon. The next two seasons were virtually identical, with the Commodores earning four seeds in

---

2 That record was set by Foster in 2001–02, and tied by Balcomb in 2004–05.

the NCAA Tournament in 25–9 and 26–9 campaigns. Those were two of Balcomb's prouder seasons as a coach, as she was able to mold her kinds of players into the unit she wanted even though there were hardships along the way.

Jennifer Risper drives to the hoop in a game against Georgia.
(AP Photo/Danny Johnston)

"When we had great teams, we had great leaders, and those two [Tina Wirth and Jen Risper] were really good leaders. They really understood the system and really were an extension of what me and my staff were trying to do and that's really the key. We ended up having some injuries . . . at one point we were really playing five guards. Tina was a guard when we got her and made her a small forward, and then Hannah Tuomi got hurt and we ended up making Jennifer Risper a post. She was a small forward as well and we had no post, so that's what was interesting with that group is we had to again adjust and at times we were as best as we could be," Balcomb recalled. "We ended up losing to Maryland two years in a row with those guys because Jen and Tina got in foul trouble.

"I think those years, at the beginning we were big . . . We got small and we started playing really well but it was hard to defend the bigger teams when we got deeper down into the NCAAs."

Again, there was the nagging question of "What might have been?" as the Sweet 16 squad of 2008–09 lost to Maryland by just four points. Years later, that one still haunts Balcomb.

"We had the lead and that year, [which was] Jen and Dee's senior year, we were beating Maryland by 18 and they both got in foul trouble and couldn't sustain it. We lost in the last possession. We had a chance to tie or win in the last possession. . . . We had 'em, and what are the chances your two best players get in foul trouble and with our subs, we just weren't deep enough to sustain it," she recalls.

With Wirth and Risper gone after that, things dropped off a bit, but the 'Dores managed to win their first NCAA Tournament game that year. Once again, VU was snakebitten in close games as Xavier eliminated VU by a 63–62 score.

For the first time in Balcomb's career, her team (20–12) failed to win an NCAA game in 2010–11. Balcomb followed up with single wins in both the 2012 and 2013 tourneys, but injuries and dismissals destroyed the 2013–14 season and the 'Dores, 18–13, again failed to win an NCAA game. Still, that team managed to get to the NCAAs and even draw an eight seed.

After all that success, it was natural for fans to have some disappointment in not getting to a Sweet 16 for five straight seasons. But could Balcomb be on the verge of another run like the ones a decade ago?

Balcomb sure thinks so.

"I'm excited. I think it's kind of like a new era's coming in. We're bringing in five kids . . . it's almost as good as the first one I brought in that won a lot of games for us. It was ranked seventh or eighth nationally, but then Rebekah Dahlman, who was a McDonald's All-American high school player, after seven games got a blood clot (in 2013–14). She'll redshirt and get to play, so she actually gets put in that class," says Balcomb, looking forward to 2014–15.

"So now you take that class, which is ranked seventh or eighth in the country, which is probably the best class I've had since that first class, and then you add a McDonald's All-American who was the 16th-best player in the country [Dahlman] coming out to that class, [and] it's probably a top-five class again. That's what I'm excited about."

"And that's kind of what happened when I first got here," she continued. "Those first couple of teams were very, very good, and that's what I'm excited about, getting that opportunity again."

With the NCAA tournament losses, Balcomb has also been disappointed in how the start of her second decade at VU has begun. But between that and the bigger picture of what's ahead, she's certainly proud of what she's done.

"I think that's the biggest thing that makes us unique is our consistency. There aren't many programs that have been consistent in getting to the tournament and avoiding losing seasons. I'd rather be doing what I have done, but I'm also excited about the future and what we could do," she said.

PART IV:
BASEBALL

2004 Baseball: Corbin puts Vandy on the map

All coaches, no matter how good, have their sanity questioned at times. Usually, though, the questions don't come from their spouses. But on February 18, 2003, Vanderbilt baseball coach Tim Corbin's wife, Maggie, was wondering if her husband had already made a career-killing mistake just three games into his VU tenure.

That was Corbin's home debut at Vanderbilt. For most athletic programs that compete at high levels—and there are fewer higher levels than Southeastern Conference baseball—there is anticipation in the air for better things when a new coach takes over. That's especially true when it's someone like Corbin, who had already begun to show signs of recruiting at a higher level than to that which Vanderbilt was accustomed.

So, when Corbin played at home for the first time in front of what should have been an appreciative audience, he and Maggie were shocked at the fact that there were more people in the opposing dugout than there were Vanderbilt fans in the stands.

"I actually thought I had the wrong time, because no one was here but, like, maybe ten people," Maggie Corbin recalled a decade later. "And I just remember thinking, *I got the wrong time.*

Since taking over in 2003, Vanderbilt coach Tim Corbin has taken the baseball program to unparalleled heights. (Mike Rapp)

"And then Tim looked at me and waved at me, and I said, 'I got the wrong time.' And he said, 'No, it's starting in a few minutes.'

"And I thought, *Oh my God, what did we do? Why did we come here?*"

It was even worse than Maggie remembered. According to Tim Corbin, his wife inflated the actual attendance by 67 percent.

"We were playing East Tennessee State and there were six people in the stands. That was it. . . . It was rainy, it was 40 degrees, there were six people in the stadium," Tim Corbin remembers.

"When we won, I remember going back that night and she goes, 'What did we do?' because it was one of those where you're thinking, *Are we running a high school program? What's going on?*"

Starting from (nearly) scratch

If there's such a thing as a baseball wasteland, this was it.

Excepting its basketball programs, the name "Vanderbilt" had become synonymous with athletics failure. Its football misery was front and center for the world to see, but the baseball program may have been equally futile. There had been zero NCAA Tournaments since 1980, when Roy Mewbourne's Commodores won the Southeastern Conference Tournament to get there.

Since that point, however, the program fell on hard times. It should be said that Mewbourne won more than he lost (a .519 overall winning percentage). But where it really mattered was what Mewbourne had done in the SEC, and in the twenty-two years since the title season, Mewbourne won at a .358 rate and failed to finish even .500 in the league even once.

Though Mewbourne's track record wasn't good, the fact that he stuck around twenty-four years made a statement about the apathy around it. But at least Vanderbilt was starting to put forth an effort. It had renovated its ballpark thanks to a generous donation from former baseball player Charles Hawkins, and the new stadium would bear his name. While Hawkins Field was not large (a capacity of about 1,550 at the time) it was certainly beautiful. It was a far cry from the time when the stadium had been surrounded on one side by a chain-link fence. That "stadium," if you could call it that, even lacked a press box, and broadcasters called games from folding chairs sitting atop the dugouts.

But decades of neglect couldn't be fixed overnight. Corbin still wouldn't have basic necessities, like the team's own locker room (baseball shared one with the football team) or a second batting cage. On Corbin's first road trip that February, the team traveled with just one uniform.[1]

Mewbourne had spent his final year in the new ballpark. That helped him in recruiting, as he landed some big-time pitching recruits in Kentucky's Jeremy Sowers (the Reds' first-round pick in 2001), Ohio's Jensen Lewis, and Nashvillian Ryan Mullins. The three would eventually form an outstanding pitching rotation, but Mullins and Sowers weren't on campus until Mewbourne was gone, and while Sowers pitched well for a freshman, it wasn't nearly enough.

Sowers and the new ballpark were about the only exciting things about Mewbourne's last season. Vandy finished 24–27 overall, 7–21 in the SEC. Corbin's contemporaries quickly confirmed whatever doubts the new coach might have had about the talent on hand.

"You could tell that we were so far away from being a relevant program, and I think the thing that stood out the most . . . was the amount of phone calls that I fielded from [programs] that wanted to schedule us to play, because we were an SEC team and they could acquire RPI points, but yet no one was really timid of us," he said a decade later.

"'Can we come there and play three games? Do you want to play a couple of games here?' I just remember it was easy to schedule but yet hard to schedule, because when I made those phone calls to bigger schools like Stanford, no one wanted to play us because they felt it would hurt their RPI. I'm talking about bigger schools, schools that were on the same level. The mid-majors, they were not reluctant to play us."

Maybe Corbin was crazy, after all.

"It was almost like the Bad News Bears, and—I don't know any other way to say it—crap," he remembered eleven years later.

---

1 That wasn't the worst thing about the road trip. "I remember going to Charleston, South Carolina, for that first tournament in '03 . . . and when we showed up in our hotel halfway there in Asheville [North Carolina], they had no room for us," Corbin said.

Laying the groundwork

College rules allow for thirty-five players. After various players were dismissed for one thing or another, VU had just twenty-seven on its roster for 2003.

"There were a lot of kids that dismissed themselves; I didn't even need to dismiss them because of the attitude of the program and the culture change, and there were still a lot of changes that needed to take place," he remembers.

Another thing that Corbin lacked was much offense. Vandy scored an average of 3.9 runs a game in 2003 and hit just 25 home runs as a team.

But there were things to build around. Sowers developed into a star that spring (a 2.50 ERA in 115 innings) and Mullins (3.48 in 88 innings) became a rare commodity: a reliable SEC starter as a freshman. Lewis was excellent (3.00 in 57 innings) as a closer and sometimes starter, as was fellow freshman Matt Buschmann (3.86 in 49). But Corbin needed more of them; starting catcher Jonathan Douillard was actually forced into seven appearances on the mound.

The arms were enough to make it interesting. Vanderbilt stunned everyone by sweeping No. 13 Florida in its fourth SEC series. Two weekends later, it took a series from eventual College World Series participant LSU, ranked seventh at the time. The following weekend it shocked No. 8 Auburn with another 2–1 series triumph.

Surprisingly, Vanderbilt was in the rare position to make the Southeastern Conference Tournament, an event in which it had not participated since 1996. There was one catch: the Commodores had to sweep arch-rival Tennessee at Hawkins Field in the season finale. With a 7–4 win in the first game and a 9–1 victory in the second, it had a chance.

The Commodores trailed 5–4 in the ninth on Sunday. The Vols' Luke Hocheaver, who'd eventually become the top overall pick in the 2006 Major League Draft, was on the hill to face Worth Scott (who was hitting .180), with Rucker Taylor on first and two out. In the words of Commodore play-by-play announcer Joe Fisher, here's what transpired next:

"Taylor with a short lead at first, the stretch by Hocheaver, the pitch . . . Scott launches it to right . . . looking up, drifting back, it is . . . outta here! Yes! Yes! Yes! Home run! Vanderbilt wins! Vanderbilt wins! They're on their way to Birmingham! How about that! Worth Scott dives into home plate, and the Commodores punch their ticket to the SEC Tournament! Unbelievable! Unbelievable! Worth Scott turns on the pitch, just inside the foul pole down the right field line, and the celebration has broken out at home plate by the Commodores! What an incredible finish!"

No matter what happened from there, the season had been a success. Vanderbilt fell to Auburn and South Carolina in the tournament, but for the first time in a long time, there had been modest results and the hint of a foundation.

"I really think [the 2004 season] was built on that confidence we got from 2003, from winning that one game against Tennessee, to going to an SEC Tournament," Corbin remembered. "We had talked about that moment at the beginning of the year in '03, about winning and being able to celebrate in the middle of the field, and it ended that way, so I think the kids were seeing some type of vision come to fruition. . . . Several kids went off in the Cape Cod League during the summer and had very, very good years.

"In fact, I can remember Maggie and I going up there to watch the All-Star Game, we had four Vanderbilt guys in it, and I think those guys came back from the Cape almost thinking that they were relevant and as we started the year in '04, we played with a confidence that didn't exist in '03 that stemmed from the moment against UT, and then stemmed from the confidence that kids got from the course of the summer."

Sowers had become a legitimate superstar. Mullins would be considered an ace on most staffs, and Lewis and Buschmann would do a competent job splitting the Sunday starter's role in 2004. Corbin found a couple of good freshmen bullpen arms in highly recruited Floridian Tyler Rhoden, and a local kid in Mt. Juliet's—Steven Shao—who, while not highly recruited, proved poised enough to pitch big innings in 2004.

But it was what was happening with the position players that would put Vandy over the top in 2004.

Nashvillian Warner Jones, an outfielder as a freshman, moved to second and immediately became a superstar. His double-play

Warner Jones shows the ball to an umpire after making a diving catch at second base. (Mike Rapp)

partner, transfer Ryan Klosterman, benefitted from constant playing time he hadn't gotten at Clemson. He'd also become a star. At third, Tony Mansolino didn't hit a lot, but was a whiz with the glove. Across the diamond was Cesar Nicolas, who had developing power. Corbin also added a couple of pieces in the outfield with the transfer of Columbia's Mike Baxter[2] and the addition of high school recruit Aaron Garza from Texas.

---

2 Baxter would also split time with Nicolas at first, and DH some.

One other piece was also coming. The Commodores rarely sign JUCOs in any sport because they're not usually good students, but there are some exceptions. One dropped in Vandy's lap that spring of 2003 when North Florida coach Dusty Rhodes introduced Corbin to Antoan Richardson, who'd man center for the 'Dores in '04.

"[Rhodes] came up to me and said, 'Tim, some day you're going to have a good program, and by the way, I have a good player for you. You're really going to need to look into him . . . he's a kid from the Bahamas who can run and is better than anyone I've ever seen. He's a great fit for your program,'" Corbin recalled.

"I remember calling [Richardson] that night . . . we got him on campus and the next thing you know, he came. He really solidified our team. It was like putting the athlete on the field that we just didn't have. . . . He was a game-changer when he put the ball in play. He was the fastest thing we had at Vanderbilt, maybe the fastest guy in the school."

Vanderbilt has always had excellent outfield defense under Corbin, but the diminutive Richardson patrolled center field that spring in a way no one's done quite the way Richardson did that spring. He saved Commodore pitchers a number of home runs in 2004.

"I think the best play I ever saw him make was at LSU in the first game of the [series] in '04 when he went into the fence and he leaped into the fence, he caught the ball, and then like Velcro, he was stuck in the fence. . . . I remember [outfielder] Billy Kleinscrodt running to him and grabbing him off the fence and ripping his shirt. It was amazing," Corbin said.

The other piece to the puzzle was catcher Jonathan Douillard. The rising senior had hit just .237/.292/.258 in 2003, but his work behind the plate was tremendous.

"He stopped the running game, he blocked everything, he was the ultimate catcher. . . . He was a very un-sung part of that team," Corbin said.

The pitching and the defense would be there. If the offense came along, ending that tournament drought was a real possibility.

The regular season

The Commodores then started the 2004 season 7–0. Granted, it wasn't against the best of opponents, but it was the way that Vanderbilt was playing that pleased Corbin.

"The games we were winning, we were winning big. We were moving away from people quick," he remembers.

That turned into a 14–2 start that included a series win over Baylor, which built some confidence as the Bears were normally an NCAA Tournament team.[3] Only two of those first 16 games were decided by two runs or less, and VU won both. But the schedule got tougher starting with a road trip to 16–1 Ole Miss, where Vandy's luck ran out. The Commodores lost the series by scores of 5–4, 6–5, and 3–1.

Losing the series was no shame—the Rebels would finish 18–12 in SEC play and go to a regional—but Corbin, sensing that VU had been complacent for too long, became angry with his team on the bus.

"I remember going back on the bus on that trip after the kids showered, in my uniform and it was one of those moments where, I just wasn't going to tolerate personally an attitude that coming close was good enough. . . . That was a key moment because we played pretty good baseball but lost and I remember telling them, obviously, that's not good enough."

He was right. Georgia, which would go to Omaha that year, came to Nashville for VU's SEC home-opening series and it got one of Vandy's best efforts all season.

Sowers was brilliant on Friday, striking out seven of the first 11 hitters as the Commodores eked out a 4–3 win. On Saturday, the Commodores trailed 4–3 in the seventh, but came back for an 8–4 win. On Sunday, the Commodores trailed 5–1 heading into the bottom of the fifth, but Baxter's two-RBI triple broke open a 5-all tie, and VU eventually cruised to a 12–8 win.

After a midweek win over Austin Peay, the Commodores had eventual College World Series participant South Carolina for

---

3 Baylor went just 29–31 in 2004 and missed the NCAAs.

three at home. The Gamecocks had beaten Vandy an incredible 21 straight times, but Sowers snapped the skid in a complete-game, 6-2 win. Garza's two-out, two-run single in the seventh and Nicolas's bomb over the Green Monster in left provided the offensive highlights. Carolina, though, recovered with 6–3 and 10–4 victories.

Vandy took a midweek game from Evansville, and then went to Tuscaloosa and nearly blew a 6–0 lead as the Crimson Tide got to Sowers for four two-out runs in the eighth. However, Sowers got the win in outdueling future Major Leaguer Wade LeBlanc. On Saturday, 'Bama got even with a 3–1 win as VU wasted a good start from Lewis and left 11 men on. The Commodores, though, took Sunday's game by a 3–2 count, snapping Alabama's seven-series winning streak against Vandy that dated back to 1992.

Tougher times were coming. Sowers would walk just 26 men in 122 ⅔ innings that year, but on the following Friday, walked four and gave up six runs in the first two innings to an Arkansas club that would also be Omaha-bound. Garza had a three-run homer, but that was all the offense, as VU fell 6–3. On Saturday, Arkansas chased Lewis in the fifth. Buschmann was ineffective in relief, and Arkansas clinched the series with a 9–4 win. Vandy took out its frustrations on Sunday as Nicolas clubbed two homers, Jones had three hits, and VU pounded the Razorbacks, 14–8.

A road trip to Florida, though, ended with a Gator sweep in three close games.

That left the Commodores at 7–10 in SEC play. There were four conference series left, three coming against teams that would go to regionals that spring. Vandy needed a confidence boost and got it the next weekend against perennial power Mississippi State.

Sowers did his usual Friday thing by scattering eight hits over 7 ⅔ innings, striking out eight and getting the win as new closer Jensen Lewis closed out a 7–2 game. Mullins, now the Saturday starter, struck out six, and walked one in a seven-inning performance as the 'Dores earned a 5–1 victory. Buschmann, the new Sunday starter, went seven and gave up three and Lewis pitched the final 2 ⅔ innings as the 'Dores won 5–4.

It was a big sweep for a number of reasons. First, MSU was one of the giants of college baseball, a program that expected to go to the College World Series every year. The Bulldogs had won the previous two seasons' series.

"I think that really, really generated some confidence in us because of Mississippi State's success and [College World Series] success as well," Corbin remembers.

Second, the new weekend rotation had success. It would be a sign that the pitching staff, which had struggled the previous weekend, had come around. The team posted a 1.93 ERA for the weekend, the fewest runs allowed in an SEC series since the Florida series the previous year, which had come thirteen weekends prrior.

Vandy went to Knoxville, where Hocheaver beat VU 5–3 on a Friday. But Mullins returned the favor on Saturday, throwing a complete-game four-hit, 2-0 victory despite the fact he'd been sick all week. On Sunday the 'Dores got to .500 in conference play by winning 3–2 in a game that Ryan Rote closed to pick up a school-record 10th save. Klosterman had a home run and scored two.

Nobody could say VU's sudden superiority over the Vols was a fluke, as the 'Dores had now won five of the last six games over UT.

The biggest stage, though, was yet to come as the Commodores headed to Louisiana State, which was debatably college baseball's best program. The previous year, the Tigers didn't take Vanderbilt seriously. Corbin recalled the Tigers kicking a couple of soccer balls around in their Hawkins Field dugout when the two met the previous season. When Vanderbilt took two of three from the Tigers in '03, that got their attention for the next spring.

LSU got its revenge early, beating the Commodores 3–2 in 10 innings on Friday and 7–6 in 11 on Saturday. Suddenly, the 'Dores were two games back under .500 with just four games left to play in the regular season.

"The last one on Saturday, we were making plays all over the field. . . . I just remember trying to build their confidence right away because I could see they were just so despondent," Corbin recalled.

The team believed it should have won both games. The next day, it took care of business. Klosterman went 5-for-5 with two solo home runs, including one to lead off the game. Buschmann, now 7–1, threw a complete-game shutout—the first anyone had thrown against the Tigers that season—as VU got an 8–0 win.

"I think that game more than anything instilled growth in our team," Corbin recalled.

Vanderbilt had played the toughest teams in the league, but it would now play one of the easiest as Kentucky came to Hawkins Field. All three wins seemed to come effortlessly, by scores of 9–1, 8–6, and 11–5. Jones broke Hunter Bledsoe's school record for hits and won the league's batting title. The slumping Richardson started hitting again, rapping five hits, scoring six runs, and stealing four bases. The Commodores set school records for wins (39) and SEC wins (16) that weekend.

More importantly, though, the Commodores were virtually assured of a regional for the first time since 1980. But the squad also wanted to do something it had not done the year before: win some games in Hoover.

Making a run at a title

Most teams go to the SEC Tournament with a bid to the NCAAs virtually clinched, and for that reason, some teams don't compete at 100 percent. That was never Vanderbilt's plan.

"We went there with the expectation of winning. I'm telling you, it didn't matter that we'd never done it before," Baxter remembers.

The SEC Tournament opener was a matchup of a pair of future Major Leaguers, VU's Sowers and Georgia's Mitchell Boggs. Sowers won in a landslide, fanning 10 of the 29 hitters he faced. The offense chased Boggs out of the game by the fourth and Vandy coasted to a 6–0 win. The Commodores had that magical 40th victory and if there had been any way the tournament's selection committee was going to keep VU out before, there was no way now.

Mullins was just as good against Florida on Thursday. The breaking ball was working and the Gators had no chance, striking out 12 times. Nicolas had the offensive highlight, a home run to dead center in the spacious Hoover Metropolitan Stadium, and Vandy won 3–0.

That earned Vandy a day off. It would need it, as the next game would be one of the longest of the season and still one of the more memorable ones of Corbin's career.

The Gators fought their way through the loser's bracket of the double-elimination event to get a rematch against the team that had beaten them all four times. Klosterman led off the game with a homer, but the Gators touched Buschmann for two in the second. Richardson and Baxter had RBI singles to put Vandy back up 3–2 after four, and then both Buschmann and the Gator tandem of O'Day and Bryan Ball held the contest there until the ninth. UF tied it when Ben Harrison doubled in Adam Davis. Rote held UF scoreless until the 11th, when the Gators got two runs.

Mansolino struck out to start the 11th, but Garza doubled and Douillard singled. Klosterman struck out for out number two, but Richardson walked. Jones, as he did all year, lined a double into the gap. Garza and Zach Simpson, pinch-running for Douillard, scored, and Jones raised his arm in celebration as Richardson came around for the apparent game winner. Vandy, though, got an unfortunate bounce, as the baseball bounded over the wall for a ground-rule double. Richardson was sent back to third, and when Baxter struck out, the game went to the 12th.

By then, Lewis, effective in his new role as the closer, was on for Rote. He struck out two and stranded a two-out runner on first. Mansolino hadn't gotten a hit all tournament, but led off the 12th with a single. Garza singled him to second and Douliard's spot was due. Corbin had Matt McGraner hitting in that spot. McGraner had three at-bats in 30 SEC games that season, but on a 2–1 pitch, he lined an opposite-field single to right. Mansolino scored, and Vandy would play South Carolina for the SEC Tournament title the next day.

Starting pitcher Jeff Sues gave VU a chance until he tired in the sixth. The 'Dores trailed 3–2 in the ninth with a man on and one out when the red-hot Klosterman smashed a ball to Carolina's Steve Pearce at first, who fielded it to start a 3-6-6 double play to give Carolina a title. Klosterman made the all-tournament team along with Jones, Douiliard, Nicolas, and Sowers, and Vandy left Hoover feeling good.

"That was one of those periods where our pitching— everyone could tell on our team that our pitching was national championship-caliber, we felt that way. We felt like Sowers could beat anyone, we felt like Mullins—that was Mullins' best year by far, he was on, he was doing things right, he was healthy, and he was pitching well," Corbin remembers.

It carried over to the next week.

Making history in Charlottesville

The NCAA always announces its field on Labor Day, and that morning, VU learned of its destination: Charlottesville, Virginia, where it would face Virginia, George Mason, and Princeton. It was the first time that UVA, which was in the process of building a program the way Corbin was, had hosted a regional.

The Commodores were the region's two seed, and faced George Mason in the start of the four-team, double-elimination tournament. Mother Nature decided that VU's twenty-four-year wait to play another regional game wasn't long enough; VU and GMU were rained out on Friday and wouldn't take the field until Saturday.

The extra day to sit and think about things made the Commodores "a little more nervous," Corbin remembers, but the steady Sowers got things going in the right direction early by striking out four of the first seven hitters he faced. VU put up two in the first when Klosternan scored on a throwing error by catcher Robby Jacobsen and Richardson crossed the plate on a Nicolas single. Nicolas hit a long home run in the bottom of the third to put Vanderbilt up 3–1. In the fifth, Nicolas and Mansolino had RBI singles, Jones scored on Garza's fielder's choice RBI, and then Garza scored on an error.

Lewis gave up two runs in the ninth, but it didn't matter; he'd come in with a six-run cushion and the Commodores got a 7–3 win, their first NCAA Tournament victory since they'd beaten East Carolina in 1974.

"You could kind of feel the magic working," Baxter said.

That might be the best way to describe it, because the Commodores caught a huge break. It's not common that a region's top seed loses its first game, but Virginia, which had future Major League stars Ryan Zimmerman and Mark Reynolds, was shut down 4–2 by Princeton pitcher Ross Ohlendorf, who'd also make the Majors.[4] Virginia would now have to get by GMU and then beat the loser of VU-Princeton, and then beat the winner of VU-Princeton twice in order to advance.

Virginia burned All-America pitcher Joe Koshansky against George Mason in a fight for its postseason life, and stayed alive.[5] Meanwhile, Vandy's Mullins was again fantastic, striking out eight and throwing a complete game while Scott went 4-for-4 with four RBI. UVA's Matt Avery came through in a big way, throwing a complete game to knock out the Tigers, meaning VU would finally meet the host team on Sunday.

Vandy was playing with house money, but didn't want to take any chances. Jones doubled in Klosterman in the first, and Garza doubled to the alley to score Jones and Nicolas. Nerves bit Vandy in the bottom of the inning, as Virginia scored three unearned runs off Buschmann, the most embarrassing being a grounder that rolled between Jones's legs while Virginia had the bases loaded.

Corbin knew something was wrong, and addressed it immediately.

"At the start of the game, I thought we were tight. I remember Klosterman and Warner Jones making errors they typically wouldn't make, and when they did, I remember them talking to the kids in the dugout and just telling them to settle down, that we would eventually win the game but we needed to settle down a little bit," he said.

---

4 It's not often that a regional has this many future MLB players of significance; Princeton also had Will Venable, who later became an every-day outfielder for San Diego.

5 Koshansky was also briefly a Major Leaguer for the Colorado Rockies, albeit as a first baseman and not as a pitcher.

That's how it happened. Jones singled in Klosterman in the second to go up 4–3. In the fourth, Nicolas singled to right to score Douillard. Garza's sacrifice fly to fight in the seventh scored Nicolas.

Buschmann, meanwhile, was money until the seventh, when Shao come on with two outs and two on. Koshansky lined to Jones, and the game moved to the eighth, where Klosterman scored Scott on a fly ball. Lewis relieved Shao and got the only two hitters he faced in the eighth, and Rote pitched a 1-2-3 ninth.

The crowd of 2,530 fans—mostly UVA rooters—sat and watched as the Commodores stormed the field to celebrate a regional title.

The reality check

Charlottesville had been the perfect setting for VU; as the Commodores found out three years later, it can be tough to host a regional for the first time. Vanderbilt would get no such luck with its next matchup, a Texas Longhorn club playing in its home park of Disch-Falk Field. Texas had been to Omaha thirty times already, including three of the previous four seasons.[6]

"I think [we were overmatched]. What I remember about that series was even before it started, there were a lot of interviews. We're going from a Regional where we were a lot like Virginia, we were the new kids on the block, and going to a team that was there every year, was used to going every year. . . . I remember Texas talking during that Super Regional like they were already making plans for Omaha and they were talking above us. It was like they had already moved on, and not that they were cocky but they were very confident that they were going to go through us and they were going to win," Corbin remembers.

There were other things amiss as well.

---

6 Texas would win the College World Series in 2005.

"I remember that Regional, they're supposed to be run in a very neutral atmosphere, but I can remember them playing their own music and their own fight song and you're not supposed to be able to do any of that, but they were doing it, and it was like, 'Yeah, you guys are in enemy territory and you should be thankful that you're here and just take your two games and get back to Nashville.' That's what it felt like," Corbin said.

Then, there was the matter of the talent on the Longhorn team itself. Texas was the tournament's top seed overall. Its top two starting pitchers, J. P. Howell and Sam LeCure, went on to become Major Leaguers. All-America closer Huston Street, un-hittable while at UT, would be closing out games for the Oakland Athletics the next season.

Jensen Lewis, who alternated between starting and closing at Vanderbilt, went on to post a 3.68 ERA in 198 innings with the Cleveland Indians between 2007 and 2010. (Mike Rapp)

The Longhorns were more known for pitching than for offense, but there was a lot of talent there, too, Right fielder Drew Stubbs would be the eighth pick of the MLB Draft two years later, and manned center for the Cincinnati Reds, and then the Cleveland Indians, for years. Three other guys in the lineup, Michael Hollimon, Curtis Thigpen, and Taylor Teagarden, made the Majors briefly.

Vanderbilt had a talented team that season, as Baxter, Lewis, Richardson, and Sowers would all make the majors at some point. But not many college teams have seven future big-leaguers on their roster at one time like the Longhorns had, and it showed.

When the teams took to the old-style artificial turf that Saturday night, it didn't take long to see where things were heading. Texas hit an endless succession of line drives that got to the gap and seemed to roll around the ballpark forever, and roughed up Sowers in a manner no one else did all season. The Longhorns got five two-out runs in the first. Sowers was done after getting just 10 outs, as Texas piled on eight more runs in the next four innings. Jones managed a two-run homer off Howell, but otherwise, Howell's breaking ball was ridiculously good. He struck out 13 over seven innings, and Texas won 15–3 that evening.

The Longhorns picked up where they'd left off the next day versus Mullins. Thigpen hit a two-out solo shot off the scoreboard in the first and got another on Thigpen's third-inning single. Stubbs hit a two-run bomb in the fifth for a 4–0 lead. Scott tripled in Mansolino and scored on Klosterman's groundout to cut it back to two, but Texas just wouldn't stop hitting. Lewis gave up a run in both the sixth and seventh, and Rote was unable to get Lewis out of an eighth-inning jam due to three walks, a wild pitch, a pair of sacrifice flies, and a single. Vandy's fifth-inning rally would be all the offense the Commodores could muster, and Texas advanced to Omaha with a 10–2 win.

"For those of you that haven't seen us play this year, you may not think that [we] are a good team, but we are," Corbin said later that day. "I am glad for our kids and especially our seniors because this is uncharted waters for the Vanderbilt program because we have never made it this far before."

Building it

The way the 'Dores were thrown around like a rag doll in Austin did little to tarnish what the team had accomplished. If you wanted to put a face on what Corbin was doing, it would probably be Baxter's. His transfer from an Ivy League school didn't make much noise, but he'd put up good numbers (.322/.354/.394) in '04.[7] Reflecting on the situation a decade later, he said it was the work that the players put in that put the program over the top.

"The stuff that we did to prepare for that season, [Corbin] kind of made something out of nothing. Now, that's not to say we had a lack of talent, because we had some guys that went on and had good pro careers. Jeremy Sowers, Mully, there were some parts there that were really good, but when you compare it to the monster squads now, it's nothing," he said.

Finding players like Baxter, whom nobody suspected in 2004 would be a major leaguer, and making them into something was the only choice that Corbin had. Texas had shown the difference between teams with elite talent, and where VU was. As he had been settling into his new job in Nashville, Corbin can recall at least one instance of a father of a recruit, point-blank, telling him that essentially his program wasn't even worth considering given the other available scholarship opportunities.

Something had to happen for the Commodores to get the kind of talent that could get them to the next level. That 2004 season did the trick.

---

7 Baxter became a legitimate collegiate star in 2005, hitting .378/.468/.607. He debuted in the majors in 2010 with the San Diego Padres and played for a few years, also with the Mets and Dodgers.

2007 Baseball: The climb to No. 1

Success breeds expectations for more success. When Vanderbilt printed the logo of the 2005 College World Series on the back of its media guide that year, it became very clear where the program wanted to go next.

For a while, it looked as if it could happen. Vanderbilt started 2005 with a 12–0 record and a spot in the rankings, but Baylor swept VU in Nashville and things slowly disintegrated from there. The 'Dores got to the end of the season needing to win a game or two against Florida, but the Gators' Matt LaPorta was a one-man wrecking crew that weekend, as the Gators swept VU in Nashville. That cost Vandy a bid to both the Southeastern Conference and NCAA Tournaments.

It was the first of two transition seasons for the program. When VU made it to Austin in 2004, a local kid named David Price, who was becoming a pitching sensation at nearby Blackman High (Murfreesboro, Tennessee), took notice of what Corbin was building. The year before, when someone had suggested Vanderbilt as a possible college destination, Price literally laughed. In 2005, though, Price was on the mound for Vanderbilt after passing up a nice offer from the Los Angeles Dodgers to turn pro. That raised some eyebrows, as did Price's 2.73 ERA in 69 ⅓ innings in his freshman campaign.

In Price, Corbin had an ace befitting a championship-level club, but he needed a whole lot more players. Corbin coveted a

David Price, the 2007 Golden Spikes Award winner as college baseball's Player of the Year, celebrates one of the 194 strikeouts he recorded that season. Price won the Cy Young Award with Tampa Bay five years later. (Mike Rapp)

broad-shouldered third baseman from the Bronx, New York, named Pedro Alvarez, who was considered the best hitter on the East Coast. There were two big obstacles to getting him to Nashville. First, there was Alvarez's family; his parents didn't speak English, and they weren't exactly rich, as Alvarez's father was a New York City cab driver. That went hand-in-hand with the second difficulty, which was that the Boston Red Sox offered Alvarez about a million dollars when they drafted him that summer. Corbin finally won that battle, but not after (literally) having an assistant walk him to class on his first day at Vanderbilt.[1]

There were others. Vanderbilt landed seven other players considered top-200 recruits in California outfielder Diallo Fon, Maine's Andrew Giobbi and Ryan Flaherty; and four top-flight high school pitchers in Ocala, Florida's Bobby Kennedy and New Haven, Connecticut's Josh Zeid, Arizona's Brett Jacobson, and New Jersey's Nick Christiani.[2] He also inked a couple of lesser-known JUCO players in Florida's Matt Meingasner and California's Casey Weathers.

It was widely considered to be the best college signing class in the country. Many of those players contributed immediately in 2006; Alvarez became the team's regular third baseman and Flaherty started at first before moving to short. A number of sophomores who'd been used sparingly in 2005, including catcher Shea Robin, center fielder David Macias, and left fielder Ryan Davis, stepped up and contributed as starters in 2006. Second baseman Alex Feinberg and shortstop/outfielder Dominic de la Osa started almost immediately as freshmen and held down jobs again in 2006.

At the midway mark of conference play, VU was unexpectedly 10–5 and in contention for a league title. Price had been downright dominant, fanning 17 against Arkansas on April 17 and earning National Pitcher of the Week honors. It was the sixth-straight start in which he'd fanned 10 or more. But teams started sitting on Price's fastball and the lefty was hit hard through much of the remainder

---

1 Under draft rules at the time, MLB teams could still sign draft picks up until the moment they walked into their first class.
2 Kennedy (Indian River Community College), Fon (Arizona), and Zeid (Tulane) all transferred after doing little at VU.

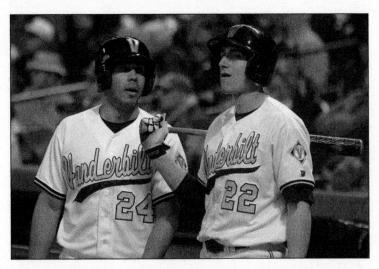

Future major leaguers Pedro Alvarez (24) and Ryan Flaherty (22) trade advice during the 2007 season. (Mike Rapp)

of the SEC schedule. The team limped to a 16–14 mark in the SEC, but got hot again in the SEC Tournament, where it finished second. The Commodores were sent to Georgia Tech for a regional, where they beat Michigan twice, but were overmatched against a Tech team that had a lot more power and played on its home field.

Finishing second in Atlanta was hardly a disappointment. Price had ended the regional on a down note, but anyone watching him knew he had exceedingly rare talent. Alvarez was a first-team All-America player, pounding 22 homers and hitting .329/.456/.675. Flaherty was emerging as one of college baseball's best all-around shortstops. Macias had become a reliable center fielder and leadoff man, and Robin, a capable hitter who'd worked hard to become a quality receiver behind the dish. De la Osa could be erratic, but had athleticism and raw power. Weathers suddenly found a new gear to his fastball to get it into the mid- to high-90s, and Corbin began to experiment with him as a closer. Christiani and Jacobson showed flashes of success.

There were enough pieces that the Commodores found themselves in the top 10 of some major preseason polls. Upon beginning the 2007 season, the team immediately proved it belonged there.

All-American closer Casey Weathers fires a pitch. (Jimmy Jones)

At last, a championship

You can often tell how good Corbin thinks his team is by looking at the team's early season schedule. He'd prepared his team to face some of the best of the best when he scheduled a season-opening, three-game trip to Houston, where Vanderbilt would play on a major league field at the Minute Maid Classic.

First up was top-ranked Rice. Price went 5 ⅔ innings and gave up three, and got shutout relief from Tyler Rhoden, Steven Shao, and Weathers. It took the offense a while to get going, as the 'Dores trailed 3–1 heading into the seventh, but Feinberg had a huge two-out hit in that inning to tie the game. A three-base error on an Alvarez line drive led to two more runs, and Meingasner and Robin added eighth-inning home runs for a 7–3 win.

The next day, the 'Dores beat No. 6 Arizona State when ASU's Ike Davis, trying to intentionally walk Brad French, uncorked a wild pitch that scored Jonathan White from third in the 10th. That ended a 4:09 marathon, as the Commodores escaped with a 7–6 victory. On Sunday, Jacobson, with help from Mike Minor's collegiate debut, helped pitch the 'Dores to a 7–4 win over Baylor.

"We played very well and it kind of sent us on our way," Corbin remembered seven years later.

A lot of national media were in attendance, and it definitely left an impression. The Commodores rose to No. 3 in *Collegiate Baseball's* rankings on Monday, surpassing the No. 6 ranking that the 1973 team had achieved. A weekend later, the Commodores had blitzed Ohio in three games by a combined 26–3 margin. On Monday, two of the major polls tabbed VU as the country's top team.

For perhaps the first time in program history, the Commodores had a target on their back. It didn't really matter. VU started 20–0 and though most games weren't close, Vandy played well with its back against the wall. That included one-run wins in 5 of those last 12 games. It nearly ended against Boston College on February 25, with VU trailing by two with two out in the ninth, but Flaherty smacked one over the wall in right-center and the Commodores prevailed, 7–6.

The last game of that streak came when Price threw 137 pitches in a 10-inning, 14-strikeout complete game victory over Ole Miss. The next day, Ole Miss's Lance Lynn, a future rotation mainstay for the St. Louis Cardinals, one-hit the 'Dores in a 6–1 loss. Vanderbilt got a bounce-back win on Sunday, when Macias singled in Meingasner in the bottom of the ninth for a 6–5 win.

After a 15–2 pounding of Western Kentucky, Vanderbilt took its first true weekend road trip to Arkansas. Corbin had played the Razorbacks four times and yet Arkansas, 9–3 against Corbin, remained the only team Vandy had not won a series against in his tenure.

Price had one of his worst outings on Friday, giving up five runs in six innings. Still, Vandy took the game to extra innings with Weathers on the mound. Arkansas had men on second and third when Logan Forsythe hit a fly ball to deep center. Macias caught it, but the outfield was wet and he'd caught it with his momentum carrying him toward the wall. Seeing this, coach Dave Van Horn waved both runners home. The relay throw skipped on the wet turf and Robin couldn't handle it, as the Razorbacks got an 8–7 win on a rare two-RBI sacrifice fly.

Vanderbilt rallied for a 6–3 win in Game 2 on an inside-the-park home run from Alvarez. But on Sunday, Jacobson lasted just an inning and a third and his bullpen was of little help, as the 'Dores dropped their first weekend series that year.

Just how good were the Commodores? In SEC play, they were now just 3–3, and two of those wins were by a run. A road trip to South Carolina would give some answers. The Gamecocks, 24–4 and 4–2 in the league, had moved a spot ahead of Vandy's at No. 2 in *Baseball America*'s poll and were always tough to beat anywhere.

On Friday, Price was solid once again, giving up three and striking out 10 before giving way to Weathers, who got Vandy into extra innings. In the top of the 12th, Davis singled to score Macias with the go-ahead run and Weathers hung on for the victory after throwing 4 ⅓ innings and fanning 7.

The Commodores, though, were having a hard time finding a consistent second and third starter. Corbin inserted Minor into the Saturday slot against the Gamecocks, and it worked as well as anyone had hoped. The freshman fanned nine in seven innings and gave up just one run. Meanwhile, the offense exploded against Carolina's normally outstanding pitching, as VU got hits from eight of its nine starters, with de la Osa's three leading the way in a 12–1 slaughter. Carolina jumped on Christiani early en route to an 8–2 win the next day, but the series win vaulted Vandy back to the top spot in the polls.

Vanderbilt provided some midweek drama, trailing Austin Peay 1–0 heading to the ninth before de la Osa, Alvarez, and Flaherty had big hits to spark a 4–1 win. On Friday, Price was back to elite form, striking out 10 and allowing just three singles in a complete-game, 3–0 win on a 38-degree evening at Hawkins Field against Alabama. Saturday, Alvarez and de la Osa hit back-to-back bombs, and Minor went 5 ⅓ and gave up just a pair of unearned runs for another win.

It was the first time in six series that 'Bama had ever lost a series to a top-ranked team. The 'Tide, though, got a game back when Del Howell stole home on an odd play against Weathers in the ninth to sneak out with a Sunday win.

After a 7–6 home win over Belmont, Vandy went to Lexington for a marathon Friday night game with Kentucky. On another sub-40-degree evening, Price had a no-hitter through five, but a meltdown between his defense and his bullpen soon had UK up, 7–5. Weathers again came on in a cold evening in the eighth, and

Dominic de la Osa earned first team All-American status in 2007 as an outfielder. Here's de la Osa as a freshman shortstop in 2005. (Mike Rapp)

started mowing down UK hitters with triple-digit fastballs. It took until the 12th for the bats to get going, but Flaherty and Feinberg had RBI singles then and VU escaped a 10–8 victor.

Minor was tough again on Saturday, retiring 14 UK hitters in a row and giving up just one unearned run. The 'Dores led 2–1 in the sixth when the game was suspended on account of rain. That made for a strange situation on Sunday. Sunday's regular game was supposed to be televised, and so to comply with the TV schedule, the remainder of Saturday's contest would be played after the completion of that one. Furthermore, the scheduled Game 3 would last just seven innings. That game was tied in the sixth, but UK's Sean Coughlin got a wind-aided homer off Stephen Shao in the sixth and UK won that one, 8–6.

In the completion of the suspended game, French, Alvarez, and Macias all had run-scoring singles to cap the big inning that had started the previous day, and VU emerged as a 9–4 winner. Carolina and VU now led the East by a game over Florida at 9–6.

Vanderbilt had won 23 in a row out of conference, but slipped up in a pair of road games at Lipscomb and MTSU before Tennessee came to town. For the first time in Corbin's tenure, the Vols had taken a series against Vandy the previous year, and now, some revenge was in order. Price was perfect through 6 ⅔ and struck out 14, and Weathers got out of a ninth-inning jam to preserve a 3–1 win. Price was now 7–0, as was Minor after a 4–3 win on Saturday night that included another Weathers save.

There was still the matter of finding a competent Sunday starter. Corbin gave Shao a try, but the lefty was bombed and exited in the third. Christiani got him out of a jam in that inning, which turned out to be important. Vandy tied the game in the bottom of the inning with Alvarez's three-run homer. The teams were tied at six heading to the ninth, and then Davis singled in Alvarez in the ninth for the go-ahead run. Weathers, who by now was having probably the best season of any reliever in college baseball, finished to improve to 8–2.

Corbin called the weekend "a confidence builder," but the continued struggles of the No. 3 starter was a worry. Shao's brief trial was over, and Vandy would now turn to other arms from there.

"[Shao] didn't handle himself well and I think that started to change some things for us. It was Price, Minor, and then [Crowell and Christiani], we went back and forth," Corbin recalled.

Vandy led Carolina and Florida by two games each. The Gators came to town in what figured to be a make-or-break weekend for their SEC fortunes, and Vanderbilt broke them quickly.

Price, who by now was staying ahead in counts and successfully working in pitches besides his fastball with regularity, fanned 13 in eight innings.

"I just think he's getting older, and that's the evolution of a pitcher who really works at his craft," Corbin said at the time.

De la Osa, who was now in the midst of an All-America season, homered and scored four times in leading his team to a 10–1 win.

Minor wasn't sharp on Saturday, blowing the 6–1 first-inning lead to which he'd been staked, but Ty Davis, using a sweeping, overhand breaking ball, came on for seven strong innings of relief. De la Osa homered as part of a four-hit day, and Alvarez and Flaherty each added three hits and two RBI in a 17–6 stomping of the Gators.

On Sunday, Florida threw up the white flag as Crowell, who struck out 11, went 6 ⅔ for the win. Feinberg and Alvarez rapped out three hits each. Flaherty had a homer and the Commodores, 13–5 winners, set a school record for runs in an SEC series with 40.

The team had captured Nashville's imagination, as Hawkins Field was packed for the entire weekend. The same program that couldn't draw flies four years previous now had hundreds of people trying to catch a glimpse from nearby parking garages and the concourse of Memorial Gym. With nine SEC games to go, the Gators were squarely in the rearview mirror and the 'Dores had also put some distance on South Carolina. Now, the competition was 14–6 Arkansas, which was tied with VU for the SEC's overall lead. A trip to Athens to face last-place Georgia was on the horizon for Vandy.

Corbin rode Price for 135 pitches on Friday, but it was obvious by the 12 hits that the Bulldogs put up that it wasn't the lefty's best night. Vandy trailed in the sixth and then Meingasner blasted a two-run homer to tie the game at 5. Weathers got the 'Dores through the eighth and ninth without a scratch and then de la Osa, the previous week's SEC Hitter of the Week, blasted a bases-loaded triple with two outs in the ninth off star closer Josh Fields. The junior had two doubles and a triple that night, and when LSU beat Arkansas, Vandy had sole possession of the SEC lead.

Vanderbilt figured to have an easy time on Saturday, with Minor facing Nathan Moreau (3-2, 5.37 ERA). But no matter how bad a season Georgia was having, the Commodores always figure to be good for one clunker each trip to Athens, and Saturday was that day. Moreau went seven innings and struck out eight and Trevor Holder finished off VU in the last two innings for a 7–0 Bulldogs win. The 'Dawgs touched Minor for three in the first, and that would be all they'd need. Arkansas won, and the pennant race was back to even.

VU, though, never stayed in a funk for long. The only time that season it would lose consecutive games was the mid-April losses to Lipscomb and MTSU following the Kentucky series. So, the 'Dores had it coming to Georgia on Saturday.

Vandy rapped out a season-high 23 hits, led by Feinberg's 5-for-5 finish, with six RBI. Feinberg and de la Osa homered, and though Crowell went just 2 ⅓ innings, Davis got him out of a jam and retired the final 13 batters he faced. It went in the books as a 15–4 romp, and when LSU won, Vandy had first place all to itself again with six regular-season games to go. That victory was the 17th in the SEC, more than any other team in VU history.

The last road trip of the year loomed at Auburn. Price wasn't great, giving up five runs (four earned) in eight innings with six strikeouts. The offense, though, just kept rolling. For the fifth time in seven SEC games, VU hit double-digits in runs, with de la Osa blasting a pair of doubles and Feinberg contributing another homer. On Saturday, Davis scored on a passed ball in the top of the tenth to put Vandy up, 6–5. Weathers had blown a 5–3 lead in the ninth, but threw a perfect tenth to move to 10–2 as the Commodores escaped. On Sunday, Weathers came in with a 2-all tie in the eighth, but gave up an infield single and then a two-run homer in the ninth. VU rallied with two in the ninth and had men on the corners, but Macias fanned to end the game.

Still, Arkansas had faltered that weekend, and now, VU needed to win just one more game to get a share of the SEC regular-season title. Already, Vanderbilt's 43 regular-season wins were the most in school history.

Because the SEC Tournament would start in the middle of the next week, the league would play the final three games on Thursday, Friday, and Saturday. Price was magnificent in Game 1, fanning 15 in 8 ⅔ innings. Robin had three hits and Meingasner added a solo homer. The Commodores, 4–1 winners, waited to see if Ole Miss could finish off the Razorbacks.

The team lingered on the field and in the dugout for the next hour as Vanderbilt broadcast the game over the public address system. A small group of fans and press waited with them. Corbin stood nervously on the top steps of the dugout as Ole Miss clung to a 5–4 lead in the ninth and Arkansas threatened to take the lead . . . and then suddenly, it was over, as the Razorbacks couldn't finish.

For the first time in program history, the Commodores were the SEC's regular-season champs!

Coach Tim Corbin accepts the Southeastern Conference's regular-season championship trophy from SEC commissioner Mike Slive in Hoover, Alabama, during that season's Southeastern Conference Tournament. Vanderbilt won that event as well. (Mike Rapp)

The reality of the moment hit Corbin, and suddenly, the perpetually poker-faced coach cracked a smile. He raised his right fist over his head and sprinted out to left field in front of the big wall to join his players as they celebrated.

Price, the team's leader, paid homage to the 2004 team for taking the first steps toward this moment before describing what it was like to be in the moment.

"It's unbelievable," he said. "It's the best time I've ever had in my entire life."

Playing with house money

Regardless of whether the Commodores won the next two days or not, they'd still be the 2007 SEC champs. No matter how they fared in Hoover, they'd be a national seed and host a super regional if they were still playing that second weekend of the NCAAs. Coasting to the finish line, though, has never been Corbin's modus operandi. Not long after Thursday was settled, he reminded the team that he expected it to continue to play well.

While the big things had been settled, there were some other items on the line. Rather than just settling for a national seed, the 'Dores wanted to be the top national seed and win the conference tournament.

And then, there's the notion of playing well just to be in the habit of playing well as tournaments roll around. Minor shook off his struggles that Friday, hurling 7 ⅔ innings of five-hit, two-run baseball and striking out six as Davis knocked in three runs and de la Osa smacked a homer. The 45th win tied the school record, and Corbin could exit the weekend feeling better about one of his starting pitchers.

In Saturday's regular-season finale, Crowell gave Corbin reason to feel good about his entire rotation. The lefty went seven innings and gave up seven hits, but just two walks and one run while fanning five. The 'Dores clung to a 3–2 lead in the eighth, thanks to de la Osa's two-run homer off the Memorial Gym roof.

Crowell went into the eighth, when Weathers took over, and when the 'Dores gave him some insurance runs, VU had a 6–2 win and ended the regular season with a 22–8 SEC mark.

With 46 wins, the Commodores were now indisputably the best team in school history. The sweep over LSU was the first in program history, and 22 league wins were the most for an SEC team since South Carolina had gone 25–5 in 2000.

Corbin and crew wanted one more thing, however: a title in Hoover.

Late Wednesday evening, that didn't look too likely. Corbin rarely diverts from a plan once he gets one, but he made an exception in the opener against Tennessee by starting Jacobson instead of Price. Jacobson was mediocre, giving up three runs before leaving in the sixth, at which point Christiani gave up a fourth on a Shawn Griffin triple. The Vols led 4–0 as James Adkins carried a no-hitter into the eighth. Vandy finally scratched in the eighth and then rallied, thanks in large part to Alvarez's two-run homer in the ninth. But by that time the Vols had added insurance runs, and prevailed by a 6–4 score.

VU would now have to win five games in four days to take home a title. Even with Vandy's pitching depth, that was unlikely, but the team wasn't folding. On Thursday, Price was perfect through six innings against Mississippi State before Jeffrey Rea led off the seventh with a single. A walk and two doubles later, the Vandy lead was cut to 3–2. Price persevered, getting through the eighth with a pair of Ks and a ground-ball out, before pitching around a ninth inning double to finish. MSU went home, and now, Vandy had a rematch against the Vols in the loser's bracket.

Unlike Wednesday's tilt, there was no drama to this one. With five runs to work with in the first two innings, Minor cruised into the eighth with a shutout before giving up a pair of runs. Those scores were inconsequential, since the Commodores pounded out 16 hits, including four Alvarez doubles, and cruised to a 15–2 win.[3] Ole Miss was next.

---

3 Vandy's romp that evening included eight ninth-inning runs in what would be the last game for Vols coach Rod Delmonico, whom Tennessee fired the next week.

Rarely do offensive fireworks like VU had put on the night before extend into the next day against a team with good pitching, but Saturday morning was an exception. Vandy scored eight in the first two innings as Alvarez, de la Osa, and Parker Hanks each homered. Crowell carried a no-hitter into the fifth, and went into the seventh with a 10–0 lead. The conference has a "mercy rule" for tournaments whereby a team with a double-digit lead after seven innings is awarded a victory.[4] A two-out Justin Henry single spoiled Crowell's chance to end it then, but after VU added three the next inning, Crowell shut down the Rebels and ended the game an inning early.

That sent the 'Dores into a 4:45 rematch with the Rebels later that afternoon. Davis got the start and gave up a homer, a triple, a double, and two walks all in the first before limiting the damage to two runs. Flaherty knocked in two with a double in the bottom of the inning to tie. Davis, though, gave up a run in the second and after another walk, Corbin's patience was exhausted.

Before the week started, many debated how hard the Commodores should exert themselves in Hoover given that the NCAAs were around the corner. It was hot and the 'Dores were in the middle of their fifth game in four days, and so Corbin's next move, which was going to seldom-used Jason Cunningham, almost made it look as if VU were waving the white flag.

Cunningham came to Vanderbilt as the team manager the previous year, but made the team during preseason tryouts. Previously, he'd pitched just three times, two coming in blowouts. On a good day, Cunningham might be lucky to hit 80 with his fastball. The sophomore, though, got a pop-up from future big-leaguer Zack Cozart to get Davis out of the mess.

Corbin was admittedly grasping for straws by throwing Cunningham. But there was a method to the madness. Though the tournament had started to take its toll, the Commodores still had about as many good arms as anyone. It was obvious that Cunningham didn't have a fastball, but if Corbin were to throw him in that spot, he must have *something* that kept

---

4 This is designed to save pitching staffs, which can easily be taxed in tournaments.

people off-balance—a hard-breaking curve or a trick pitch of some sort.

The truth is, Cunningham had none of the above, but by virtue of leaving virtually no scouting footprint, Corbin's gamble was that the Rebels would keep waiting for that something that Cunningham was holding back, allowing the sophomore to win the mental game for a few outs until Corbin could figure out an appropriate next option.

"The only thing was I thought he might be nervous. I went to the mound and I told him I had an extra pair of underwear and asked if he needed them. He laughed and said, 'No.' Then he pitched," Corbin said.

Cunningham had one attribute that caused Ole Miss problems: he was left-handed. Four and two-thirds shutout innings later, Ole Miss still hadn't scratched and Corbin summoned Weathers as Cunningham left to a standing ovation.[5]

The All-American pitcher retired two hitters to get out of the inning and stranded Cunningham's man, but Vandy hadn't scored since Flaherty's double. The game went to the ninth, and the 'Dores were three outs from being sent home, but Macias's sacrifice fly in the ninth sent the game to extra innings.

Weathers started the 10th by whiffing Henry, but Cody Overbeck blooped a single to center, and Cozart and Logan Power followed with infield singles to load the bases. Rebel coach Mike Bianco had Peyton Farr attempt a suicide squeeze. Farr failed to get the bunt down, which left Overbeck hanging out to dry about 30 feet off the bag.

Robin did what catchers are trained to do and ran toward Overbeck with the ball in his throwing hand. It should have been an easy second out, but Robin's throw sailed over Alvarez's head at third and into left. Overbeck and Henry scored easily.

Later in the at bat, Farr came home on a fielder's choice, and perhaps should have scored on a teammate's double off the top

---

5 That would be the only real shining moment of Cunningham's career. He pitched four innings and gave up four earned runs in 2008, and didn't play his senior year. His teammates gave him a great send-off that day. As Cunningham boarded the team bus, they formed two lines facing each other as they held bats above their heads with the bat heads touching each other to form a mock canopy.

of the wall later in the inning. Perhaps Bianco held him because there was just one out at that point, but Weathers fought back by striking out Brett Basham and Jordan Henry to end the inning. Still, it didn't seem to matter, as a 6–3 lead with an ace closer on the mound could have been safe for Ole Miss.

De la Osa, leading off the inning, fought back after getting down 0–2 in the count before jacking a 2–2 pitch over the wall to the alley in left-center. Alvarez singled sharply up the middle, and Flaherty followed with the same. Corbin had Meingasner bunt toward first, not a bad idea since Overbeck, the second baseman who'd cover on the play, had three errors in the first game. Overbeck came in to field, and then overshot Farr as his teammate scrambled to cover first. Alvarez scored and Flaherty took third.

Flaherty stood 90 feet from home, and Meingasner on second, when Robin had his shot at redemption. The infield was playing back, willing to give VU the tying run with no out, but trying to keep Meingasner from beating them. All Robin wanted was a ground ball to pull VU even, but instead, he got a line-drive single past Farr.

An amazing comeback was complete in the blink of an eye. Vandy now had a shot against Arkanasas—the only team to take a series from the 'Dores all year—for a title.

"I've been coaching for twenty-three years and that's probably as—I'm not going to say well-played—but as good a baseball game as I've been involved in for a myriad of reasons," Corbin said afterward.

No team had ever lost the first game of the SEC Tournament and won five straight for a title. Vanderbilt needed a big boost from starting pitcher Tyler Rhoden, who hadn't been asked to pitch for long in key situations, if it were to pull it off. The Floridian was shaky through the first two innings, but his teammates had staked him to a 4–3 lead and he settled down to retire 13 of the last 14 hitters. The one hitter he didn't retire would score in the seventh, but by that time, Robin had added an RBI single and Alvarez scored on an error in the top of the inning and the 'Dores were up 6–4.

Jacobson found himself in trouble in the eighth, as Wayne Hrozek lined a two-out single to left that had Matt Willard racing home from second. Meingasner, though, picked it up from left field and threw a strike to Robin to end the inning. Meingasner then tripled to left-center with one out in the ninth, and then scored on a sacrifice fly from Ryan Davis.

In the bottom of the ninth, Jacobson started by striking out Tim Smalling and Jake Dugger, and even though Ben Tschepikow bounced a liner off Jacobson's leg, the right-hander fielded and threw to French to end it.

The team sprinted out of the dugout to celebrate. Not since Alabama in 1996 had the same team won both the SEC's regular season and tournament titles. Robin, Flaherty, de la Osa, and Alvarez were named to the all-tournament team, with Alvarez taking home Most Valuable Player honors.

"I'm proud of them. . . . It takes a special makeup to do what we did," Corbin said.

Earlier in the day, the NCAA confirmed what everyone already knew, which was that the 'Dores would host a regional for the first time. The Commodores took a happy three-hour bus ride back to Nashville and waited to see who was up next.

Home, not-so-sweet home

There weren't a lot of surprises when the NCAA announced the pairings on Labor Day. First, the Commodores were the tournament's top seed, which hadn't been hard to figure since they'd been No. 1 in the polls for all but three weeks. Nor were the opponents unfamiliar.

First up would be Austin Peay, a familiar midweek rival with a campus about an hour down I-24 from Nashville. Another in-state foe, Memphis, would participate in the Nashville Regional as the three seed. Finally, Michigan, the Big Ten Tournament champs— the same Michigan that VU had beaten twice in last year's Atlanta Regional—would be the two seed.

At no point did anyone remotely consider that VU wouldn't advance to play a super regional in its park the following weekend.

The thought that VU would even need beyond Sunday to clinch things didn't seem likely, either.

Corbin, though, knew better from experience. The Commodores had been the beneficiary of Virginia's first-time hosting experience just three years earlier, and the veteran coach knew full well that a team in VU's position had cracked on many an occasion.

"It was just a feeling we hadn't been exposed to yet. I don't know how, in retrospect, we handled it. We may have been a little uneasy in that environment—first time we've hosted a Regional, ranked No. 1 in the country a long period of time, we won the SEC outright and then we go ahead and win the tournament—so we were coming in as the gladiator and we're hosting this big tournament with Austin Peay and Memphis and Michigan certainly as the team that was supposed to go on and get to Omaha," he recalled a decade later.

Michigan beat Memphis on Friday afternoon, and would play the winner of Vandy–Austin Peay on Saturday. Vanderbilt had brought in bleachers in right and right-center and the crowd that night and the park, which normally seated about 2,400 fans, drew 3,532 that evening. That didn't include dozens more who watched from the parking garage that stood diagonally from the right-field foul pole. Every one of them got their money's worth that night.

In one of the more epic pitching matches that Hawkins Field has ever seen, Price faced off against APSU ace Sean Kelley, who'd been the Ohio Valley Conference Pitcher of the Year.[6] The fans would see Price's power against Kelley's finesse, and even though Price would strike out 17 that night, Kelley matched him pitch-for-pitch, keeping VU hitters off-balance time and time again while fanning nine, walking none, and yielding five hits.

APSU threatened in the fourth. Jacob Lane singled with one out and Trey Lucas lined a ball to the gap in right-center that looked as if it would score Lane. But de la Osa came out of

---

6 Despite a quality career at APSU, Kelley wasn't drafted in 2006 and came back for his senior season. That night at Hawkins Field did a lot to help his professional prospects. He was drafted in the 13th round a few weeks later by Seattle, and actually made his major league debut in 2009 before Price, the No. 1 overall pick that year, did.

nowhere to make a spectacular catch and keep the Governors off the board. It was one of several nice defensive plays that evening. Until the ninth, the game's only run came when French scored on a fifth-inning wild pitch.

Price trotted out for the ninth determined to finish things off, but Nashville native Tyler Farrar homered over the big wall in left to tie the game as the leadoff man in the ninth. Price settled down, but VU couldn't score in the ninth, so the game went to extra innings.

Weathers was now on, and he whiffed the side in order in the 10th. Vanderbilt failed to score again, but Weathers got two strikeouts and a groundout in the eleventh for another perfect inning.

In the bottom of the eleventh, the Govs brought in closer Ben Wiltshire with Flaherty on second and Meingasner on first with two outs. His wild pitch moved runners over. Wiltshire got exactly what he wanted, jamming Robin and forcing a weak grounder back to the mound. But Wiltshire's spikes got caught in the ground and he couldn't field it. Flaherty raced home from third and the crowd exploded.

"A crazy set of circumstances, but a great atmosphere and was just glad to get out of it," Corbin commented seven years later. "I remember when they took out Kelley, there was a sigh of, we were just lucky. Lucky to get him out of the game."

Many experts had pegged this as the easiest regional in the country, but that night was a sign of things to come.

Perhaps that game got in the Commodores' heads a bit, for the tension carried over to the Saturday evening tilt with Michigan. Hanks homered to right-center in the fifth for the game's first run, but Nate Recknagel blasted a bases-loaded double off Minor in the top of the sixth as the Wolverines took a 3–1 lead.

But as it always did, Vandy punched back. Meingasner smacked starter Mike Wilson's 3–1 pitch over the short wall in left around the 375-foot sign, also scoring Alvarez. The game was tied after eight.

Farrar's homer may not have beaten Vandy the night before, but it may have played a role in Vandy's loss on Saturday. Minor was done and Corbin would have normally gone to Weathers immediately in the ninth in this spot. Instead, he went to Jacobson, who gave up a lead–off single to Adam Abraham.

Now, Corbin went to Weathers, but he wasn't as sharp as the night before. Doug Pickens sacrificed him over a base, and Derek Van Buskirk lined to right. Weathers walked Jason Christian, and No. 9 hitter Kevin Cislo grounded to Flaherty at short. The sophomore went to the ground to field it, but Christian beat the throw to second as Abraham scored, and the Wolverines now led by a run. In the ninth, Abraham, now on the mound to close, fanned Flaherty on a high 2-2 pitch with two on and two out.

An air of shock and uncertainty now hung around the ballpark that evening. Why hadn't the team that had had so many comebacks had one on Saturday? Maybe the team that had run roughshod over others in the nation's best conference—South Carolina, one of the country's best programs, had finished 5 games back in the East—was no longer invincible. VU had to win 3 straight from here just to survive the weekend.

The hangover carried into Saturday's early-afternoon elimination game with Austin Peay. Vandy, the visiting team that day, trailed 3–0 in the third before Feinberg had an RBI single, Alvarez bounced a two-RBI single off the wall in right, and Flaherty lined a homer to right-center. VU led 5–3, but Peay got a run back in the fourth to chase Crowell. De la Osa, though, hit a wind-aided homer to right-center in the fourth to extend the cushion to 7–4.

Vandy finally got things right on the mound, with Ty Davis finishing off the game with 5 ⅓ scoreless innings, and Meingasner added a two-run insurance homer in the sixth. Flaherty went 5-for-5, extending his hitting streak to 33 games as VU eliminated APSU with an 11–5 win, and now, the 'Dores had to beat Michigan twice, starting with that evening's game.

The positive momentum carried over. Vandy exploded for seven second-inning runs, including a rare home run by French, who hit only one other in 165 at bats that season. Michigan cut the lead to 9–5 in the fourth when Jason Christian hit a three-run double, but Jacobson, who threw five innings in relief, kept the Wolverines off the scoreboard from there en route to a 10–5 'Dores victory.

Everything was back to even, and that had to favor the Commodores. That "team of destiny" feeling was back. The Commodores were hurting a bit on pitching, and would need to start Rhoden, who had a 5.66 ERA in 20 ⅔ innings. But Rhoden had pitched reasonably well in Hoover, and Michigan's Chris Fetter, with a 4.71 ERA against a much weaker schedule, hadn't exactly been an ace. On the other hand, there was some potential hidden in the numbers, as Fetter had been the Big Ten's ERA champion the previous season.

Michigan got to Rhoden early, scoring in the second on Eric Rose's sacrifice fly and again on Recknagel's homer. It got another in the fifth when Brad Roblin knocked in Jason Christian with a double. That chased Rhoden after four.

Vandy, having thrown 11 more innings than the Wolverines coming into Monday, was on the wrong end of a war of pitching attrition, but did its best. Crowell gave Corbin a perfect fourth, striking out two, and Minor did the same in the fifth. Weathers threw the seventh and eighth, allowing a hit and two walks, but nary a run.

The other problem was that UM's Fetter was giving coach Rich Maloney the 2006 version. Despite being 6-foot-8 and 230 pounds, Fetter was a soft-tossing control artist, and that's what most gave the Commodores fits that season. As a result, Fetter pitched seven innings, surrendering seven hits, two walks, and posting just three strikeouts. More importantly, he gave up just two runs. One came in the second on Alvarez's homer. Macias scored Vandy's second run in the eighth, leading off with a walk that chased Fetter for Abraham, who gave up a double to de la Osa and then a sac fly to center that scored Macias to get within one.

But there were now two outs, and Vandy had its backs against the wall with Meingasner at an 0–2 count. The left fielder fouled off three pitches and took two pitches out of the strike zone before blooping a two-out single to score de la Osa and tie the game heading to the ninth.

Of course, nobody expected to see Price, who had thrown 130 pitches on Friday, again. Coming into that day, even Corbin did not consider him an option. But the hyper competitive lefty had left a note on Corbin's desk that morning that simply read this: "If the game is tied, I want the ball."

Running out of options, Corbin sent Price and Mark Lamm to the bullpen to get ready. Lamm would have also been an interesting choice, as the freshman had not played all year and was in line for a redshirt. But Lamm, too, had told Corbin he was ready to take one for the team if needed.

In case Corbin hadn't gotten the morning memo, Price was there to tug on his jersey as crunch time approached. When Weathers walked Cislo on a 3–1 pitch to start the ninth, Corbin gave the call for the National Player of the Year to pitch. The stadium exploded as Price charged to the mound ready to go.

"All those pictures you see of David Price with his head back and his mouth wide open yelling, that was the moment that it occurred," Corbin remembered later.

Maloney had Rose bunt Cislo over a base, but it was useless. Christian and Roblin followed next, and both may as well have been carrying a flyswatter to the plate instead of a bat. Price fanned each on three pitches, as neither came close to making contact.

Vanderbilt was tough enough to beat without giving it anything, and when Robin reached to lead off the ninth on an error, it seemed inevitable that a Commodore victory celebration was coming. French got Robin into scoring position with a bunt. Macias blooped a ball to right and for a moment, it looked like that might win the game, but Cislo, the second baseman, made a fantastic, over-the-shoulder grab well into the outfield. That was out number two, and when Feinberg flied to center, things headed to extra innings.

Price came out to start the eleventh. The concern was Recknagel, who led off, but when Price retired the guy who'd be the Big Ten Player of the Year the following season, everyone could breathe a sigh of relief.

·Up next was Zach Putnam, a good hitter in his own right, and one who Corbin had recruited aggressively as he assembled the Flaherty-Alvarez class. The fact that Putnam was a right-hander helped a bit, but Maloney didn't like something about the matchup. He shocked everyone by going to his bench for freshman

Alan Oaks, who was hitting below .200. Maloney knew he needed one big hit and felt that the freshman had the best chance of hitting Price's fastball.

Corbin, perhaps never unprepared for anything a day in his life, knew this also. For that reason, he had Price mix in a pair of curve balls on his first four pitches.

"He didn't bite on two breaking balls that were down. He's supposed to," Corbin said after the game.

The next pitch brought on what was arguably the biggest heartbreak in Vanderbilt sports history.

The end

In 133 ⅓ innings of work that year, Farrar's blast on Friday had been just the second homer against Price all season. The chance that Oaks would deliver here was remote. Price got a fastball down in the zone, which is probably what he wanted to do. But he left it slightly in, and bat met ball.

"He crushed it. He absolutely crushed it," a somber Corbin said afterward.

The ball went over the wall in left-center, and Michigan led, 4–3. It would be the last pitch of Price's great career as Corbin called for Jacobson, who got VU out of the inning.

The 'Dores had a chance in the bottom of the 10th, and they had the guys they wanted—de la Osa, Alvarez, and Flaherty—due. De la Osa had started to press, and grounded the first pitch to short for out one. Alvarez, though, hit a 2–2 pitch deep to left-center. The crowd came to its feet as the ball soared toward the wall. It was going, going . . . caught by Michigan's Derek VanBuskirk (who at 6-foot-5 was, and still is, perhaps the tallest left fielder to play at Hawkins Field), just inches from leaving the park.

Flaherty kept the dream alive with a single, but when Meingasner tapped back to reliever Michael Powers, the pitcher gloved and threw to first to end things.

Everyone was stunned. Other than the voices of the celebrating Michigan fans and players, all that could be heard was the sounds of peanut shells crunching beneath the feet of 3,500 departing Vandy fans.

"I still, to this moment, thought we were going to win. I just thought we were going to win. I did not visualize sitting in front of you talking about a loss tonight. I still think it's a bad dream," Corbin told the media afterward.

Michigan had done the impossible. Vanderbilt, with 54 wins, two conference titles in the toughest league in the land, and a consensus No. 1 ranking, was done in the tournament's first weekend at the hands of the champs from the lowly Big Ten.

A bittersweet parting

Price would be an instant millionaire in a few days, when Tampa Bay would pick him first in the 2007 MLB Draft. Everyone knew this, including Price, but it was no consolation. The junior was a no-show for the postgame press conference, said to be too distraught to face the media.

If you've been around the program, it wasn't hard to understand. Corbin had built a family atmosphere, and Price felt he'd let his family down. Years later, former players still come back in droves to work out at VU and hang together. Those same players often describe the college experience as the most fun years of their lives. Corbin shares that feeling, especially on that team.

"It was one of the most fun seasons that I've ever had as a coach, to be honest with you. I just thought we were tough. We came from behind. We had good players. The locker room was phenomenal. . . . I would put it second to the 2013 team in terms of locker rooms, but the locker room was so good because of guys like Price," Corbin said in 2014.

In the days that followed, Price talked of coming back for a senior year. That would have been ridiculous, and when his

David Price high-fives Pedro Alvarez (24) after a big moment at Hawkins Field in 2007. (Jimmy Jones)

emotions settled down, Price inked a six-year, $8.5 million deal with the Rays.

Lamm remembered how Price and several of the upperclassmen conducted themselves.

"It was really special. I think the best part for me, on my end, was just seeing how they handled things. You had a guy [Price] that you knew was going to go out there and make $8 million when the draft came. You couldn't tell that at all. You had other guys obviously in the next couple of years that would be doing the same thing, going high in the first round," he said.

Several from that team would go on to the majors. Price, of course, won a Cy Young with Tampa in 2012. Alvarez, whom Pittsburgh took second overall in 2008, was the National League's home run champion in 2013. Flaherty would become a valuable utility infielder for Baltimore, and Minor, a rotation staple for the Atlanta Braves.

Their first claim to fame, though, was establishing the Commodores as a national power. Because of that, the 2007 team will be as fondly remembered as any group of players that ever played any sport at Vanderbilt.

2011 Baseball: Reaching the promised land

Heartbreak still lingered in the air following the shocking end to the 2007 season. The 2008 team lost David Price but returned the core of its lineup, and was certainly good enough to reach the College World Series. But third baseman Pedro Alvarez hurt his wrist early in the season, which sapped his power, and something was generally amiss about that bunch. By the time the NCAA Tournament rolled around, the Commodores, who finished just 41–22 overall and 15–14 in the Southeastern Conference, were sent packing the first weekend after losing twice to an Oklahoma squad that barely made the tournament.

With most of those key faces gone, Corbin had to overhaul almost his entire offense for 2009. The team just barely made the NCAAs, thanks mostly to another nice run in the Southeastern Conference Tournament, where Vanderbilt dropped the title game to eventual national champion LSU. The 'Dores, playing out of the loser's bracket, rallied back to get to the title game of the Louisville Regional against the home-standing Cardinals, where Mike Minor, pitching on short rest, lost the last game of his stellar career.

That set 2010 up as a season with some expectations, as a bunch of the previous season's freshmen—namely, pitcher Sonny

Gray, third baseman Jason Esposito, first baseman Aaron West-lake, and outfielder Joe Loftus—had shown promise in full-time roles. Sophomore arms like Grayson Garvin and Jack Armstrong had flashed potential. Junior catcher/designated hitter Curt Casali had been tremendous as a first-time starter in 2009 and senior Andrew Giobbi had also become competent behind the dish.

The defensive-minded Corbin had also brought in a pair of fleet-footed freshman outfielders in Connor Harrell and Mike Yastrzemski and a freshman shortstop in Anthony Gomez, who could flat-out hit. Juniors Chase Reid and Taylor Hill had also at times shown good things on the mound the previous spring, and freshman Will Clinard had been excellent in relief.

It figured to be a team that would get better as the year progressed, and sure enough, a six-game SEC winning streak toward the end of the conference season helped the Commodores to a 16–12 regular-season conference mark. This time, the Commodores upset Louisville in its regional when Harrell's suicide squeeze scored Casali from third in the tenth inning of the title game. Vanderbilt then went to the Tallahassee Super Regional, where it gave host Florida State a scare before dropping the decisive Game 3.

All-Southeastern Conference center fielder Connor Harrell rounds the bases. (Jimmy Jones)

At one game short of the Omaha, it was the closest Vanderbilt had come to reaching college baseball's biggest stage. With memories of 2007's heartbreak still fresh, it may have seemed to Vanderbilt fans that Omaha would never be in the cards. But if you could step back from the emotional ledge and see how that 2007 season had brought greater talent to the program—talent that was mostly returning for 2011—it wasn't a leap to think that bigger things might be in store that spring.

"I thought that super regional had a lot to do with where we were headed once we got started the next year," Corbin remembered years later. "I felt like after the conclusion of that season, that team was very determined and destined to take another step, and that was a year that was, I'm not going to say easy—that's not the right word—but it was seamless, it was smooth. You had talent, No. 1, from a baseball standpoint—it was a very talented team—but you had talented leadership."

According to Gomez, the team didn't speak much about expectations for 2011—"Everyone kind of knew what was going to happen next year, but nobody really spoke about it. We just kind of practiced our way through the fall and spring and hoped to see what would happen," he'd say later—but Harrell knew full well that the specter of Omaha would hang over the program until the Commodores could get there.

"Whether you wanted to acknowledge it or not, there were lots of expectations for that team. After 2010, getting to where we got—I think we almost won fifty games that year[1]—to come in with the same nucleus of guys, a lot to be gained but at the same time there was some pressure," he said.

A trip for a fall series to perennial power Texas, which would play in the College World Series the next spring, raised the bar. The Commodores got the best of the Longhorns that October weekend, which only served to make the four months between then and the start of the 2011 season seem even longer.

It would be worth the wait.

---

1 The 2010 team went 46–20.

Arms, defense lead the way

Corbin builds his teams around power pitching and defense, and this team would be no exception. The staff's headliner was junior Sonny Gray, who'd flashed triple-digit velocity as a freshman and a wipe out curve to complement it. Gray had been a second-team All-SEC pick the previous year, going 10–5 with a 3.48 ERA and 113 strikeouts in 108 ⅔ innings. Gray, who was an obvious pick to start Friday night games, was also a spectacular fielder. He often had early-inning control problems, but in 2011, he'd elevate his game a notch to finish 12–4 with a 2.43 ERA.

"With Sonny, when we were facing another team and he got on the mound, I would tell guys, 'Listen, if you don't get to him the first few innings, you might as well just go up there and put your spikes and your bat in the batter's box, because once he gets rolling, that's it,'" Gomez recalled.

As talented as Gray was, he wasn't the staff's best starter that year—or, at least he wasn't according to the league's coaches, who named Grayson Garvin the league's Pitcher of the Year after 2011. The big lefty had missed much of 2010 with an injury, but threw well in the 2010 Louisville Regional and used that to spring board into the 13–2 season of 2011, which saw him post a 2.48 ERA with 101 strikeouts and just 25 walks in 112 ⅔ innings. Garvin was even better in SEC play, where he was 9–0 with a 1.83 ERA.

Garvin didn't have Gray's stuff, but what he did have was an uncanny ability to mix pitches and keep hitters off-balance.

"I thought he was the right guy to pitch after Sonny. He was a lefty, he was a different look. . . . Change-up, change-up, and fastball. You couldn't hit the ball well," Corbin remembers.

Finding a reliable third starter is tough for any team, even in the Southeastern Conference, which historically has had arms as good as anyone's. Even for Corbin, this had sometimes been a problem; even as talented as the 2007 staff was, six different guys took turns starting SEC games. Corbin nabbed senior Taylor HIll as the Sunday starter from the start, but his career numbers coming in—13–8 with a 4.62 ERA in 195 innings—were just ordinary.

The one thing the Mt. Juliet (Tennessee) pitcher always had was an ability to throw strikes. That solidified his hold on the job at the start of 2011. But when Hill suddenly started pumping the fastball up four or five miles per hour higher and into the mid-90s, he started to dominate on the same level as the other two.[2]

"[It was] movement and velocity. . . . It was his downhill plane to his ball. I think his slider command was good, it was sweeping and it was late. His fastball, though, his angle to the plate—that's when I looked at him and thought, *This is a different pitcher*," Corbin recalls.

Indeed, Hill wound up with Garvin-like numbers, throwing 99 innings that fall, striking out 92, walking 26, and going 6–1 with a 2.73 ERA.

There was no let up once those guys left the game. Vandy's bullpen was deep and talented. Closer Navery Moore hadn't been healthy and Corbin wouldn't use him for long stretches, but in 28 appearances, he'd go 4–2 with 11 saves with a sparking 1.21 ERA. The 'Dores had flame-throwing setup men in right-hander Mark Lamm and lefty Corey Williams. If Corbin needed a righty to go a little longer, there was Clinard.

Even if you stopped there, it was a great staff. What made this one special, though, was that Corbin had recruited a pair of highly regarded freshmen in righty T. J. Pecoraro and lefty Kevin Ziomek, who would combine for a 1.59 ERA in 85 innings.

Ziomek summed up the situation nicely a couple of years later.

"That was one of the coolest things, it seemed we could match up with anybody. . . . One thing I'll always remember is a guy like Clinard or Corey Williams, they'll be throwing the ball well and next thing you know after two or three hitters they're out of the game," he recalled.

"You kind of sit there as a fan and say, 'What the heck? Why are you taking them out?' But you've got someone who's just as good who can come in and pick it up. . . . To have that many guys who can pitch in that many situations is unbelievable."

---

2 A member of the staff also caught Hill tipping some of his pitches; once that stopped, the results improved also.

Curt Casali puts the ball in play against North Carolina in the 2011 College World Series. (Jimmy Jones)

The staff would register about a third of the year's outs on its own. As for the rest of those outs, it relied on a defense that fielded a terrific .973 (.977 in the SEC) and didn't have a weakness in the field. Corbin's teams have always been good behind the plate and with veteran Curt Casali, that was the case in 2011.

"He was like a brick wall back there. . . .When you have a catcher who's not letting anything get past him, you have a pitcher who's more confident to throw their curveball and they spike their curveball like someone's gonna stop it," Gomez says.

Starting with the left side of the infield, Esposito had a shortstop's ability—that's where he'd start the year—but was indirectly pushed to third because Riley Reynolds was as steady as you could get at second. Reynolds bumped Gomez to short and Bryan Johns, who'd played second the year before and knocked the cover off the ball, from third to the bench. At first, Westlake wasn't a terrific athlete, but made just two errors and his ability to, quite literally, do the splits to stretch in order to get to a teammate's throw, helped save a few errors and register an extra out or two.

And then, there was that outfield that essentially consisted of three center fielders. Yastrzemski had played center through part of

2010, but he'd be in right the next spring. Harrell stuck in center, where he'd also played some as a freshman, and speedy (and often spectacular) freshman Tony Kemp would be stationed in left.

Gomez called it "the fastest outfield in the SEC." Obviously, that made pitching even easier for the Commodore hurlers, as Ziomek recalled.

"It just seemed like every single ball that went to the outfield was caught. It was unreal as a pitcher. I'd never seen anything like it. And then you've got those guys up the middle, with Gomez and Riley Reynolds, I don't know if Riley made an error all year.[3]

"He was unreal." Ziomek said later. "Just seeing the plays that Tony would make out there in left field, I'll never forget those diving plays he'd make.

"I found myself going to pro ball just wishing I had those guys behind me, still, as crazy as that sounds."

No easy outs

There would be many comparisons to the 2007 team. Both squads were ranked No. 1 at one point in the season, and both would win or share the SEC's regular-season title. But the biggest difference was in the lineup: while the '07 team was top-heavy with bats, this would be Corbin's most balanced lineup yet.

"I was talking to one of my buddies that goes to South Carolina, and I asked, 'So, what was your scouting report for our 2011 team?' And they were like, 'Well, we had a scouting report, but you have like green, you have yellow, and you have red for their hitters and they said that one through nine, everybody was green,'" Kemp said.

At the top of the lineup was Kemp, the rare freshman who established himself as an every-day player well before opening day (he played in 65 of the team's 66 games, and started 64). Corbin knew he had something special well before the regular season began.

---

3 Ziomek was nearly right; Reynolds made one error that season in 60 games.

"I knew we had a leadoff hitter in him, though, when we went to Texas. We played well on Friday night and beat them up and we got into Sunday's game and I went over to Tony and I said, 'Hey, listen, Tony, I know you didn't play the other night and you got a pinch hit. What I want to do is just test you a little bit tonight and have you lead off,' and he goes, 'Cool,' and just shook his head. All I said, 'All I want you to do is get on base as many times as you can. Don't worry about how you get on, just get on,'" Corbin remembers.

"And he went 4-for-4 with two doubles and almost hit a home run, and I thought, *That little booger's gonna be a really good player*, and he was."

Kemp would justify Corbin's faith in him with a .329/.434/.417 stat line that fall, and he'd also steal 17 bases in 22 tries.

Gomez would start the season lower in the order, but wound up in the 2-hole. Corbin was looking for a guy to put the ball in play in that spot, and nobody was more qualified than the sophomore from New Jersey, who struck out just 14 times in a still-school-record 286 at bats.

Westlake, the tall, broad-shouldered lefty, would hit in the 3-spot from start to finish. That's where you want your best hitter, and Westlake, who led the team in on-base percentage (.463), slugging (.640), home runs (18), total bases (160), and ranked second behind Esposito in RBI (56) was certainly that.

Casali, Yastrzemski, and Esposito would generally follow in some order. Casali was dangerous because he rarely chased pitches out of the strike zone, made consistent contact, and had power. Esposito had perhaps the best power-speed combination on the team. Yastrzemski was an instinctual player, someone who could get on base in a variety of ways and efficiently make things happen (23-of-26 on stolen bases that season) once he was there.

That was more than enough for most opponents to contend with, but the bottom of that order made the Commodores quite unique.

In the No. 7 spot was Conrad Gregor, a pure hitter who had exceptional strike-zone judgment and on-base ability for anyone, much less a freshman. Gregor started the season on the bench but forced his way into the lineup, and hit .382/.446/.517 in Southeastern Conference games that fall.

Behind him was Harrell, who, with nine homers and 12 doubles and a triple in 197 at bats that year, may have been the most powerful 8-hitter in the country that year. Reynolds (.331/.383/.373) was incredibly effective to be the last guy in the lineup and saved his best for the SEC (.344/.398/.411).

It was a lineup that hit so well from start to finish that talented players like Johns and Loftus, who'd be lineup fixtures in most places, spent most of the year in the dugout.

Gomez shared a funny story that demonstrated not only how tough it was to pitch to that lineup that year, but about how unified the team was that season.

"A short anecdote, we were at Kentucky and so obviously [Sam] Selman didn't pitch much that year, and it's Thursday night, and he considered himself the Thursday night starter because he was throwing Thursdays, we'd have a little scrimmage on Thursday night practices," Gomez recalled. "So sure enough, he gets up and Tony leads off, he gets a hit, Espo might have hit a home run, Westlake gets a hit.

"So sure enough, he pitches to like nine guys, doesn't record an out, I think[4]— and . . . so he comes off the mound and Corbs goes, 'Sam, what do you think?' and he goes, 'Corbs, honestly, I think you should start every one of those guys tomorrow.'

"That's just proof that he wasn't getting his innings in yet, but he was still making a joke about having a good time. Whether you were playing or not, everyone was having a good time."

Great start leads to big things

Any questions about where the season was heading were answered when the Commodores won nineteen of their first twenty games. Lots of teams have fast starts in out-of-conference play where teams can schedule some easy wins, but the first twenty contests included a three-game series against a Stanford club that

---

4 Harrell, present for that conversation, said, "I think we had two home runs."

would go to a super regional and Mississippi State, which made a regional. There was also an early midweek game against a decent Belmont squad that VU would see again in the postseason.

A trip to San Diego for three games against the University of San Diego, as well as one with San Diego State, resulted in a 4–0 start. The win over Belmont, plus Friday and Saturday home wins over Stanford, pushed Vandy to 7–0 before VU couldn't solve Stanford pitcher Jordan Pries in a 5–2 loss on February 27. However, the Commodores would beat Stanford's Mark Appel, who'd eventually be the first overall pick of the 2013 draft, by a 2–1 count on Saturday. Vandy would rip off twelve more wins before losing to Mississippi State on Sunday, March 20.

"When we got back from [San Diego], I felt like we had a pretty good team because we played everybody at their place and handled them well. Sonny pitched against San Diego and it was a well-pitched game, and everybody felt pretty confident then," Corbin recalls.

The MSU loss was tough to swallow at the time. VU led 8–4 at home after seven innings, but uncharacteristically gave up five eighth-inning runs to blow that one.

"I probably was [upset], but it was easier to get over after the fact. I felt like Mississippi State was good. In retrospect, I thought they were really good," Corbin remembered just before the start of the 2014 campaign.

Vandy rebounded for an easy 11–2 midweek win over Tennessee Tech before heading to Arkansas, which is one of the toughest places in college baseball to play. Gray was terrific that night, recording 12 strikeouts in an eight-inning complete game. However, UA's James McCann, hitting with two out and men on second and third, hit a ground ball to Gomez, whose throw home bounced off the mound and resulted in the Razorbacks' only two runs, and Vandy fell by a 2–1 count.

Garvin pitched VU to a 4–1 win on Saturday, putting Vandy in a position to do something that Corbin had never done in his previous five series against the Razorbacks: win one of them. Kemp remembers what Hill did from there.

"I think these guys were pitching in 20-degree weather, I don't know how they got grip, I don't know how they got anything, I

Taylor Hill, who had an outstanding 2011 season as VU's No. 3 starter, fires a pitch at the College World Series. (Jimmy Jones)

just remember him going five or six innings and pitching a gem and I think we won the game by one or two, and he held their offense to one or two runs and I think that's really what solidified Taylor's role as Sunday starter the rest of the year," he said.

Officially, Hill threw five scoreless innings that day, and Westlake provided the offensive highlight with a mammoth home run off the right-center-field scoreboard in a 4–1 win. Moore closed the door with a save. VU returned home with a 4–2 SEC mark and a series win over another eventual NCAA Tournament team.

"We were flawless. I remember meeting [their athletics director], Jeff Long, after that series, and he said, 'You've got a World Series team,'" Corbin said.

The Commodores next drilled Tennessee-Martin at home and then grabbed a road sweep at an Auburn squad that would go 14–16 in the conference, but not make the NCAAs. Vandy came home and had no problems with Alabama, which had an identical SEC mark as Auburn but made the NCAA Tournament. Two wins over MTSU sandwiched the 'Bama series.

By any measure, a 31–3 start is special. But how did the Commodores stack up against the nation's really elite teams? That would soon be revealed.

Facing the best

The Southeastern Conference has been the standard-bearer for college baseball, and South Carolina was slowly becoming the league's preeminent power. Starting with the 2000 season, the Gamecocks hadn't missed an NCAA Tournament. The previous season, the Gamecocks won a national title.

The Commodores got the better of Carolina for a while, winning each season series between 2005 and 2008. However, Carolina had taken the rivalry back with series wins the previous two years. But being 28 games above .500 just 34 games into the season and being ranked No. 1 in the country got VU fans' attention, as did the fact that both teams were 10–2 in conference and tied for the SEC lead.

Terrific pitching was in store for the fans on Friday; the Commodores would throw Sonny Gray (1.54 ERA at the time) against Michael Roth (1.25), the brainy, off-speed control artist who would end his career as one of the Southeastern Conference's greatest pitchers.

Carolina Stadium was packed, and Gray got well into the eighth, but so would Roth. The Gamecocks scratched out runs in the third, fourth, and seventh off Gray, the last being Peter Mooney's solo home run that made a two-run lead seem like double that on a night where the 'Dores couldn't solve Roth (eight strikeouts in 7 ⅔ innings) or ace closer Matt Price. Even the hot-hitting Gomez, who came in with a 29-game hitting streak, couldn't manage a hit against Carolina; Vandy registered just three that evening and lost, 3–1.

Garvin evened the score the next day and the bats took off quickly against USC's Colby Holmes. Kemp doubled and scored on Westlake's groundout in the first, and Yastrzemski led off the second with a solo homer. Carolina got three in the bottom of the inning, but Esposito's solo homer tied it in the fourth. In the fifth, Gregor singled, Harrell was hit by a pitch, and Kemp and Gomez singled both in to chase Holmes.

VU then smacked around lefty Brian Harper, on to pitch to Westlake, who lined an RBI single to right. Yastrzemski's two-out walk put Vandy up 6–3. Brady Thomas hit a solo homer off Garvin

Shortstop Anthony Gomez takes a hack in Omaha. (Jimmy Jones)

in the sixth, but that would be all the scoring for either squad as Armstrong, Ziomek, Lamm, and Moore all did their part to close it out on Saturday for a 6–4 win.

The Commodores looked in charge early on Sunday, carrying a 3–1 lead into the seventh thanks to two Esposito homers and one by Westlake. Hill had been great to that point, but gave up a leadoff double to Steven Neff to start the inning. That's when the bullpen collapsed.

Williams came in to face the lefty Mooney and walked him. Clinard, summoned to get right-hander Robert Beary, slipped trying to field a bunt. The bases were loaded with nobody out and Ziomek, now on, hit pinch-hitter Greg Brodzinski with an 0–1 pitch. Outfielder Jackie Bradley, who'd be a first-round MLB pick that June, hit a liner to Harrell in center that he just missed catching. Wingo's ground ball off Ziomek scored the go-ahead run, and after an intentional walk to the powerful Christian Walker, a sac fly to deep center plated Thomas.

It was now 5–3 in Carolina's favor. VU had men at second and third with two out and a 3–2 count in the ninth, but Price got the favorable call on a letter-high pitch to Kemp near the outside part of the plate, and the Gamecocks had the series.

Meanwhile a few hundred miles south, Florida was fielding a special team in its own right under coach Kevin O'Sullivan, who'd been an assistant at Clemson with Corbin. Due to the ties between the coaches, the Gators may have been an even bigger rival than Carolina, and O'Sullivan had his Gators tied with Vandy for second in the East after taking two of three games at Georgia.

Deep down, according to Gomez, the team realized there was a silver lining even though it had just lost two of three to Carolina.

"You looked at those teams, we weren't giving up any stupid losses, they weren't giving up any hiccups," he remembered in early 2014. "So we knew once we got past each other, it was going to be a walk in the park for the rest of the teams, as bad as it sounds."

All eyes were on the three-team race between the programs. The Carolina disappointment seemed to light a fire under the Commodores as Gomez's thoughts turned out to be prophetic.

Vandy spanked LSU by counts of 11–2, 10–1, and 10–7 the following weekend in Nashville, and stayed at home to destroy Tennessee in two 10–1 games, followed by Sunday's 19–3 pounding. Kentucky's future first-round pick Alex Meyer completely shut down the Commodores on a Friday afternoon, 2–0 game in Lexington, but Vandy got the Wildcats back with 6–3 and 5–1 wins. After a 5–1 midweek win over Louisville— another good team—it was time for a showdown with the Gators in Nashville.

UF came to town at 18–6 in the SEC, tied with Carolina, which had just lost two of three against Ole Miss. The Commodores were now in the driver's seat, one game ahead of each.

Friday night got off to a great start, with Gray throwing six innings of two-hit ball to stake the Commodores to a 4–2 lead after 5 ½ innings. Vandy hit UF starter Hudson Randall hard, with Esposito, Gomez, Yastrzemski, and Gregor all connecting on RBI singles. With the bats going and VU's bullpen fresh, it looked like VU would end the night two games ahead of UF. But a rainstorm blew in and umpires stopped play at 7:43.

After a 1:03 delay, the game was postponed and would be resumed on Saturday, if possible. That had started to look dubious, with rain forecast for much of Saturday.

The delay changed everything. VU wasn't going to give Gray the ball in the restart, so Corbin went with Pecoraro. A two-run home run by Florida's Nolan Fontana tied the game in the seventh. Harrell's two-out RBI single in the ninth scored Jack Lupo with the go-ahead run, but Josh Adams led off the ninth with a bomb off Moore, who then seemed to lose confidence in his fastball. The Gators had a pair of one-out base runners and then Yastrzemski made a rare misplay of Bryson Smith's line drive to right.

UF now led by one, and Mike Zuninio's sacrifice fly scored another. Infielder Austin Maddox, who doubled as the Gators' closer, retired Vandy in order in the ninth.

Game 2 started about 45 minutes later. It started as another tense affair, with VU clinging to a 2–1 lead in the bottom of the fifth. The dam burst from there. Westlake hit a grand slam into the right-center field bleachers off Florida starter Brian Johnson, and Gregor added a two-run double later in the inning. The hitting became contagious. VU rapped out 18 hits en route to a 14–1 smacking of the Gators, who hadn't given up that many runs in a game all year. Garvin improved to 11–1, giving up six, walking two, and fanning six.

At 19–6, VU was a game up on both the Gators and Carolina, which had split with Arkansas in its first two games of a weekend series.

Once again, VU carried a lead into the middle innings, with RBI doubles by Casali and Harrell and Esposito's solo homer putting VU up 3–1. Zunino, who'd be a high first-round pick in the June draft, homered off Hill in the seventh to bring the Gators within one.

Again, the bullpen collapsed. Vandy's Williams came in for the eighth, and with one out, he gave up an 0–2 single to Fontana. He also had Smith at 0–2 but hit him with a pitch. Preston Tucker, who'd been a Commodore killer throughout his career, hit the next pitch to right to load the bases. Zunino's sacrifice fly off Lamm scored the tying run, though Armstrong got VU out the inning without further damage.

Vandy had a chance to win in the ninth, but Gregor and Lupo struck out after Yastrzemski stood at second with one out. The Commodores had men at first and second with nobody out in the

10th, and a man on second with one out in the 11th, but each time failed to score.

Armstrong got Vandy through the 10th and 11th without allowing a run. In the 12th, Armstrong walked Fontana to lead things off and Smith bunted him over. Corbin then rolled the dice and walked Tucker to get to Zunino and bring in Moore to face the right-hander.

Corbin was hoping for a double play. Instead, Zunino muscled a pitch in to the bleachers in right-center. Moore had given up one earned run all year, but had now given up three on Saturday alone. The Commodores went quietly in the 12th against Tommy Toledo as Florida boisterously left Nashville with the series win.

Vandy's lead on the field had vanished, and now, the Commodores had confidence issues with a bullpen that had been talented, but had now blown leads in seven of VU's nine league losses.

"I feel like those kids are pretty darn good," Corbin told the media, trying to put a positive spin on things after Saturday's games. "They have good stuff and I know right now it doesn't look that way because of the outcome, but I have a lot of believability in those kids, and they're going to have to believe in themselves, too."

With one weekend to go for a shot at a title, they'd certainly need help from their bullpen.

Bringing home the prize

Three games remained for each team to decide who'd be the league's champion. The Gators, with a home series against lowly Kentucky (7–20), were in the driver's seat as VU went to Georgia to face a team that would go to the NCAA Tournament, and Carolina went to Alabama to take on a Crimson Tide squad that would also make the NCAA's postseason event.

The SEC always starts its final regular-season series on Thursday. Georgia threw experienced junior Michael Palazzone, who had a 3.22 ERA in SEC starts in 2011, to begin a beautiful weekend in Athens. The Commodores roughed him up in the second on RBI singles by Casali and Harrell, and then Kemp's bunt single that scored Harrell. VU had a chance for more, but Gomez hit into an inning-ending double play.

That would be costly. Both pitchers had great breaking balls, and the difference was that Palazzone controlled his from there on, while Gray didn't. Chase Davidson hit a home run over the batter's eye in center to get UGA to within two. Westlake got that run back with a bomb of his own to right in the third, but No. 9 hitter Peter Verdin took Gray deep in the bottom of the inning. Three two-out singles by the Bulldogs in the fourth made it 4–3.

In the sixth, Gray got the first two outs, and then gave up a double to Curt Powell, a former Commodore.[5] Two singles loaded the bases, and a walk to Levi Hyams on a 3–1 pitch knotted the game at 4.

In the seventh, Corbin brought on Clinard, who'd been perhaps the most reliable reliever of late. Clinard loaded the bases with two outs and then uncorked a wild pitch that scored Kyle Farmer with the go-ahead run.

Palazzone, now in a groove, retired 13 VU hitters in a row until Westlake led off the eighth with a single. But that would be it; Palazzone finished the game with no other base runners and ended with a 5–4 win.

The 'Dores looked like a team feeling the weight of what was at stake. VU looked impatient, never making Palazzone throw more than 10 pitches in an inning from the fourth on. It had been a pattern over the years; in the last four regular-season-ending conference series, including this one, VU was now 1–9.

Arkansas had done its part by beating South Carolina that evening, but the Gators had beaten Kentucky, 9–6, and now were in the driver's seat.

It had already been a rough week without baseball. The players had been in exams all week, and on top of that, as

---

5 Powell, the Tennessee High School Player of the Year from Farragut High in Knoxville, signed with Vanderbilt in 2009. After fall practice, Powell was lower on the depth chart than he liked and he transferred to nearby Volunteer State for the spring. He transferred to Georgia the next fall and routinely wore Vanderbilt out his whole career.

Yastrzemski put it, "All those [Georgia] frat guys were calling our hotel at 3 in the morning.[6]" That may have explained why Garvin, who'd exhibited Greg Maddux–like control for most of his career, even while staked to a 4–0 lead after one (a two-run homer by Harrell, the big hit), couldn't find the plate and quickly cut the lead to a run.

Corbin yanked Garvin (5 walks) after 2 ⅔, went to Pecoraro with two outs in the third to get Hyams looking. He'd get out of a jam in the fourth. Pecoraro threw a perfect fifth, while Ziomek came on and kept Georgia off the board in the sixth.

Meanwhile, the 'Dores had precariously clung to that one-run lead against talented UGA starter Alex Wood, who'd be picked in the second round the next year before breaking into the Atlanta Braves' rotation in 2013 at the age of twenty-two. Wood pitched through the sixth. Despite his 105 pitches with the top of the VU order up to start the seventh, Perno left him in.

It was a bad move. Gomez and Westlake singled with one out and Casali walked to load the bases. Yastrzemski then got perhaps his biggest hit of the year, a single up the middle on a 2–1 pitch that scored two runs and stretched the lead to three. Perno then went to lefty Earl Daniels, who gave up an RBI double to the struggling Esposito. Chase Hawkins got the Bulldogs out of that jam, but Casali touched him with a two-run homer into the trees in left in the eighth.

By that point, Ziomek was in a groove and shut Georgia out the rest of the way for a 9–3 win.

Meanwhile, Carolina had beaten Arkansas 6–5 to stay even with Vandy, but in a shocker, the lowly Wildcats had pounded UF by a 14–1 count that afternoon. It was back to a three-way tie with one game to play, and what happened next was a journey

---

6 It wasn't the first series of prank calls VU had gotten from opposing rooters. "That still doesn't beat the Mississippi State [fan] having the number to the bullpen," said Lamm as he listened to Yastrzemski recall that story. "They'd call and the phone rings in the bullpen and I was in charge of the phone, and, 'Hello, Hey, get 46 [that was Lamm's number] up in there.' Actually, they're a little bit country, and I was like, 'This is not [pitching coach Derek Johnson], who is this?' And they were like, 'Ha, ha, bye!'"

Freshman relief pitcher Kevin Ziomek throws a pitch in the 2011 College World Series. Two years later, he'd be Vandy's No. 1 starter. (Jimmy Jones)

from euphoria to heartbreak and back in what seemed like the blink of an eye.

With VU ahead 6–1 in the sixth, the roof suddenly caved in on Hill, who gave up three hits. An Esposito error added another base runner. Three runs were in and after Clinard couldn't help, Corbin used the quick hook for Williams, who'd keep the lead at two before another long homer from Davidson in the seventh tied the game. Next, Jonathan Hester added a long bomb into the trees in left, and the Commodore bullpen had blown its fourth lead in six games.

But as bad as VU's bullpen had been, Georgia's was about to collapse even more spectacularly.

Yastrzemski led off the eighth with a single against Brian Benzor, and took second and third on wild pitches. With a 2–0 count on Gregor with one away, Perno made the rare move of pulling his pitcher in the middle of the at bat and turning it over to closer Tyler Maloof, who had converted each of his 16 save opportunities. Instead, Gregor singled to tie the game.

Next, Reynolds singled off Powell's glove into center. Kemp bunted for a single to load the bases. Gomez chopped a ball to the pitcher, but the go-ahead run scored. Casali fouled off a pair of two-strike pitches and then singled in two more, and the lead was 10–7 going into the bottom of the eighth.

Lamm held Georgia scoreless in the eighth. In the ninth, Esposito led off with a homer over the trees in left, Gomez had a two-RBI single, and Westlake hit a homer a country mile to right that nearly hit someone's house.

The 'Dores closed it out in the ninth for a 17–7 lead. Florida and Carolina would also win, but Vandy had a share of a league title for only the fourth time in school history.

As soon as it was over, it was clear that Corbin still hadn't quite recovered from seeing his bullpen implode again, but that didn't dampen the players' enthusiasm.

"It feels pretty good," said Casali, a senior who hadn't been a part of a title team, after the game. "It's one of those days you think about when you were recruited, and you come in as a freshman, it just seems like a far and a distant home. But for it to come true is pretty special. We're really excited about it."

Aaron Westlake heads for home after one of his three home runs against Oregon State. Vandy's victory that night launched the team into its first College World Series appearance. (Jimmy Jones)

Let's make it two titles

With the three teams finishing at 22–8, the conference tournament in Hoover, Alabama, loomed as an opportunity to settle the score. On that note, the Commodores did their best to settle the score with Palazzone and Georgia, whom they pounded by a 10–0 score that resulted in the game being called after the seventh due to the league's "mercy rule." VU had 11 hits off Palazzone, and the big blow was Esposito's home run. On the hill, Pecoraro and Ziomek combined to one-hit Georgia.[7]

Vandy now had a chance to get even with South Carolina, ranked No. 1 in the polls, on Thursday night. Gray returned to form with 6 ⅓ good innings, striking out seven with five hits and just one walk. VU clung to a 3–2 lead after his departure, and Williams, Clinard, and Moore made things interesting as they scattered six runners over 2 ⅓ innings of work. But none scored, and the Commodores added four insurance runs in the ninth on three bunt hits, including one by Westlake, who hadn't bunted all year, and a successful suicide squeeze by Yastrzemski. Moore picked up his 10th save and VU got a bye on Friday before a Saturday game with Arkansas.

Vandy had just five hits against the Razorbacks, but one was a two-run homer by Harrell. Garvin had a shutout through five, but gave up a run-scoring triple and an RBI groundout in the sixth. When he gave up a one-out single and a walk to start the seventh, Corbin went to Clinard, who got a couple of big strikeouts. Ziomek, Lamm, and Moore (who got his 11th save that season, establishing a school record at the time) went the rest of the way, as the Commodores, who sealed the 3–2 win, would advance to the tournament's title game for the fifth time in the Corbin era.

The opponent would be Florida and unfortunately, VU turned in perhaps its worst performance of the season in the Sunday heat.

---

7 Pecoraro left the game with what was called a "forearm strain" but turned out to be a torn elbow ligament. A second-team Freshman All-America player that year, Pecoraro returned to pitch very well at the end of next season thanks to a consistent ability to throw strikes, but his velocity started to fade. So did his margin for error, and by the start of 2014 he seemed to have completely lost his feel and confidence.

The Commodores made a pair of errors that led to two unearned runs, stranded nine men in scoring position, and couldn't solve UF's mound combination of Alex Panteliodis, Greg Larson, Nick Maronde, and Austin Maddox. Vandy fell 5–0 and Hill suffered his first loss of the season, even though he gave up just one earned run in seven innings.

It was the first time VU had lost a game by more than three runs all season, and only the second time it had been blanked.

"Their pitchers were keeping the ball down for the most part," Casali said. "You've got to give them credit for that."

Westlake, Reynolds, Esposito, Gregor, and Gray made the all-tournament team, but the Commodores felt the pain of losing the title game for the fourth time in those five tries. But now, VU (47–10) knew it would have something to look forward to that it didn't have after those other three title-game defeats: NCAA Tournament baseball in Nashville.

"Everyone's [upset] right now, but you know what? You should be if you're a good team, you should be if you lose a championship game. But we will put it to bed tomorrow and move on to other things . . . play at home. It'll be good to sleep in our own beds and put the attack on someone else besides other people in this conference," Corbin said.

Staying home

VU was curiously made the No. 6 national seed, which seemed low for a team that had been so dominant. In the Nashville Regional, it would face Oklahoma State, Troy, and Belmont, with VU facing its crosstown rival in its opener on Friday night.

Memories still lingered from the last time the Commodores had played on such a stage. The fact that VU played an in-state rival with nothing to lose in an opener once again didn't make fans any less nervous, but there was a different attitude around the team. Corbin recalls a conversation about where the team would stay for the weekend—generally, teams would hole up in a local hotel as part of the experience—but the players didn't care where they were. They were just eager to play.

"We stayed in the hotel across the street in the Marriott for that Regional, and I remember talking to Mark Lamm and he goes, 'Corbs, you don't have to worry about this group. If you want to save some money, you can put us in the dorms, it's not going to matter.' He goes, 'We got this.' And we did," Corbin recalls.

Belmont was playing its first NCAA Tournament game ever, and it showed that evening. Vandy got to BU ace Matt Hamann (2.22 ERA coming into Friday) in the first on Casali's two-RBI single. In the fourth, VU put six runs on the board on a Reynolds single, a Kemp sacrifice fly to right, Gomez's suicide squeeze, Westlake's RBI single, and Casali's run-scoring groundout. Coach Dave Jarvis left Hamann in for the sixth, and Yastrzemski and Esposito had RBI singles.

Meanwhile, Gray didn't allow a base runner until Greg Brody singled with two outs in the fifth. He'd go six and Clinard and Armstrong would finish as the Commodores breezed to a 10–0 win. The next evening they'd play third-seeded Troy, which had scored a mild upset of Oklahoma State earlier in the day.

This one had more drama, at least for most of the night. Gomez lined a sac fly to center off freshman lefty Jimmy Hodgskin to open the scoring in the third. Troy climbed ahead in the bottom of the fourth, as Todd McRae singled in Tyler Hannah and Adam Bryant on a single to left, where Kemp slipped and fell on the throw home. In the top of the fifth, Hodgskin hit Gregor with the inning's first pitch and then walked Harrell on four tries.

Troy brought in soft-tossing lefty Nathan Hill with Reynolds up; the runners moved up a base on the second baseman's bunt and then Kemp singled to center off the glove of second baseman T. J. Rivera on an 0–2 pitch. Gregor scored and Rivera, trying to catch Harrell at the plate, threw a couple dozen feet wide of home. Kemp was already on second and took third. After a sacrifice fly from Gomez later, a one-run deficit was now a two-run lead.

Garvin took that 4–2 lead into the seventh, when Corbin brought in Clinard to get him out of a two-out, men-on-the-corners jam. Clinard did that, but VU couldn't do anything against Hill until Yastrzemski tripled to right in the eighth. Troy walked Esposito intentionally to pitch to the lefty Gregor, but Gregor had never seemed to have trouble hitting lefties and didn't this time, either.

Esposito stole second and Gregor lined a single up the middle, and the 'Dores led 6–2. Westlake hit a three-run homer in the ninth for insurance, and Casali deposited another pitch to the bleachers in left. Vandy left the night in the winner's bracket with a 10–2 victory.

Late on Sunday afternoon, Belmont eliminated Oklahoma State on a hot, humid day. It had to turn around to face the Commodores that night on about an hour's rest. Belmont got to Hill early on a solo home run by Tim Egerton to tie the game at 1, but an Esposito double and Gregor's sac fly put Vandy up 3–1 after 2 ½ innings.

In the fifth, Gomez added an RBI double to left and Casali lined out to right to add another run. Esposito's solo homer to the bleachers in left-center ended the scoring, as Hill went on to record 13 strikeouts. VU won the regional by a 6–1 score.

"I'll never forget that game [Hill] threw in the regional," Ziomek recalled later. "He was just so dominant."

Ironically, it was Lamm, the man who warmed up to finish for Price in '07, who finished this one with a scoreless ninth.

"What I remember about that regional is that we played well and we handled it well," Corbin recalled just before the start of the 2014 season. "It was just a calmness that existed on the team, when we beat Belmont, it could have been a mid-week game because I remember the celebration, there was none. The guys just walked off the field and it was like, Okay, let's take the next step. They were just shaking hands, they were very calm, they put their uniforms up. 'When are we going to work out again, coach?' ''I'll give you a day off and then I'll see you here.'"

Espositio was named the Nashville Regional MVP, and was joined on the all-tournament team by Gray, Westlake, Reynolds, Gomez, Yastrzemski, and Gregor. It was the first time VU had won a regional in its park, and now, Vandy would host a super regional for the first time. Oregon State, which beat Georgia in the title game of the Corvalis Regional, would be the opponent.

The Beavers, national champions in 2006 and 2007, were used to the spotlight, but they'd be no match for Vandy this year.

Oregon State pitcher Sam Gaviglio had been the MVP of the Corvalis Regional, but took it on the chin that night of June 10. Yastrzemski hit a solo homer, followed by an RBI single by

Esposito and a two-run single by Harrell, and VU led 4-0 after one. In the fourth, Casali's RBI single made it 5-0, and then
Yastrzemski homered just over the wall in deep right-center to
score three more. Gray, again, was great, throwing 6 ⅔ innings and
giving up just one run en route to an 11-1 VU victory.

Vandy needed one more win to get to Omaha, but everyone in the
park sensed that the die had been cast. Coach Pat Casey's No. 2 starter,
Josh Osich, was out with arm trouble and James Nygren, whom most
people suspected would go in his place, had thrown in relief.

The way Vandy's bats were going, it didn't seem as if it would
be an issue no matter whom the Beavers threw.

"At this point, I don't think it matters, and I don't mean that
in a disrespectful way," Corbin said. "I just think that when you're
playing at this point, the kids have approached just about everyone
the same way, whether it's right-handed or left-handed, whether
it's a speed-up guy or a slow-down guy."

The pitcher would be freshman Ben Wetzler, who kept OSU
close. The Beavers trailed 3-2 heading into the sixth, until the dam
burst.

Westlake had already homered off Wetzler in the top of the
first, and after Gomez's two-run homer, he added a solo shot off ace
lefty Matt Boyd (1.45 ERA coming in) for a 7–2 margin. Westlake
connected for a third two-run homer in the seventh, this one also
coming off Boyd. It was the first three-homer day for a VU player
since Jeff Martin had done it roughly a couple of decades previous.

Clinard, who'd gotten Garvin out of a first-and-second, one-
out jam in the fifth, went 4 ⅔ innings and struck out eight. When
he fanned Parker Berberet to end the game, the junior tossed
his glove and was mobbed by teammates for a celebration like
Hawkins Field had never seen.

As it was with Lamm ending the regional, there was also a
touch of baseball karma with Clinard being on the mound to
close. He and Gray had been in the stands right behind home
plate, watching VU lose to Michigan four years prior.

"They didn't get up after we lost [to Michigan]. They
stayed right there until the dugouts cleared because they were so
bummed. . . . What comes around, goes around, and that was
very ironic," Corbin said.

It was an unusual moment for the program. Corbin has never been one for living in the moment, but this time, the Commodores carted two-liter soda bottles onto the field, shook them up, and removed the tops for their own version of a champagne celebration. Players hoisted Corbin on their shoulders and paraded him around the infield as the coach grinned from ear to ear.

"I'll never forget that as long as I live. That whole game was great and it was just one of those feelings, you just hope you get a chance to repeat again. The best feeling of it all was that we came up into the classroom here, the coaches, the kids, everyone, and we didn't leave until sundown the next day," Corbin said.

"It was one of those things where no one wanted to leave. Everyone was still in uniform. We just stayed up here. . . . It was almost like, you know you only get those moments once in a while. I guess I just didn't want it to go, either."

"I remember seeing the sun rise," added Hill.

The sun would set on the season in Omaha, but not before Vandy made a few more good memories.

First-timers

The College World Series field would soon be set. The Commodores, the only first-timers in the field, would be sentimental favorites along with Cal, which was supposed to have its baseball program dropped after the 2011 season because of the state's budget crisis, but had gotten a stay of execution a couple of months before. North Carolina, Texas, Texas A&M, and Virginia would join the field.

That was a tough field already, but the bad news was that Florida and South Carolina were in Omaha as well. The news got worse from there: the field was split into two four-team, double-elimination brackets, with the Gators and the Commodores in the same bracket. Still, Corbin was optimistic.

"I knew we had something special, and I felt like we were going to go to Omaha and have a chance to win it all," Corbin said.

The Commodores would have a lot of company while they were there. Many fans in Omaha without a dog in a hunt pick a team to follow, and VU, a first-time participant, picked up a lot of supporters.

"The personality that our team had won over a lot of fans. There were a lot of crowds that were heavily in our favor and I thought that was pretty cool to see how we could move people in our favor," Yastrzemski remembered.

VU also made history in another way. The city of Omaha had just put the finishing touches on brand-new T.D. Ameritrade Park, and the Commodores faced North Carolina in the first game there.

"I remember walking into the empty stadium right when we got there. . . . We were just so excited walking through the gates. I think we all got chills when we walked down the steps and checked out that new stadium," Ziomek said.

Gray picked a bad time to have his worst start of the year, but North Carolina stranded an incredible 16 men thanks to some help from Williams, Clinard, and Ziomek, who combined to throw 4 ⅓ scoreless frames. Vandy trailed 3–2 early, but Gregor doubled off the top of the wall in left center in the sixth, and Harrell hit a long two-run homer—the first in the history of the park—two batters later. Kemp and Gregor added RBI singles in the eighth and ninth, respectively, and Esposito and Kemp both had great defensive plays to prevent runs as VU won 7–3.

"Some very, very good two-out hits today were the story," Corbin said.

Unfortunately, Florida—the only team in the country to have a winning record against Vanderbilt—was up next on the night of June 20.

Garvin was brilliant that night, striking out nine and giving up five hits and just one walk. Unfortunately, his timing was awful, as one of those hits was a three-run homer by Tucker. Vandy came back in the fifth when Gomez singled home Harrell, but at 9 that evening, tornado sirens sounded and the game was suspended, with the resumption scheduled for 10 the next morning.

When things resumed, Vandy had two outs in the bottom of the sixth, trailing 3–1 with Esposito at the plate. As had been the case in Nashville, the restart was not kind. The Gators left left-handed reliever Stephen Rodriguez in the game, and that was the worst thing that could possibly happen to VU.[8] He'd hold Vandy hitless the rest of the morning, and the Commodores were in a do-or-die situation in the loser's bracket.

The Commodores got UNC again after the Tar Heels beat Texas, 3–0. Harrell again had the big hit, a three-run homer in the second that broke the game open. Gomez added a sacrifice fly in the first and Casali homered in the third. That was more than enough. Hill was up to the task, throwing seven innings of one-run ball, and Williams pitched two more scoreless frames. Vandy, 5–1 winners, now got another shot at Florida on the 24th.

Westlake homered in the top of the first to put VU up a run, but Gray, who wasn't at his best, gave up an RBI groundout to Tucker in the third and Fontana's two-RBI single in the fourth put UF up by two. Smith's RBI groundout in the sixth extended that lead by a run.

But Vandy rallied. The 'Dores got to reliever Tommy Toledo in the seventh as Harrell singled home Yastrzemski, and after Nick Maronde relieved Toledo, Kemp took a bases-loaded walk to bring home a run. In the eighth, closer Austin Maddox hit Gregor with a pitch to score Casali.

It was tied at four, and when Harrell crushed a pitch headed to center, it looked as if VU would lead by two. Instead, Fontana, the shortstop, made a fantastic, diving grab to end the inning.

Gray had not retired UF in order all day, and with 123 pitches under his belt, it didn't look like he'd come out for the eighth on a hot summer day. Corbin and Gray had that conversation in the dugout, but Gray told Corbin he wasn't tired and wanted to pitch the eighth.

"I don't care what the number of pitches was," Corbin said. "He wanted to go back out there. That's all there is to it. You're not

---

8 Rodriguez, who now goes by "Paco," was tough for anyone to hit. His 2.19 ERA was the best in Gator history. Drafted by the Dodgers a couple of weeks earlier, he made the majors on September 5, 2012, becoming the first player in that draft to make his MLB debut.

Sonny Gray, Vanderbilt's ace in 2011, throws a pitch at the College World Series. Within two years, he'd be in the starting rotation for the Oakland Athletics. (Jimmy Jones)

going to take the ball away from him or else you're going to fight him; rather give him the ball and let him pitch."

Pigott led off the bottom of the eighth with a single. No. 9 hitter Cody Dent bunted to third, Esposito fielded but hesitated, and Dent was safe at first. Next, Fontana laid a bunt that Gray couldn't field.

That was it for Gray, and Clinard came on to get Smith to pop up. Corbin went to Williams against Tucker, a lefty, and Tucker crushed a pitch Kemp's way in left. The freshman just missed grabbing Tucker's hit, but grabbed the ball bare-handed as it hit off the wall, and fired to Esposito at third as Dent, who'd been on second, had to unexpectedly scramble back to third. Lamm came on next and he struck out Zunino, but the ball got by Casali and scored Dent for a two-run Gator lead.

Westlake doubled in the ninth with two outs, and Casali sent a ball to left for a potential tie. Instead, it settled into a Gator fielder's mitt.

The dream had died.

Tim Corbin sits in the dugout at the College World Series in 2011.
(Jimmy Jones)

Retrospect

The decision to go to Gray is one that will be talked about for years. Corbin stuck with his junior because, as he later said, Gray's the team leader and if he didn't let him pitch when he wanted the ball, it might have sent the wrong message to his team. It didn't feel like the right move at the time, but had it happened again, who knows, it might have worked.

The blow that was the real killer was the bunt. The irony is that Gray was, even then, one of the best-fielding pitchers on the planet and was spectacular at fielding bunts.[9] But that's the way baseball goes, and as VU learned the hard way in '07 with Price on the mound, even the best can fail when the chips are down.

---

9 Kemp had this to say on Gray's ability to field bunts: "We rated our pitchers 1 to 3 on fielding bunts, and 1 (which Gray was) is the best. No matter if I tried to lay a bunt down third or first base, the guy throws the pitch and he's right in my face any time I tried to bunt, so he was definitely one of our best defensive bunt fielders.

The worse break was catching the Gators in those circumstances. The Commodores went 1–5 against Florida in 2011, but 53–7 against everyone else. Had Carolina been on that side of the bracket, it may well have been Vandy and the Gamecocks in the title series, since the eventual national champions handled UF four of five times that year.

An argument even existed that the Commodores were the best of the three. VU out scored SEC opponents in regular-season games by a staggering 234–96 that season, a margin that neither Carolina nor Florida came close to matching even though those teams tied for the regular-season title.

However you slice it, it was a special year between those three clubs, which were three of the last four standing in Omaha that year.

"If you look at our three teams—us, South Carolina, and Florida—it's kind of like a 'Who's Who' in the Big Leagues," Gomez recalled in early 2014. "You had Sonny, you had Jackie Bradley, Jr., you have Maronde, Roth, Paco, Zunino.[10] We were facing the best of the best on the weekend and it kind of got to the point in the season where I was like, 'I hope one of these guys gets rained out and we'll slip by and win the title.'"

It was certainly a special year for VU. The argument for the best four teams in school history comes down to Corbin's '07, '11, '13, and '14 teams. The 2007 squad was ranked No. 1 most of the season and was the top overall seed in that year's NCAA Tournament. The 2013 team set a conference record for wins that will probably stand for decades.

But neither of the other two teams had a weekend rotation that was quite this good from start to finish, and while the '07 lineup was more top-heavy, it wasn't as deep 1-to-9. Those other two teams didn't dismantle SEC regular-season foes the way this one did, either; the 2007 team out scored SEC opponents 193–130, while the '13 team did it 204–103. Of course, the '14 team also did the best in the postseason.

---

10 All six players made the majors by the end of the 2013 season.

No doubt, all four teams were special, and trying to pick a winner between the four is sort of like asking a parent to pick a favorite child. SEC fans certainly won't forget any of those historic teams any time soon, and all four were elite by any standard. It appears, though, that based on overall depth and postseason accomplishments, this was Corbin's best team.

The 2011 team poses in front of the famous statue in front of TD Ameritrade Park in Omaha. (Jimmy Jones)

2013 Baseball: Making Southeastern Conference history

When the Commodores had a Southeastern Conference record twelve players drafted by major league teams in 2011, 2012 set up to be a rebuilding year.

Yet Corbin hadn't rebuilt; he'd simply reloaded with more top freshmen as he landed what some national publications considered to be the country's top class. When pitcher Tyler Beede, the gem of that class, spurned a $2.4 million signing bonus from the Toronto Blue Jays—he'd be the only first-round pick not to sign—that got everyone's attention. The news was out: the Commodores, ranked 10th in *Baseball America's* preseason poll, would be pretty good again in 2012.

Or maybe not. An ambitious early-season slate nearly killed the season as well as the team's confidence.

After losing 1–0 to Georgia on the night of March 23, the Commodores were riding a five-game losing streak—the program's longest since 2008—and had a 7–15 record, by far the worst at any point in Corbin's tenure. The easiest opportunities for wins were behind Vanderbilt. The schedule from there was brutal; of the 32 remaining regular-season games, 17 came against teams that would make the NCAA Tournament that May.

Sometimes, though, all a young team needs is a break. In the next day's game, Vandy trailed 4–2 heading into the ninth, but rallied to beat Georgia. Slowly, the 'Dores started to climb back toward .500, but the killer schedule wasn't helping. At 16–21 on April 22, the 'Dores were on the verge of being swept by lowly Alabama, but turned a 7–2, eighth-inning deficit into a victory.

From that point until the NCAAs, nobody in the country played better baseball than Vanderbilt. Vandy lost Friday night games to Kentucky, Tennessee, and LSU, but took each series. It swept Ole Miss the final weekend, which not only secured a bid to the Southeastern Conference Tournament, but also ensured that the 28–25 Commodores would finish at least a game over .500 in Hoover. Vanderbilt then went and did what it almost always does in Hoover—made a run at a title—but lost 3–0 to Mississippi State in the final. From there, VU was sent to the Raleigh Regional, where it came within an inning of advancing to a super regional, but instead blew a 7–3 eighth-inning lead.

That night ended in disappointment, but everyone knew that 2013 could shape up as a special season. However, there were a lot of variables between that May and the next February. The Commodores were bringing in their second-straight No. 1 recruiting class, but they'd have to make a good argument to counter the money that major league teams would throw at those recruits.

Mike Yastrzemski slides in safely with a stolen base. (Jimmy Jones)

Even if they came to campus, the first half of 2012 had shown the dangers of relying on freshmen right away.

Perhaps the bigger matter was the return of several draft-eligible upperclassmen. Starting outfielders Connor Harrell and Mike Yastrzemski would almost certainly be drafted, as would starting shortstop Anthony Gomez. Draft-eligible starting pitcher Sam Selman had suddenly become an ace, and there was no doubt he'd be a high pick. Key relievers Will Clinard and Drew VerHagen would also have professional options.

It would be an anxious summer for Corbin.

Building on a solid foundation

The one thing you hear constantly from Corbin's former players who come back to visit is how much they miss college; everyone, of course, loves the idea of getting paid to play baseball, but it's different at the professional level. Teammates are transitory, always moving up or down a level or getting released altogether, and the bonds between teammates are rarely like they are when you spend years with the same people.

On the other hand, there are times that finances and opportunity dictate a player's decision. For Selman (second round, Kansas City), VerHagen (fourth, Detroit), and Gomez (sixth, Florida), the draft positions were high enough that each should (and did) leave. As for Clinard (nineteenth, Detroit), the redshirt junior wasn't on a full scholarship, and paying for a fifth year of VU would be tough.

Harrell (thirty-first, Detroit) and Yastrzemski (thirtieth, Seattle), though, had the chance to better themselves with another year. Neither signed, and the Commodores headed into '13 with the rare luxury of an all-senior outfield.

"I was feeling good as long as the right guys came back. When Yastrzemski and Harrell came back I said, 'Okay, our recruiting class is complete,' because it felt like those were two old souls who were very mature who could help coach," Corbin said.

With those two on board, it was going to be a great year anyway. Things soon got even better.

Eleven of the thirteen players in that recruiting class reported to Vandy, and a bunch of them could help right away. Pitchers Walker Buehler (Lexington, Kentucky) and Carson Fulmer (Winter Haven, Florida) were two of the top high-school hurlers in America, and were good enough to challenge for a spot in the rotation right away. Corbin had three immediate-impact bats in Rhett Wiseman (Cambridge, Georgia) and Xavier Turner (Sandusky, Ohio), big-bodied kids who had all the tools. Dansby Swanson (Marietta, Georgia) was also a major catch, and showed right away in fall practices that he could compete to take over Gomez's job.

The lineup looked like this: Spencer Navin, who had become a defensive wizard and a good hitter, was behind the plate. Conrad Gregor, an extraordinarily polished hitter, manned first. Kemp had moved to second and that worked very well. Sophomore Vince Conde returned to start at third, and shortstop would be either Swanson, who turned a lot of heads with his play in the fall, or veteran Joel McKeithan.

Conrad Gregor takes a rip at a pitch. (Jimmy Jones)

In the outfield, Harrell was flanked by Yastrzemski in right and Jack Lupo, who hadn't hit much but had center-fielder-like abilities. The DH spot was wide open, but Turner looked like an option.

On the hill, Kevin Ziomek was coming off a rough season, but the talent was there. Beede would obviously return to the rotation after pitching there for most of 2012. The third spot was unsettled; it might be T. J. Pecoraro, or highly regarded sophomore Philip Pfeifer, or perhaps even Buehler or Fulmer.

Sophomore Brian Miller, who'd been almost untouchable with his odd arm angles and off-speed stuff, would return to anchor the bullpen and have plenty of help from the guys who didn't make the rotation, like junior lefty Steven Rice and sophomore southpaw Jared Miller.

"I couldn't imagine trying to hit our pitching staff," Navin said. "You're coming in with Beede throwing 96 pretty hard, and then we'll throw Steven Rice throwing right after him, throwing from different slots, different angles, making batters look dumb. And then to finish off with a hard Fulmer and a soft Brian Miller coming from the side, the rubber band that he is."

It had potential to be a special team, and it was.

Men on fire

Corbin scheduled a home series with perennial power Long Beach State to open the season. Though the Dirtbags[1]—had fallen on harder times, having not played in a regional since 2008, they'd still be able to put up a fight.

Ziomek threw six innings of one-run ball and was backed up by an 11-hit offense, as Vandy won 10–4. Saturday's game was one of the flukier ones ever at Hawkins Field: Vanderbilt was out-hit 8–5, but won 12–2 thanks to four Dirtbag errors, 10 walks, and

---

1 Yes, that's their real nickname. Lacking a real practice field in 1989, Long Beach State played on a local all-dirt field and the team would end practices covered in dirt. It was given as a term of endearment and when that bunch made the College World Series that year, the name stuck.

four hit batsmen. Beede walked five and gave up five hits, but picked up his first win. Sunday's game was shortened to seven innings, and Long Beach State scored nine in the first three innings, including six off Pecoraro in 1 ⅔, for a 13–9 victory even though the Commodores pounded out a weekend-best 14 hits.

The next ten games wouldn't be challenging. Central Arkansas, which VU beat 10–2 in a February 20 midweek game, would be the only opponent that made a regional. Vandy won each, with an extra-inning, 3–1 win over Illinois-Chicago being one of the few real tests.

But, there was already one major bump in the road. Swanson, who was supposed to be the team's shortstop, had been sidelined with a variety of injuries and though Corbin at this point had hope that he'd return, the freshman wasn't able to contribute much from that point forward.

"Dansby was the one kid on that team that I thought could have played a lot for us, had he stayed healthy. I thought he was one of our better players, but he just didn't get the chance," Corbin said.

McKeithan was supposed to be the other option at short, but he wasn't hitting. At that point, Corbin moved Conde to short in the Sunday game of the Monmouth series in the season's second weekend and installed Turner, who'd been serving as a designated hitter, at third.

The previous season, Conde had struggled both in the field (an .899 fielding percentage) and at the plate (.195/.280/.297), but the move seemed to relax him. In the next seven games after the switch was made, Conde went 14-for-25 (.560) with three home runs and didn't make an error.

It might not have been what anyone had in mind, but it was a combination that would work for the remainder of the season.

"I give Vinnie a lot of credit because Vinnie was that guy, going into the season, that I really didn't think was going to play shortstop, and he took off to the point where we thought, *That's our shortstop*," Corbin said.

SEC play was just around the corner. With that, Corbin scheduled a true test to prepare for that with a weekend series at Oregon from March 8–10. The Ducks would be the No. 8 national seed in the 2013 NCAA Tournament, but they had their hands full with the Commodores that weekend.

Ziomek had been on a real tear, and struck out 13 Ducks in a complete-game effort while giving up just two hits as Vandy won the Friday game by a 4–1 count. On Saturday, Oregon couldn't hit Beede, either, as the sophomore went 6 ⅔ innings while allowing just one unearned run with seven strikeouts.

The 13-game winning streak was the longest for the program since 2007, but the Commodores threw it away on Sunday. Pfeifer wasn't sharp, but managed to stake his team to a 4–2 lead before hitting the leadoff man in the eighth. Relievers Carson Fulmer, Jared Miller, and Brian Miller, all brought in during the eighth, each struggled with control, and a huge two-run throwing error by Conde also contributed to the downfall. By the time the eighth was done, five runs were in and the Commodores lost 7–5.

A 4–2 midweek win over Buffalo got things headed in the right direction again as VU traveled to Auburn. Once again, Ziomek was brilliant, carrying a no-hitter into the seventh before giving up two runs in the eighth. Gregor and Harrell homered, and Vandy won its conference opener, 5–2. Beede took a no-hitter into the seventh on Saturday and got the win as the 'Dores cruised to an 8–1 victory. The next day, VU's pitching was a little shaky but the offense wasn't, scoring in each of the first four innings on the way to an 8–6 win.

For one of just two times during the regular season, the Commodores lost two in a row as they fell 4–1 on the road at MTSU and then 7–1 to Florida in the conference home opener at Hawkins Field. Beede picked Vandy up on Saturday as he surrendered just two hits in 6 ⅓ as the offense gave him 15 hits in a 6–1 win.

Sunday's game was one of the stranger ones ever played at Hawkins Field. Vanderbilt trailed 4–2 in the fifth as a thunderstorm hit Hawkins Field and caused a 49-minute rain delay. The SEC has always tried to govern Sunday games in a way that gets the visiting team back to campus before too late on Sunday evening and for that reason, umpires announced that no new inning would start after 3:15. The game had started at noon, and it became clear that it wouldn't go nine innings.

After play resumed, VU scored on a balk to inch to within a run and then tied it on Turner's two-out infield hit in the sixth. The tie held until the seventh, when Yastrzemski scored from second on an infield hit. It was now 3:13 as Navin came to the plate.

Corbin could have had Navin step in and out of the box or call time-out, but chose to play it straight. The catcher worked the count to 3–2, and on the seventh pitch of the at bat, Navin fouled a ball off into the stands. He'd strike out on the next pitch but just before it, the clock struck 3:15 and the game was over.

The Commodores were now 21–4 and led the SEC East with a 5–1 mark, even though Corbin didn't feel great about how Sunday's game was won.

"It was a weird game. It didn't feel right. It was a win and I understand it, but it just feels awkward, still, to end the game, people cheering at 3:15, and we end the game on a strikeout and we walk off. I've never been a part of something like that," he said.

The ending may have lacked style points, but it was about to launch the 'Dores into another hot streak.

Vanderbilt beat Lipscomb in a midweek game, and then battled both the rain and the Volunteers in Nashville on Friday as Navin's 12th-inning single drove in Yastrzemski for the winning run in a 4–3 game. Beede threw 7 ⅓ strong innings and got great help from his defense on Saturday in an 8–3 win on another wet day. On Sunday, the Commodores played from behind all day until freshman Kyle Smith belted a seventh-inning grand slam to put the Commodores up 10–8 in an eventual 12–8 victory.

A midweek victory against MTSU pushed the winning streak to seven. In Oxford, Ziomek again pitched deep into a game, throwing 7 ⅓ innings against Ole Miss. His offensive teammates, though, couldn't do much against Rebels ace Bobby Wahl, either. Finally, the 'Dores broke through on Navin's sacrifice fly to right in the eighth and Harrell's two-out RBI single that scored Kemp, and that was good for a 3–1 win as Brian Miller shut the door in the ninth.

Saturday's game was more of the same. Beede went six and struck out six to go to 8–0 as Kemp and Yastrzemski had RBI singles, and that was enough offense for a 2–1 win. Vanderbilt trailed 3–1 on Saturday, but rallied for four runs to take a 6–3 lead in the fifth. Ole Miss eventually tied the game in the ninth, but Harrell singled and scored on a wild pitch in the 11th for the go-ahead run. Brian Miller threw a 1-2-3 ninth and the Commodores were an incredible 11–1 in the SEC, which beat the 1972 team's 10–2 start to league play as the best in school history.

Next, Vanderbilt crushed Tennessee-Martin by a 10–3 score. The winning streak stood at 11 with Missouri, playing in its first season as a member of the SEC, coming to Nashville.

Ziomek was shaky early on Friday, but Harrell hit a three-run homer in the bottom of the first to tie the game at three. After Missouri took the lead in the second, Smith's homer to dead-center to lead off the second tied it again. Ziomek settled down and pitched into the seventh and by that time, another Harrell homer and a Conde double in the fifth had him in the lead. Conde added run-scoring hits in the sixth and the eighth and VU walked away with an 11–5 victory.

On Saturday, both Beede and the offense were on. The right-hander improved his record to 9–0 when he gave up three hits and struck out 10, and his offense pounded out 19 hits, 18 of which were singles. On Sunday, Pfeifer once again had trouble making it out of the middle innings, but it didn't matter, since the offense mashed Tiger pitchers again and the Commodores cruised to a 16–4 win.

The wins were piling up now. The Commodores were ranked second in America coming into the weekend, and now stood at

Vanderbilt coach Tim Corbin moved Vince Conde from third base to shortstop early in the 2013 season. The move worked wonders, and Conde became dependable as a hitter and in the field. (Jimmy Jones)

33–4 and 14–1 in the league. Even great teams can't continue to play that well, and after Friday's game was rained out, the streak came to an end in the first game of a doubleheader on Saturday afternoon at Georgia, when the lowly Bulldogs picked up a 3–1 win in the series opener.

Corbin wasn't happy with the way the team played and decided to bench Gregor in game two, for what would be the only game that Gregor would miss that year. As for the rest of the team, nobody was fazed.

"I don't even know what it was, we just lost—and then the best thing, I think, was that we went into the batting cages and people started taking naps. It just made me realize that people cared about the game, but they weren't worried, which was really important because when you stress about the game, that's when it turns south," Kemp remembered months later.

Benching Gregor turned out to be a huge blessing in disguise. Redshirt freshman Zander Wiel, who'd gotten just eight at bats all season, homered twice and also crushed a double in Gregor's place. Conde, Navin, and Yastrzemski also homered as the 'Dores blasted the 'Dawgs, 15–4. On Sunday, Pecoraro, Fulmer, and Brian Miller held Georgia to seven hits in a 4–1 win to take yet another series.

If you wanted to pick a "flaw" with the 35–6 start (and 16–2 conference record), it would be this: VU hadn't exactly played a murderer's row of a schedule. Of the weekend opponents to this point, only Oregon, Florida, and Ole Miss would make it to a regional. Mississippi State, up next in Nashville the next weekend, would be a much better test for the Commodores. MSU would eventually be one of the final two teams standing in Omaha before it bowed out to UCLA.

But first, Vandy had a rare midweek road trip to face an excellent Louisville squad. It was probably the team's best performance of the season against what had become its biggest out-of-conference rival. Buehler was excellent in his 5 ⅓-inning start, and by the time he was done, Wiel's two-run homer, followed by RBI singles from Navin and Conde, staked him to a lead. The team's 14 hits included a three-run bomb by Conde. The defense was also outstanding, and the 'Dores came home with a surprisingly easy 10–2 win.

Tony Kemp, the 2013 Southeastern Conference Player of the Year, heads for third in the 2012 College World Series. (Jimmy Jones)

On Friday, Ziomek and Brian Miller held MSU to six scattered hits, and Yastrzemski came up big with a two-RBI single in the second, as the Commodores won 3–1. On another of what seemed to be an endless stream of rainy weekend games, Vanderbilt endured a five-hour rain delay as Beede gave up two runs and Kemp went 4-for-4 in a 5–2 win. Gregor homered as part of a three-hit Sunday and Pecoraro gave one of his best performances of the season, holding MSU to one run in five innings in an 8–3 Commodore victory.

Vanderbilt was now an incredible 19–2 in the league. It wouldn't be long before talk shifted from whether the 'Dores could win the league, to whether they could win it in a manner in which nobody's ever won the SEC before. In the thirty-game-season era, South Carolina's 25–5 mark stood as the best in the league's amazing history.

Could Vanderbilt challenge the Gamecocks for history? The players had started to quietly talk about it among themselves.

"I know that when we looked back and we knew that South Carolina had the 25–5 record—we never even looked at that record at the beginning of the year—you're going through and we're like 20–2 or something like that and we're like, 'Oh, what's the [SEC] record, just curious?' and we see that and then I think everybody kind of had in mind, *We could really do this*," Kemp remembers.

Guess who was up next?

Into the record books

No road trip to an SEC school is ever really easy, and going to South Carolina had always been a particularly tough task for Vanderbilt. In five road trips there under Corbin, the Commodores were 5–10 in Columbia and were 1–5 in their last two trips. On top of everything else, the Gamecocks had won two of the last three national titles.

Ziomek was up to the task on Friday night in front of a full house on a beautiful evening at Carolina Field. He wasn't overpowering, allowing eight hits in eight innings and striking out four, but like every other pitcher on the staff, he knew he could trust his defense. Navin's two-run homer in the second staked him to an early lead, and Yastrzemski came home on Gregor's line-drive single in the sixth. Brian Miller gave up a two-out, two-run homer in the ninth, but pinch-hitter Curt Britt chopped harmlessly to Gregor to end the evening with Vanderbilt up, 3–2.

Vanderbilt was now in the incredible position of being able to clinch a share of the SEC East title, and Beede had saved perhaps his best game of the season for Saturday. He went 6 ⅓ innings and was just about untouchable, giving up just two hits (though four walks) in 6 ⅓. Once again, he had a no-hitter until L. B. Dantzler broke it up in the seventh, and made quite an impression on the Gamecocks.

"The story of the game was Tyler Beede. He was terrific. Big-league stuff. There's a reason why he's going to be the first or second pick in the draft next year. He kind of overpowered us there for six-plus innings," Carolina coach Chad Holbrook said.

With that kind of pitching, VU didn't need much hitting, but Wiel (three hits, one run, two RBI) and Yastrzemski (three hits, one run) provided enough as Vandy came out on top 5–2. About the only lowlight was a two-out error by Gregor in the ninth, which snapped the team's eight-game errorless streak.

With 23.3 percent of the league schedule remaining, Corbin's club had once again written itself into the league's history books as an SEC regular-season champion. Vandy had its first series win at Carolina since 2007. It would not get a chance at a sweep, as cold and rain moved in and doused Columbia that morning. That denied the 'Dores a chance to extend their three-game lead on LSU, but there would be plenty more chances.

A home win over Presbyterian pushed the overall mark to 41–6 with a road trip to Kentucky ahead. Vandy fell behind early on Friday, but Harrell and Wiel blasted second-inning homers to go up 3–1. A seven-hit third extended that lead to 10–1, and with Ziomek on the hill, there was little doubt about the outcome as VU cruised to an 11–3 win.

Control troubles, which were becoming quite frequent for Beede, forced him from the game with one out in the sixth. Vanderbilt clung to a 3–2 lead when Fulmer came in, and he'd go 3 ⅓ and give up a run. Yastrzemski added a double for two insurance runs and VU had a 5–2 win.

One more win, and the 'Dores would have a title. Vandy trailed 2–1 in the second, but Kemp's sacrifice fly in the third tied the game. In the fourth, Harrell doubled in Yastrzemski and then after Gregor walked, back-to-back sacrifice flies from Wiel and Conde scored Harrell. Navin's single brought Gregor home, and the lead was 5–2.

The third starter's spot had been an adventure, and was again on Sunday. Pecoraro gave up home runs to Brett Kuhn and A. J. Reed, and the game was again tied.

But lefty Steven Rice, who'd been an afterthought coming into the season, came on and would not allow a run the rest of the day while striking out five. Gregor hit a two-run homer in the sixth, Turner knocked in Kemp in the seventh, and singles by Conde, Navin, and Lupo produced two more eighth-inning runs.

With a 10–5 win, the Commodores had their sixth SEC title in school history, and their fifth outright.

As Harrell said at that point, "We might as well set this record." With home runs from him and Smith in the first two innings, coupled with solid pitching from Buehler, Vandy was well on its way in Thursday's series opener against Alabama. After Conde's double in the fourth, the lead was 6–0, and when Yastrzemski scored on a sixth-inning balk, it was 7–1.

A seventh-inning single from Alabama's Chance Vincent cut the lead to five, and then in the ninth, Brian Miller gave up a one-out grand-slam that stunned the crowd at Hawkins Field and cut the lead to a run. Miller, though, got the next two hitters and tied Ryan Rote for the school's all-time lead with 19 career saves. More importantly, the Commodores had conference win No. 25.

"It's very difficult to do," Corbin said. "If you had asked me before the season, 'can you pull that off,' who's ever thinking about that? You have to have some luck and you have to play well, and you have to be very, very mature and play consistently to pull that off."

Maturity and consistency didn't stick around for Friday. VU led 2–0 in the third with Ziomek on the hill.[2] A series of walks and errors helped Alabama score three runs and after 7 ½, 'Bama led 4–2. VU sent the game to extra innings, but Georgie Salem's 10th-inning single off Brian Miller dealt Vandy a 5–4 loss.

Corbin, of course, wasn't going to give his bunch a free pass no matter how much had been accomplished.

"We lost, and I just remember Corbin flipping because he knows how close we are," Kemp said months later. "And I remember [Saturday] before the game, we always have pre-game meetings and we're meeting and he's like, 'If you guys really want it, go get it. If you really want it, go get it.' And so we go out there, we had a phenomenal game."

It was one of the odder games of the season. Vanderbilt nearly blew a six-run lead on two occasions and was outhit 14–9,

---

2 Ziomek was pitching because Corbin wanted to keep him throwing on Fridays, consistent with his usual routine.

but just as the Commodores always did, they kept fighting back. Vandy scored seven in the second, five in the sixth, and two in the eighth, and Kemp led a balanced offensive attack with two hits.

It should have been an easy win, but Corbin admittedly left a struggling Beede, who was trying to win his 14th game in 14 starts, in longer than he would have if he weren't trying to make history himself. Pecoraro also struggled, but Rice was huge, throwing 2 ⅓ scoreless innings in the game's middle innings to get a win in a 14–10 game.

Going 26–3 in any major conference is incredible, if not unthinkable. But as Ziomek reflected later, Corbin had planted the seeds for that kind of thing months earlier.

"The pretty cool thing about the record: I remember coach Corbin kind of touched on it at the end of the year, he was always stressing to us that he wanted us to be the best team ever, and he's said that in a couple of meetings. I think a lot of us, when he said that, we kind of looked at him and we said, 'What do you mean? What are you talking about, the best team ever? What does that even mean?'" Ziomek said.

"He always said he wanted us to be the blueprint. He said it and we kind of understood it, but we really didn't know what he meant by it. As we started to move forward during the year when we were getting close to that record, I think we all started to understand that we could be something like that. We could be one of the best teams ever.

"To have the ability to do that was pretty unbelievable. Everything that he said at the beginning of the year ended up coming true, which was really cool for all of us."

The numbers were almost unthinkable. VU was now 48–7 overall and had won every weekend series. It was 66–13 since the last time it had lost a weekend series, which was to Alabama the previous season. It was 40–7 in games involving SEC teams, including the previous season's SEC Tournament, in that span. Now, it would head three hours south to Hoover in an attempt to add another title to its résumé.

Going for a tournament title

Between its stunning conference record and its remarkable consistency in Hoover over the last decade, VU headed to the Southeastern Conference Tournament as the favorite. The Commodores faced Texas A&M, a team they'd not played all season, in the opener.

The sluggishness that plagued them in the Alabama series carried over into Wednesday evening. The Aggies' Parker Ray kept VU off-balance all day, getting 11 fly-ball outs in spacious Regions Park and allowing just three hits. Buehler had a great freshman year and could mow through a lineup for innings at a time, but he also had a tendency to leave a ball or two up in the zone in every outing. That was the case that night, as Buehler allowed three homers in six innings. The Commodores lost 5–0 and their coach wasn't too pleased, but his tone changed a bit later.

"I've got to give credit to Ray. I thought he really pitched well. That was one of those, too, that at the end of the game you thought, *we were flat*, but when you saw [the replay], it made a little more sense. This guy was hitting both sides of the plate and changing speeds. . . . They were befuddled and thought the cutter just got to them," Corbin remembered.

As had been the case in '07, Vanderbilt would have to play its way through the loser's bracket in order to earn a title.

Things looked good early on Thursday as VU built a 3–0 lead on South Carolina, thanks to three unearned runs in the second. Fulmer, who threw 4 ⅓ innings in relief of Ziomek and entered with a 3–2 lead, gave up a wind-aided homer to right to L. B. Dantzler in the seventh to tie the game. It went to extra innings tied, and Kemp started the bottom of the 10th with a single to right. Turner showed bunt early in the at bat, and then slapped a single past first. With Kemp now at third, Carolina brought on lefty Tyler Webb to pitch to Gregor, but the junior bounced the first pitch into right field to send Carolina home.

A Friday night rematch with the Aggies was in order. Beede was untouchable and didn't give up a hit until there was one out in the eighth to improve to an astonishing 14–0. Brian Miller went the rest of the way while keeping A&M off the board to extend his single-season saves record to 14. Kemp, Harrell, and Wiseman each had an RBI as the 'Dores made it to the weekend and an appearance in the semifinals with a 3–0 win.

The pitching had been great, but the hitting had not. Drawing Mississippi State that morning was just what the team needed. Turner, Gregor, Wiel, and Harrell all had three hits and Vandy scored seven runs in the second and five in the third. Though neither Pecoraro or either of the Millers threw well, they pitched well enough for a 16–8 win.

Vanderbilt was now set to take on LSU, the league's runner-up, for the first time all season. Wiel summarized what a lot of people were thinking about the title tilt at Saturday night's postgame press conference.

"It's SEC baseball. It's the best two teams in the conference that happen to be the best two teams in the country right now. This is what the people want, and it's going to be a good match-up," he said.

It was everything a baseball fan could have hoped to see.

LSU hit Pfeifer hard early, but stranded five men in the first three innings. Ravenelle and Steven Rice came in to shut LSU down in the middle innings. That kept VU within striking distance at 4–2 and Conde singled in the tying runs in the seventh. Navin hit a fly ball to right that looked as if it would score another, but LSU outfielder Jared Foster gunned down Wiel at home on a close play. Vanderbilt had a man on with one out in the ninth, but the Tigers brought in ace closer Chris Cotton and their ace shut the 'Dores down.

Meanwhile, Brian Miller was pitching as well as he had in weeks. He'd come on in the seventh and proceeded to hold LSU hitless as he took the mound for the 11th. With one out, he hit Foster with a pitch, but appeared to recover by striking out pinch-hitter Chris Sciambra with a pitch.

But Miller didn't get the strike-three call, and that was huge. By now, Foster had swiped second and when Sciambra drove a pitch up the middle and through the infield, Foster scored the go-ahead run. Rice came on to keep the score at 5–4, but Cotton was untouchable and got the 'Dores 1-2-3 in the ninth.

It was another frustrating ending to an SEC Tournament. Under Corbin, the 'Dores had been to the title game seven times, and lost six. It was the third year in a row that VU had fallen in the final, and the fourth time in five seasons.

"LSU played very good defense at opportune times, inopportune for us," Corbin said afterward. "But we kept coming back and I thought the game was in our favor. When we tied it up, I thought we were going to win it. We had a couple of chances to do so. We just couldn't crack the safe."

There wasn't much time for the Commodores to feel sorry for themselves. A regional was around the corner and for the second time in three years, Vanderbilt would be hosting.

Coming home

Two-seeded Georgia Tech, third-seeded Illinois, and fourth-seeded East Tennessee State were the invited guests to the Nashville Regional. There was an eerie feel about the regional, as it brought back some memories of that ill-fated 2007 regional. First, the Big Ten champ came to Nashville, just as it had when Michigan did that year. Second, the Commodores were slated to face another in-state team with a conference Pitcher of the Year in ETSU's Kerry Doane.

Quickly, though, circumstances changed and VU fans could breathe a small sigh of relief before the Commodores took the field for their opener. Not long before the first pitch, ETSU coach Tony Skoale announced that Doane wouldn't throw against Vandy for two reasons. First, Doane had strep throat earlier in the week. Second, the innings were piling up for his ace. Doane had already logged 140 innings, which included a nine-inning outing two Wednesdays prior and then a complete game in the Atlantic Sun championship game on Sunday.

Vanderbilt would instead see Jimmy Nesselt, and threw the knockout blow early. Vandy led 5–0 after one, thanks to Gregor's two-RBI single, RBI singles from Wiseman and Navin, and Conde's line out to left. Ziomek had been remarkably consistent all season, and was again that night. He'd go seven, strike out five, and give up just an unearned run because of his error. The Vandy bats went quiet after that outburst but warmed up again late, which included a two-run homer from Harrell. The final was 9–1, and the 'Dores now would see Illinois on Saturday after it beat Georgia Tech earlier in the day.

While the ETSU game had no cause to give VU fans nervous moments, the Illinois contest would. Beede couldn't find the plate, walking five, giving up four runs (but just two earned) and had to yield to Fulmer in the fifth. That prevented him from winning his 15th game in 15 starts, even though big hits by Kemp, Turner, and Yastrzemski had given VU a 5–4 lead by now.

It nearly took a bad turn for VU immediately. Fulmer got a strikeout as Justin Parr broke for second. Navin's throw went into center field and Michael Hurwitz jogged home. However, umpires ruled that Brandon Hohl's momentum on the swing-and-miss carried him out of the batter's box and into Navin's way.

It was a controversial call, and it was also the difference between VU leading by one or trailing by two, and perhaps more.

"I'm not going to talk about it. I prefer to keep my money," Illinois coach Dan Hartleb said later.

Unable to break the game open, Corbin turned to small-ball in the eighth. With two, Kemp bunted and Illinois botched the play as David Kerian threw the ball over second baseman Reid Roper's head. Two runs scored and so did Kemp, with Turner singling him in. Wiel's sacrifice fly made the score 10–4 and Fulmer shut the door from there.

Vandy was every bit in the driver's seat. Georgia Tech had to beat VU twice and was throwing sophomore Josh Heddinger, who with a 5.75 ERA in 36 innings wasn't exactly setting the college baseball world on fire. But Georgia Tech coach Danny Hall had a hunch that it was the right call, saying he was Tech's "most-rested guy."

He was proven correct. Hedinger threw a complete-game, two-hit shutout, and the stunned Commodores, the nation's No. 2 overall seed in the tournament, were on the brink of elimination.

Monday night's game had a nervous feel about it. The 'Dores had been almost flawless all season long, and yet some cracks had emerged, starting with the Alabama series two weekends ago.

Vanderbilt was clearly the best team in the regional, and yet Georgia Tech, with a thinner pitching staff and one more game under its belt, had forced one more contest. It also was bringing back its ace, Buck Farmer, to throw on Monday.

To make things dicier, when you surveyed the roster and looked at who could start, there weren't a lot of great choices based on recent performances. After watching some film of the Yellow Jackets, Corbin went with Pfeifer because he was a lefty and saw that Tech had difficulty with southpaws. It turned out to be a great move.

The sophomore's start to the game was rocky. He walked the leadoff man in both the first and second, but both times his teammates erased the damage by double plays. In the third, Tech had men on the corners and two out, and Thomas Smith blasted a line drive to center. Harrell, though, got a great read on the ball and speared it for the third out.

Pfeifer was done after five, and left with a 2–0 lead thanks to Gregor's RBI infield single and Turner's RBI groundout in the first. Farmer was done after four and was replaced by Alex Cruz. Wiseman extended the lead to three with an RBI single in the fifth. In the sixth, Turner had another RBI groundout to put VU up 4–0. Tech's Daniel Spingola grounded a ball between Conde's legs in the seventh to score A. J. Murray, but in the eighth, Lupo bunted in Wiseman and Turner added a two-out single to score Lupo.

The lead was 7–1 and when Brian Miller recorded his 16th save with three punch-outs in the ninth, the Commodores had won their fourth regional in the Corbin era.

"Proud of the kids," Corbin said afterward. "They just responded like I thought they would. Tough, tough group. I said that last night and I'll always stand by that."

Yastrzemski was named the Nashville Regional MVP and Gregor, Turner, Navin, Ziomek, and Kemp joined him on the all-regional team. Of the five, all but Turner had been a part of that first team to win a super regional and advance to Omaha, and now, only Louisville stood between VU and a chance to do it again.

Running out of gas

Louisville was certainly a good team, but nothing about the matchup seemed to tilt in the Cardinals' favor. The Cardinals were 49–12, but it was a 49–12 record against a weak schedule in the Big East Conference, which placed only one other team, Connecticut, in the NCAA's field of 64 teams. Even then, the Huskies only got in by virtue of winning the conference tournament. Outside the Big East, the Cards were just 7–4, and of course that included the earlier blowout loss to VU in Louisville.

On the other hand, while it might be a stretch to say that the Commodores were limping into the super regional, the team that had started 47–6 was now just 7–4 in its last 11 games. Beede had control issues from the season's start, but he'd been so dominant—teams hit just .187 off him that year, with only 13 extra-base hits in 101 innings at season's end—that it hadn't really mattered.

But Beede's problems were accelerating as the schedule got tougher. There still wasn't a reliable third starter. Closer Brian Miller had a great season, but teams had started to crowd the plate against him and that took away much of his breaking ball, which was now plunking right-handed hitters instead of catching the inside corner of the plate.

There was also one huge distraction that week: the Major League Baseball Draft. Scouts were very, very familiar with this Vanderbilt club. Yastrzemski and Harrell were seniors and would be leaving regardless, but somewhere in the back of their minds, they had to be thinking about who'd pick them and when.[3]

A bunch of key juniors also figured to have their names called. Kemp, who'd been named the SEC's Player of the Year, had started to make a big impression. Gregor's year had been disappointing

---

3 Louisville was also dealing with the same distraction. The Cardinals had seven players selected, with the round in which they were picked in parenthesis: Dace Kime (3), Jeff Thompson (3), Ty Young (7), Coco Johnson (11), Chad Green (11), Cody Ege (15), and Adam Engel (19).

from a power standpoint, having homered just three times, but not a lot of players had his plate judgment and contact ability (54 walks, 29 strikeouts in 227 at bats in 2013), and that could have made him attractive to someone. Navin, with his tremendous defense and competent bat, figured to go in the first 10 rounds. Ziomek's terrific season (2.12 ERA, 115 strikeouts in 119 innings) had him in the late-first-round discussion.

The worst thing was that part of the draft ran concurrently with the games. Ziomek got his part of the drama finished when the Tigers took him in the second round on Thursday, and Gregor (Houston, fourth round), Kemp (Houston, fifth), and Harrell (Detroit, seventh) also knew their fates by the super regional. But Navin (Dodgers, eleventh) and Yastrzemski (Baltimore, fourteenth) were literally being picked as the 'Dores warmed up for the Saturday opener on a sunny, humid, mid-80s day.

Vanderbilt got to Louisville starter Chad Green in the first as Turner scored on Gregor's single to right. The Cardinals answered when Jeff Gardner, who'd been hit by a pitch, scored on a Zak Wasserman sacrifice fly. In the third, Turner singled and later scored on Yastrzemski's groundout. Vandy threatened for more, but Coco Johnson threw Harrell out at the plate on Conde's single to left.

Vandy clung to that 2–1 lead until the seventh. Gardner singled and took second on Cole Sturgeon's groundout. Wasserman's two-out single tied the game at 2. Sutton Whiting singled, and a tiring Ziomek uncorked a wild pitch to put two men in scoring position. A walk to Adam Engel loaded the bases and spelled the end of Ziomek's day.

Fulmer had been the ideal guy in this spot; nobody had been able to touch the freshman with the high-90s fastball and the A-plus slider. But while warming up in the bullpen by stretching him arm with some large rubber bands, one snapped and struck Fulmer in the eye and he was no longer available.[4]

Vandy now turned to Brian Miller. Pinch-hitter Matt Helms hadn't gotten a hit since April, but singled through the hole to left to score two. Vandy now trailed 4–2 and in the eighth, the Cardinals tacked on another run after Miller hit Johnson and

---

4 The fact that Fulmer pitched on Sunday said a lot about his competitiveness. The injury turned out to be severe enough that he'd miss summer ball.

Kemp failed to properly apply a tag on his stolen base attempt. Johnson would later score on a sac fly to center.

Vandy had men on second and third with two out in the eighth, and Yastrzemksi scored when third baseman Ty Young couldn't handle a ground ball from Conde. VU loaded the bases in the ninth, but couldn't score off ace closer Nick Burdi, whose 100-mile-per-hour fastball was untouchable that day. The Cardinals walked away with a 5–3 win.

"It was a good ball game, tough ball game for us, but we put ourselves in a position to win at the end. After the last couple of innings, we just didn't get the big hit," Corbin said.

Louisville coach Dan McDonnell was now on to something; despite the fact that VU had a terrific lineup from top to bottom, a deep pitching and talented pitching staff could match up with the Commodores. Four guys had already thrown effectively on Saturday and there were plenty more in reserve.

Sunday would be Beede's worst start of the season. It was obvious early where things were headed when Beede unintentionally threw behind Sturgeon, the game's second hitter. Perhaps over correcting for that, Beede grooved the next offering right over the plate and Sturgeon drove that for a single. It caused no harm as VU got a strike-'em-out, throw-'em-out double play to end the inning, but there was more to come.

To lead off the second, Beede plunked Johnson in the head. Navin gunned him down trying to steal a few moments later, but Kyle Gibson singled and later scored on Wasserman's single. Once again, Beede got some help from his defense, as Yastrzemski threw out Wasserman at third later in the inning.

Beede trotted out to start the third, but it didn't last long. He walked Sturgeon, gave up a single to Johnson, and walked Jeff Gardner to load the bases. There were two outs and the bases were loaded and Corbin had to have Fulmer throw now. It worked, as Gibson grounded out on the first pitch and the inning was over.

Vandy, though, couldn't hit Jeff Thompson. The right-hander had been outstanding that year, going 10–1 with a 2.06 ERA coming into the weekend. However, the 6-foot-6, 248-pounder had gotten stronger as the season progressed and his fastball now could reach the mid-90s, which VU had not expected. The Commodores loaded the bases off him in the first and couldn't score, at which point Thompson settled into a groove for several innings.

In the sixth, Wiel hit what looked like a foul pop-up to left, but it kept carrying and crashed off the foul pole for a solo home run. In the seventh, VU stranded a runner and it finally chased Thompson (who went seven and struck out nine) from the game in the eighth. With two men on, Vandy had a chance against Joe Filomeno and Kyle Funkhouser, but couldn't break through.

Meanwhile, Fulmer had been nearly unhittable himself, even though there were some control issues (two walks, three hit batsmen in 5 ⅓ innings). Time and time again, the freshman pitched himself out of jams, and kept his teammates in position to win in the ninth.

There was hope when Norwood singled with one out. Turner singled with two outs and Yastrzemski, perhaps the guy Vanderbilt most wanted at the plate in that situation, was now up. The good news is that O'Donnell had burned Burdi earlier in the inning; the bad news was that lefty Cody Ege, who had a sparking 1.26 ERA with 44 strikeouts in 28 ⅔ innings coming into the weekend, was now on to face the left-handed-hitting Yastrzemski.

As outstanding as the senior had been that season—he'd hit a torrid .407/.500/.574 mark in SEC regular-season games—he hadn't looked like himself that day, fanning twice in four previous at bats. On the last pitch he saw as a collegiate, Yastrzemski struck out swinging.

A stunned VU team and Hawkins Field crowd stared blankly at the scoreboard, which read, "Louisville 2, Vanderbilt 1." Two weeks earlier, the Commodores had been on the verge of posting one of the greatest seasons not just in conference history, and maybe in college baseball history, too. Now, it was over a step short of Omaha.

Retrospect, in the words of those who lived it

As it had been with the 2007 season, it was just so hard to make sense of the 2013 campaign because it ended sooner than most anyone expected. Early in 2014, I sat down with a number of players from that team and asked them to rehash the season in their own words. Yastrzemski seemed to sum up the final weekend better than anyone.

"I think we just ran into a couple of good arms. There's nothing that anyone did wrong. Sometimes, the ball falls that way, and when you have guys who can keep their consistency of their velocity and those guys were both throwing harder than they threw all season—our scouting reports from a lot of teams and from watching a lot of video, those guys would throw lower-90s or upper-80s but they were hyped-up and they were throwing mid-to-upper-90s for the whole game," he remembered.

"Their staff had a really good weekend and sometimes that just happens . . . but after going through a season like that, you almost feel like it must not have meant to be, because we had such a fairy-tale story to get there, and it was almost too perfect."

Several members of the team still feel as if the better team didn't prevail that June weekend.

"It's not always who's the best team that wins, but who's playing the best—with all respect to Louisville—at any time in the season. To me—we have SEC bias—but I think the best two teams in the country that year were Vanderbilt and LSU, and unfortunately we didn't get to play again. We just weren't the best team at the time," Harrell said.

"They just got that timely hit right when they needed, every time," Kemp remembers. "And we were smoking balls, hitting balls right at people and you've got to keep your confidence: We're going to get it, we're going to get it, we're going to get it. But we never gave up to the end. We did a phenomenal job.

"We were always on the gas pedal, always on the gas pedal the whole year and at the end, we just ran out of gas, I guess."

Was the team's level of previous success, and the pressure that came with it, an issue? Baseball is a high-variance game, and unlike football, even the elite teams are going to lose several times a season. The curse of a season like that is that it can be hard to recover from losing when you rarely lose. When you lose once in the postseason and face the reality that one more loss can do you in, it has the potential to create extra pressure, if not mild panic.

Harrell said it was still "hard to put a finger on why" the well ran dry against Louisville that weekend, but insisted that the stress of it all was not the reason.

"I didn't ever feel pressure. The first time there was pressure was when we lost to Georgia Tech. I think there's three games like that this season, there was Georgia, there was Texas A&M in the [SEC] Tournament and then there was Georgia Tech. Those three games were almost carbon-copies of one another. I remember going home after we lost the [Tech] game and having an elimination game here at home against [Tech] on Monday, and everyone was talking about it. No way! We're not going to lose. It wasn't going to happen and even after we lost that game against Louisville, there was no way we were going to lose," Harrell said.

As Ziomek put it: "We were just so good throughout the year and we really had never faced any adversity, and going in there at the end of the year when we did face adversity a couple of times, I really don't think there was panic. We didn't know how to deal with it. It was almost a foreign thing to us because we hadn't faced it, and when we finally did, I didn't feel like we panicked.

"It just didn't work out. That's the game of baseball, and that's the thing. That's why it's better than a lot of other sports, in my opinion, crazy things like that happen."

As for the draft, it weighed more heavily on some than others.

"Honestly, everyone knew that Kevin and Conrad and Tony were going to get drafted," Harrell said, "and so there's almost a relief when it happened. . . . As far as it affecting the games, I never thought once about my draft position when we were playing Louisville. I think it was actually pressure off us after it happened.

"Probably the tendency for a fan would be to connect our loss to Louisville to the draft and say, 'Those guys are over it,' or whatever, but that had zero bearing on our performance."

It was easier for Harrell to put behind than it was for Yastrzemski, who had maybe the worst game of his season the day he was picked.

"To be honest, I didn't want any of that draft stuff to be going on then. That stuff weighs so heavily on everyone because it's your future and you've got to put it past you. For a lot of us, it's hard to. You're anxious, you want to know what's going on, but you're in the middle of something and it's just hard to balance both things at once," he said.

The strange thing about the ending was that the circumstances were so similar to the 2011 season, which also had a lot of players drafted. Corbin talks about how the chemistry of both teams was outstanding. There was nothing lacking in the work ethic of both teams, either.

"It was all business. We didn't have as much talent, per se, as the 2011 team on the field, so when in 2011 we would play a midweek game, and we could just show up, and just by showing up we could beat teams. But 2013, we never even put ourselves in that moment. Everyone showed up to the field like it was every other day because they wanted to be there. It wasn't work, it wasn't like, Oh man, we've got to go to the field and play a game," Yastrzemski remembered.

As for Corbin, he saw the final weekend this way.

"[We were] a little bit inconsistent," he said. "We didn't hit the ball as well. I do think the draft weighed on some kids' minds. I'm not going to use it as an excuse, though, I just think it was another factor that may have taken their attention away at a certain time. I can remember the kids—some of the kids were really pressing hard at that moment, wondering if they would get drafted and when they did, and when they didn't, that was unfortunate.

"But Louisville had to do it, too. They deserved it. They came to Vanderbilt and beat us two games, and I hand it to them, because if you do that to a team that's played this well all year and never lost a series, you have to come in there and beat them and they did, they beat us. They just played better than we did."

Despite the way it ended, the Commodores' incredible SEC regular-season mark is one that should stand for decades to come.

"It's not thinkable, let alone doable. You just don't set out to do that. You don't, you can't, and you wouldn't. You just set out for small victories and those small victories start to accumulate to the point where we just played well every week. We didn't drop off at all. We didn't drop off on a weekday, we didn't drop off on a weekend, there was no time where as a coach I'm going, I wish these guys would play better," Corbin said.

"I think the only negative of all of that is you know, because of the percentages of the game, that you just can't play that well for that long of time. I've never been around a group who's done that before."

2014 Baseball:
Dreams do come true

The 2013 super regional loss to Louisville signaled a changing of the guard. Almost all the old, familiar faces that VU fans knew well had left; only T. J. Pecoraro and Steven Rice remained from the 2011 College World Series club, and neither had played in Omaha. With catcher Spencer Navin, first baseman Conrad Gregor, second baseman Tony Kemp, left fielder Jack Lupo, center fielder Connor Harrell, and right fielder Mike Yastrzemski all gone, VU would be rebuilding most of its lineup.

Sure, coach Tim Corbin had some solid remaining players; Zander Wiel (15 career starts), Xavier Turner (51), Rhett Wiseman (11), John Norwood (9), Vince Conde (65), Tyler Campbell (2), Kyle Smith (7), Chris Harvey (13), Dansby Swanson (4), and Will Cooper (1) had combined for 178 career starts. But contrast that with the 1,040 that the departing six had made, and it was clear that Corbin had his work cut out for him.

The pitching was in better hands. The team had thrown 596 innings the season before and the players who threw 69.1 percent of them were back.[1] Despite a lot of experience, though, VU lost its most valuable arm from 2013 when Kevin Ziomek (2.12 ERA,

---

[1] Rising Junior Philip Pfeifer, who had pitched 63 ⅔ innings in 2013 and made 12 starts, was among the group of departed players. Pfeifer sat out 2014 to take care of some off-field business but should return for 2014.

119 innings, 115 strikeouts) turned pro after Detroit picked him in the second round.

However, it was no secret that Corbin had recruited amazingly well with a pair of recent No. 1–rated recruiting classes, the bulk of the players that composed them still on campus. Many of them— especially hitters like Norwood, Wiseman, and Harvey, and pitchers Carson Fulmer, Walker Buehler, Adam Ravenelle, and Tyler Ferguson—had star potential, but all had to sit and watch as the veterans accumulated most of the playing time when the Commodores took the big stage in previous years. Swanson had been in the plans for 2013 as Corbin felt he'd be his shortstop that year, but injuries sidelined the freshman most of that season.

Corbin's class of newcomers for 2014 wasn't ranked in the same stratosphere as the previous two, but Corbin liked it nonetheless. He didn't know exactly who would help, but he liked a trio of out-fielders in switch-hitters Bryan Reynolds and Ro Coleman, and lefty Nolan Rogers. Two more freshmen, Karl Ellison and Jason Delay, were pushing Harvey for time behind the plate. VU was loaded on the mound, but Corbin felt that lefties John Kilichowski and Ben Bowden might be able to help, as well as right-hander Hayden Stone.

It was enough that the Commodores started the year in the top 10 of the major polls. Meanwhile, back in February, Corbin had a quiet assuredness that he might have something with this bunch.

"The part that I felt most positive about was the experience in the pitching staff. I knew that if we needed to grow from a position-player standpoint, I thought our pitching staff could stabilize us for a certain amount of time where we could start to make some headway offensively," Corbin said.

Still, there were elements that had nothing to do with talent, and those were the things that could be the difference between greatness and an early end to the season.

"Before the season started, I said, 'I've got one issue, and this is the part that we're gonna need to develop if we intend to play in Omaha, and it's our mental toughness.' We needed to mature, because we just lost so many quality seniors, an older fiber of our team," he recalled after the season.

The roller-coaster ride of Corbin's lifetime was about to begin.

A torrid start

Corbin took his bunch out west for a three-game series against Long Beach State to open the season.[2] Friday night starter Tyler Beede, a preseason All-America honoree who struggled down the stretch with control issues in 2013, had an encouraging five-inning, no-earned-run, seven-strikeout performance with just one walk in the opener as VU won by a 5–2 count. Lefty Jared Miller and Ferguson, a right-hander—each surprise additions to the rotation—went 6 and 5 ⅓ innings, respectively. Neither starter surrendered a run as the 'Dores left Long Beach 3–0.

"I thought that was a huge series for us in a lot of different ways. We were going on the road, a lot of new faces, and just to play a very good team, one that was filled with a lot of experience, I knew it was going to be tough to win a couple of ball games there, and we end up sweeping," Corbin said.

Walker Buehler gave VU another five-inning, no-earned-run performance to beat Lipscomb on Wednesday in the home opener, and then Beede, Miller, and Ferguson all picked up wins as Vandy topped Illinois-Chicago by a combined 28–2 margin at Hawkins Field that weekend. Western Kentucky got to Buehler early and handed VU its first loss, 3–2, the next Tuesday and then Evansville pounded Pecoraro for six earned in 1 ⅓ innings in another 8–3 loss.

But all three weekend starters were again brilliant in a three-game sweep of Stanford. Midweek wins over Tennessee Tech and Middle Tennessee State followed (with Buehler throwing six innings of shutout ball against one of the nation's highest-scoring teams in the first) and then Buehler, Miller, and Ferguson were nearly untouchable again as Vandy romped over Wofford in three that weekend. After an 11–2 pounding of Eastern Illinois, the Commodores were 16–2 heading into a big conference-opening three-game series against LSU at Hawkins Field.

---

2 The 49ers, after a few down seasons, finished 34–26 and were runners-up in the Gainesville Regional in 2014.

It was hard to tell how tough the Tigers would be because they'd faced a weak schedule up to that point.[3] But what everyone knew is that LSU's Friday night pitcher Aaron Nola, whom the Philadelphia Phillies would take seventh in the upcoming Major League Baseball First-Year Player Draft, was the real deal.

The showdown between the two aces was everything it had been billed. Vandy touched Nola for a second-inning run on Coleman's sacrifice fly and the lead stood at 1–0 heading into the eighth. Beede had retired 11 in a row with one out until Christian Ibarra reached on an infield single, and Beede issued his first walk of the night to Tyler Moore. At 105 pitches, Corbin pulled Beede for Brian Miller, who got another out before Jake Fraley reached on Turner's error on a high throw from third. Andrew Stevenson singled for two runs and then Swanson couldn't field a grounder that took a sideways hop on him; the sophomore was charged with an error and two more scored.

By the time the inning was finished, LSU led 4–1 and though Conde knocked in an eighth-inning run, VU fell by two.

It looked like a hiccup. In the second game of the weekend, Miller went 6 ⅔ and gave up just two hits, two walks, and a run to the Tigers as he improved to 5–0 in a 5–3 win. Ferguson struggled on Sunday and was lifted before he was out of the fourth, but Stone was magnificent, fanning 10 and giving up just one run in 5 ⅓, while Swanson (3-for-4, two doubles, two RBIs) and Reynolds (2-for-4, three RBIs) carried the offense to a 9–3 win. After an 8–4 win over Belmont that included a home run by the diminutive Coleman, Vandy now stood at 19–3 and 2–1 in the Southeastern Conference.

It looked like a national championship–caliber team. The staff ERA was 1.38, with Beede seemingly having licked his control issues and Jared Miller and Ferguson justifying Corbin's decision to put them in the rotation instead of Fulmer and Buehler. The offense, with the sophomores developing nicely and Reynolds becoming an immediate-impact bat, was averaging 5.8 runs per

---

3 They were plenty tough; LSU earned one of eight national seeds for the NCAA Tournament and finished 46–16–1.

contest in what was a new, lower-scoring era of college baseball. The defense, which might have been the biggest concern with so many players playing full-time roles in the field for the first time, was instead brilliant, as the team was fielding .979.

"I thought we were progressing okay. We were still trying to find an offensive identity, though," Corbin said. "We were starting to see what kind of player Dansby was developing into, and starting to see what was coming out of Bryan Reynolds, what kind of player he was. We quickly moved him to the top of the lineup, and we were looking for the catcher. Chris Harvey was playing pretty well, but we were also using Jason [Delay] and Karl Ellison in spots.

"I think we were just playing good, solid baseball without beating ourselves, and those numbers would tell you that. So it wasn't a necessity that we needed to score a lot of runs, but I felt as the season progressed, we were going to have to get a lot better offensively."

It looked as if this team could be as elite as the 2007, 2011, or 2013 teams, but the one thing those teams never faced was a lot of adversity. This team was about to get enough of that to test everyone's faith, and then some.

Getting exposed

On Friday, March 21, Vanderbilt traveled to Starkville, Mississippi, to face Mississippi State for its first SEC road series. The previous year, VU had swept MSU in four games by a combined 32–14 and yet the Bulldogs not only made it to the College World Series, but finished second there. With a lot of key players back, MSU was in the top five of the preseason polls but the Bulldogs had scuffled early, going 15–8 against a schedule that included no teams that would even make the NCAA Tournament in 2014.

But that night, it was VU that struggled. The Commodores made five errors that night behind Beede, and then suddenly the wheels came off for Beede too. MSU scored four in the first against

Tech, two in the second, and five in the third—all off Beede, though just five were earned—and 11 hits, five walks, and a hit batsman later, Beede was done. Once the evening was over, VU had been spanked by a 17–2 score, the worst loss Corbin had experienced as a Vandy coach.

It proved to be contagious. The next day, Jared Miller also couldn't find the strike zone against the Bulldogs, giving up five walks and four hits in 4 ⅓ innings before being chased. The defense made two more errors and the offense couldn't solve Ross Mitchell in a 6–3 loss. Vandy did manage some redemption on Sunday as Ferguson and Fulmer combined for a three-hitter in a 5–1 win that afternoon to salvage the last game of the series.

"I really thought [those losses] were anomalies. . . . We had played pretty good baseball against LSU and then we go on the road and made five or six errors and throw the ball around and the game starts to speed up a bit. We're dropping balls in the outfield, we're mis-playing balls in the outfield, I know we made a couple of errors behind the plate. Dansby, one play I remember, just over-ran a ball," Corbin said.

"It seemed like anything that could go wrong, did, and we were doing it behind one of our better pitchers [Beede]. We were getting handled, but we were committing a lot of crimes ourselves. . . . We were spiraling after that loss on Friday night."

Buehler pitched a seven-inning gem back at home on Tuesday, fanning 10 as VU beat Belmont, 2–1. Kentucky lefty A. J. Reed befuddled Vandy in a 4–2 win on Friday to open the three-game series, but a bigger concern than the offense was Beede (five innings, five hits, three walks, three hit batsmen, three runs), who once again fell apart as Kentucky got three in the sixth. On Saturday, Jared Miller was also wild (three walks, two hit batters) but gave up just three runs as Fulmer and Brian Miller nailed it down from there in a 9–3 win. Ferguson was great on Sunday, firing six innings of one-run ball while Norwood connected for a big homer in a 6–2 win.

The series win over Kentucky was nothing to sneeze at as the Wildcats were ranked in the top 20, and after a 5–0 win over Tennessee-Martin, all seemed right again. When VU went to

Knoxville on Friday, Beede struggled through a three-run first inning but was masterful from there, going eight and giving up just four runs in a 6–4 win over Tennessee. It was the fourth win in as many games.

But the 'Dores' fortunes ultimately changed in game two. On Saturday night, Vandy staked Jared Miller to a 3–0 lead after 2 ½, and even though Miller gave up two in the third, Vandy responded with a pair in the fourth and four in the sixth. But the defense again imploded. The normally sure-handed Swanson made errors on a couple of routine balls. Wiel was hurt in a collision at first and Smith, filling in for him, also had a miscue. Miller and Ellison, the latter getting a rare start behind the plate, had one error each. In spite of that, VU led by a run going into the ninth and with Fulmer on the hill, it looked as if it would escape.

That's where once again, everything went wrong. Leading off the ninth, UT's Scott Price took first after Fulmer evidently licked his hand with three balls in the count, prompting an automatic ball four. He quickly got two outs before walking Christin Stewart and then hitting Tyler Schultz. He appeared to recover, twice throwing what he thought was strike three to light-hitting freshman Nathaniel Maggio, but got neither call. Forced to groove a 3–2 pitch, Maggio reached out and touched one to left, scoring the 9th and 10th runs in a 10–9 win.

That wasn't the worst of it, though. Wiel had hyperextended his elbow and would miss a week. Turner, hit in the back of the head with an errant throw, would also be sidelined for a week. Ellison spent the night in the hospital with an injury. On Sunday, with three regulars gone, the 'Dores came out and were dominated by freshman Kyle Serrano and a pair of relievers in a 7–0, two-hit loss to the Vols.

"I think you have those games in every season, but that was a low point. . . . Saturday's game, we had command of it and lost command of it. Again, a lot of mistakes like the Mississippi State Friday night game. The way it ended was dramatic; the first baseman shanks a ball over the shortstop's head in a situation where we thought we were going to take the van and win, especially with the guy on the mound," Corbin remembers.

"But we didn't. And then it was just a comedy of injuries from there. The next day, we're playing people that we didn't [normally] play. We weren't complete, that's for sure, by any stretch. . . . And at that time, Norwood and Wiseman weren't really swinging the bat well. It was a recipe for [a] 7–0 game."

Again, Buehler was masterful in a seven-inning, 10-strikeout performance that resulted in a 6–2 win over 21–8 Indiana State. But Texas A&M, with a middling offense, came to Nashville next and smacked the Commodores for 23 runs—this time, all but two of them were earned—in taking two of three that weekend. Beede walked four men and hit another, giving up four runs on Friday and not getting an out in the sixth. Jared Miller went four and gave up four and even the normally dependable Ferguson gave up five earned runs in his six innings of work on Sunday.

There was no doubt about it: the Commodores were reeling. The same program that had won an incredible 23-straight regular-season series dating back to mid-2012 had now dropped three of the last four. The team was hitting respectably, but the team's defense and starting pitching were no longer reliable.

Putting the pieces in place

By now, Corbin knew he had to make some changes. Fulmer had nine saves, but he wasn't pitching much, as the Commodores trailed too often. With Jared Miller struggling, the logical move was to send Fulmer, who'd shown the ability to pitch for longer stretches of games, into the rotation in place of Miller. It also made sense because Fulmer was the team's toughest competitor, a guy unafraid to take the ball any time under any conditions.

On Saturday, April 19, in Fayetteville, Arkansas, Fulmer started a night game against the Arkansas Razorbacks and Corbin's plan worked brilliantly. The sophomore dominated Arkansas in six innings of six-strikeout, six-hit shutout baseball. In the fourth, Norwood hit a two-run home run and once Stone, Bowden, and

Carson Fulmer's move from the bullpen to the rotation was a catalyst in Vandy's late-season 2014 run. (Jimmy Jones)

new closer Brian Miller got the Commodores through the last three innings, Vandy had a much-needed 2–1 victory.

"I thought the Arkansas series was a turning point with Saturday's ballgame. . . . I felt like [Fulmer] ignited our pitching staff, and that was what we needed. We just needed something different to take place," Corbin recalled.

Still, all was not well. The previous night, Beede had given up six earned runs in seven innings to a light-hitting Razorback club. A win on Sunday would have given Vandy a huge boost, but Ferguson struggled through his four innings of work, giving up three runs in a 3–1 loss. The offense didn't hit the ball badly—Reynolds hit a home run and VU had seven hits that day—but they never came at the right time.

An SEC title was out of the question barring a miracle, but worse, the 'Dores were starting to run the risk of not making the NCAA Tournament. The 29–12 overall record would be good enough to get most major conference teams in Vandy's position into the field of 64, but the problem was that thirteen of the league's fourteen teams still had some shot at earning an NCAA Tournament bid.

An easy way for the NCAA to weed out some teams would be to exclude the two teams that didn't qualify for the Southeastern Conference Tournament. At 8–10 in a tightly packed league, the Commodores were in the top 12 at that point, but only by one full game.

The good news, though, was this: as bleak as things looked, VU figured to get the benefit of the doubt if it continued to put itself in good position. The NCAA relies heavily on the Ratings Percentage Index (RPI), which combines win-loss outcomes with strength of schedule, and the Commodores still ranked in the top 15 there due to a tough schedule.

Vandy also had a chance to rack up some wins over the next two weekends with Georgia (7–10 in the league at that point) coming to town preceding a road trip to Missouri (6–12 in the SEC).

Sure enough, the 'Dores cashed in on both occasions.

Vandy ripped Georgia for 29 runs in a three-game sweep, with Fulmer (seven scoreless innings) and Ferguson (five innings, no earned runs) providing the pitching highlights. The next weekend in Columbia, it was the pitching staff's time to shine. Beede gave up three runs in the first three innings, but the rest of the VU hurlers, led by Fulmer (six innings and once again, no runs), gave up just two runs the remainder of the weekend.

With those six quick wins, the 36–12 Commodores knew they wouldn't have to sweat an NCAA selection provided there was no spectacular collapse from there. Now, Vanderbilt turned its attention to earning postseason baseball in its own park; with a top-10 RPI at that point, that now seemed to be a very real possibility. But with a road trip to Florida combined with a home series against South Carolina, Vanderbilt would have to earn it.

In a nationally televised Thursday night game, UF freshman Logan Shore outdueled Beede in a 1–0 shutout as the Commodores got just two hits. On Friday, Vandy scored just three fifth-inning runs, but those were enough because Fulmer was brilliant in a complete-game, four-hit shutout. In Saturday's season finale, Vanderbilt torched UF's Karsten Whitson, A.J. Puk, Justin Shafer, and Ryan Harris for 16 runs in the first seven innings, including eight in the first inning alone as Swanson and Conde both homered.

Ferguson threw five shutout innings and at the end of that long afternoon, the Commodores came back to Nashville 16–2 winners.

"That was certainly the highlight [of the regular season].
That got us going in the right direction psychologically," Corbin
said.[4] At 16–11 in the SEC, the 'Dores still had a mathematical
chance at tying UF for the league's regular-season title, too. That
aside, if the Commodores could just win the series over Carolina,
it appeared that they'd get one of the NCAA Tournament's eight
national seeds, which meant that VU would be guaranteed to play
in its home park all the way to the College World Series, provided
it kept winning.

The title shot went by the board late on Thursday. Beede had
a great outing, but Corbin perhaps left him in too long in the
ninth. With Vandy leading 3–2 and Beede well past 100 pitches,
Carolina's Gene Cone walked to lead off the inning. Corbin went
to Brian Miller to shut the door, but Max Schrock singled on a 2–2
pitch with two out to tie the game. In the 10th, Joey Pankake lined
a homer to left and Carolina got a 4–3 win.

It took until his fifth try, but Fulmer finally gave up a run in
an SEC start in the second game against South Carolina, when
the Gamecocks touched him for one each in the second, fifth,
and sixth, but thanks to a pair of four-run innings that included
a two-run homer from Wiel, Vandy prevailed by a 9–3 score. In
Saturday's finale, the game was tied in the eighth until Carolina,
which had left 10 men on base to Vandy's none, exploded for four
runs (two earned) off Kilichowski and Ravenelle, walking out of
Nashville with a series win.

At 40–16 and 17–13 in the SEC, Vandy was going to get
an NCAA Tournament bid, and probably even host at least one
weekend. But with conference tournaments on the horizon across
the country, the Commodores didn't want to give the NCAA's
selection committee a reason to think otherwise, especially after
the weekend's events resulted in five SEC teams getting seeded
ahead of the Commodores in the SEC Tournament.

---

4 After the season, Corbin said this was the first time he thought his team might
be good enough to win a national title.

In their tournament opener, the 'Dores had a chance to deliver a potential knockout blow to Tennessee's tournament hopes in the single-elimination stage of the tournament. Thanks to a great outing from Buehler, Vandy went to the ninth with a 3–2 lead as Corbin put Fulmer in to finish. Tennessee's Nick Senzel led off with a double to left and then Fulmer balked him to third with nobody out. UT's Taylor Smart scorched a grounder to Turner, where VU's third baseman made a great play. As Turner's momentum carried him into foul territory, he noticed that Senzel had wandered too far off the bag and tagged him out. Minutes later, Fulmer picked Smart off first. When Vincent Jackson fanned swinging, VU advanced to the double-elimination portion.

A win over LSU, coupled with perhaps one more somewhere else, would have likely sealed a national seed for Vandy. Instead, the Tigers bombed Jared Miller, knocking him out in the fourth, and even touched Stone, who'd been unhittable all season, for six runs. Thanks to the SEC's mercy rule, LSU prevailed 11–1 in just seven innings.

Still, a victory over Ole Miss on Thursday could potentially give Vandy the boost it needed to secure a second weekend at home in the NCAAs. Instead, Beede's control abandoned him as the weather got hotter (he walked five and hit two) and Ole Miss knocked Vandy from Hoover by a 7–2 score.

Afterward, Corbin was so upset that while the rest of the players showered and changed clothes before the bus ride home, the coach remained in uniform. For all the Commodores knew, they might have even blown their chance to host a regional, as other teams across the country would have more days to pad their résumés.

There was perhaps a silver lining, though. Corbin had often been criticized for taxing his players too hard in Hoover in games that generally had little bearing on VU's postseason fortunes. Quite often, NCAA Tournament disappointment had followed. This time, the 'Dores would get eight days' rest before there would be baseball games again.

Within three days, Corbin said he knew that bowing out early had been a good thing for this bunch.

"We got back to Nashville about 5 p.m. [Thursday], it was the earliest we'd been back to Nashville in a while, and I leveled with them. . . . I was emotional and I explained to them how I felt and how I thought they should feel at this point, but after I was done, I told them they had two days . . . and they're not [to get] anywhere close to a baseball or anywhere close to a glove . . . I just felt like they needed to decompress after what I had to say to them," he remembers.

"I told them just to get out of here and go, and get back on Sunday, and when we got back on Sunday we had two practices, one that afternoon and one that night, and we continued to do that Monday, Tuesday, and Wednesday, and then we had our regional practices [on Thursday] and I thought we had our best practices we'd had since prior to the start of the season. At that point, I thought we were rejuvenated."

Rarely had the veteran coach been so dead-on in his assessment of his team.

Coming home

It's common for members of selection committees to refer to whether or not a team "passes the eye test" as they evaluate teams for the postseason. Anyone watching the Commodores for the last two weeks probably hadn't been impressed. Of course, playing the elite of the elite can certainly make anyone look bad, and the fact that nine of VU's last eleven games had come against teams to which the NCAA would later award those sixteen coveted hosting bids had to factor in.

With a 41–18 overall record, an RPI of 8, and a strength of schedule of 5, common sense prevailed; the NCAA did not award Vanderbilt a national seed, but the Commodores would host a regional at Hawkins Field, with Oregon, Clemson, and Xavier all traveling to Nashville. If they got out of the weekend, they would likely travel to Bloomington, Indiana, to face the Big 10 champs, the Indiana Hoosiers.

"I thought it was a tough, tough regional. I thought we were going to have a hell of a time trying to get out of it. You never know about a team like Xavier, because they won a conference tournament. Clemson was Clemson; it didn't matter how they finished [the season] . . . they know what it's like to be in that situation.[5] And I can tell you, once we got done with Oregon, I thought it was an Omaha team. I thought Oregon had everything. . . . I thought they could pitch, they could play defense, and they could put enough pressure on you offensively where it just made it very, very difficult to play them," Corbin said.

Fourth-seeded Xavier came first. As Shaun Kelley and Austin Peay had shown Vandy in 2007, a No. 4 led by an ace can be a tough match, and with right-hander Vinny Nittoli (1.98 ERA in 82 innings) on the hill, the Musketeers might not be a push-over.

Beede was as electric as he'd ever been that Friday evening. The right-hander threw 114 pitches, walked just two, and struck out a career-high 14. Nittoli was tough the first time through the lineup, but walked Conde with one out in the fourth and then hit Wiel, before Turner lined an RBI single. Vandy clung to a two-run lead heading into the bottom of the sixth, and then Norwood chased Nittoli when he ripped a single with nobody out in the inning. Reliever Eric Steine couldn't get the job done, walking or hitting all of the three hitters he faced, and Brad Kirschner gave up two more hits in the inning.

By the time it was over, VU had seven runs in the inning. It would add two more in the seventh and coast to an 11–0 win.

"[My goal was] honestly just to enjoy the moment," said Beede, who was sitting between 94 and 97 miles per hour on the radar gun that evening. "The season was what it was, and we all wanted to refresh and get a new season."

Oregon, which smoked Clemson by an 18–1 score earlier that day, was next. The Ducks were a bit of a scary match for Vandy because they had a lineup full of line-drive hitters, the kind that you don't necessarily want to face at Hawkins Field, with its 375-foot

---

5 Clemson went 36–23 in the regular season and was thought to be perhaps the last at-large selection to the NCAA Tournament.

power alleys. That's exactly what OU had done to beat Clemson on Friday, but as Ducks coach George Horton warned fans when asked about carrying momentum into Saturday night's winner's bracket game, "In baseball, momentum is only as good as the next day's starting pitcher."

By that count, Vandy had all the momentum on Saturday. Fulmer went eight innings and threw 122 pitches, giving up just two runs before being pulled for Ravenelle, who pitched a perfect ninth. Meanwhile, Oregon's starter, the soft-tossing Jeff Gold, wasn't as good. Vandy hit the ball well early, but only had a run on a Norwood double high off the wall in the second that scored Wiseman. Then the fifth inning came, and the 'Dores erupted for five runs thanks to RBI singles from Reynolds and Conde and a two-RBI double from Wiseman, with the other run scoring on an error.

Once it was done, VU had an easy 7–2 win.

"We were just seeing [the ball] really well, letting it get really deep and just trying to barrel it up," said Reynolds, who had three of Vanderbilt's 13 hits.

Vanderbilt needed just one more win to get to the next weekend. Xavier had earlier eliminated Clemson, Corbin's former employer, and threatened to upset Oregon as well once it led by five runs heading into the eighth. But the Ducks got three in the eighth and two in the ninth before tacking on three more in the 10th for a wild 11–8 win earlier on Sunday, earning a spot with Vandy in the title game. The Ducks, of course, had to beat VU twice to advance.

It figured to be to Vanderbilt's advantage that Oregon had already played a long game in the June heat, while the Commodores had almost 24 hours to rest, before the teams played that night. However, it didn't turn out that way.

Oregon led 2–1 as the Commodores struggled against freshman fireballer Stephen Nogosek that evening. Nogosek used a breaking ball and a change up that complemented his fastball, and kept Vandy guessing through seven innings, with the Ducks clinging to a 2–1 lead. But Nogosek had thrown just 28 ⅔ innings all season and after 109 pitches, Horton decided he was done.

So, the Ducks' coach went to ace reliever Garrett Cleavinger to start the eighth, but Cleavinger had trouble locating his pitches within the strike zone. He hit Ellison with a pitch to start the eighth and after Cooper pinch-ran, Delay moved him up a base with a bunt. On Swanson's grounder to third, Cooper took off when he shouldn't have, but shortstop Kevin Minjares threw wildly to third. Reynolds followed by nearly hitting into a double play, but he beat the throw to first as Cooper crossed home with the tying run.

Meanwhile, Vandy's Buehler had also been brilliant, keeping the score knotted at two heading into the bottom of the ninth. The sophomore had fanned eight and walked just one and stood to pick up his 11th win of the season if Vandy could get him some runs.

Cleavinger walked Wiel to start the ninth and so Horton called for closer Jake Reed, who had 13 saves and a 1.96 ERA. The first hitter was Turner, whom Reed hit with a pitch. Wiseman, next up, dropped a perfect bunt down third, and VU had the bases loaded with nobody out.

Norwood was in position to win the game and got ahead in the count, but Reed rebounded to strike him out. Ellison was due up next, but instead, Corbin went to the bench and got Coleman.

Coleman had struggled to hit for much of the year, but the decision made sense for two reasons. First, Coleman was the smallest man on the roster,[6] and Reed was struggling with his control. Second, Corbin knew that if Reed couldn't throw strikes, he'd have to come back with a fastball at some point—and, as Corbin said later of Coleman, "He's a good fastball hitter."

That's exactly how things played out. After Reed fell behind 3–0, Coleman, a switch-hitter who was batting left-handed, took strike one. Coleman got his fastball, slapped it through short and into the outfield, and once Wiel touched home, Vanderbilt players sprinted from the dugout where they mobbed Coleman, who after shaking his fist began to grin from ear to ear.

---

6 Vanderbilt lists Coleman at 5-foot-5; having stood next to him, that's probably generous by two inches.

"I was just trying to make them come in my zone and when it came to 3–1, I knew I was getting a fastball," he said.

Vanderbilt fans could breathe a sigh of relief. For just the fifth time in school history, the Commodores would be playing in a super regional. Buehler, Swanson, Reynolds, and Conde were selected to the all-tournament team and Beede was named the MVP.

"I thought the dramatic, walk-off win really, really lifted us," Corbin said after the season.

After Stanford played three close games against No. 4 Indiana and came out with two victories, the Cardinal would be Vandy's next opponent.

This Stanford club was a better version than the one the Commodores caught in February. However, the extra baseball had also taken its toll on the Cardinal pitching staff. Freshman ace Cal Quantrill had been needed to throw the final 2 ⅓ innings in the last Indiana game, that coming just after he'd thrown 104 pitches in a complete-game effort against Indiana State.

So on Friday afternoon, Stanford went with John Hochstatter, who'd picked up the loss in the previous Saturday's game with Indiana. Hochstatter fed Vandy a steady variety of off-speed stuff, which the Commodores had difficulty in squaring up. However, most of it was out of the strike zone and so Vandy just waited out the lefty. With 1 out, he'd loaded the bases with 3 walks, and with two outs, a walk to Wiseman forced in a run. A wild pitch scored Wiel and when Norwood lined a single to left, Vandy had a 4–0 lead after one.

Ellison walked to lead off the second, spelling the end for Hochstatter. Singles by Swanson and Reynolds off Chris Viall loaded the bases and then Conde walked in a run. A sacrifice fly by Wiel and a groundout by Turner scored two more. In the third, Ellison and Delay led off with singles and an infield single plus a throwing error by Stanford first baseman Danny Diekroeger scored another. After Wiel's run-scoring single, Vandy led 10–0 through three.

Beede had cruised through three, but gave up a pair of singles to start the fourth. With two outs, Taylor tripled in two. Beede walked two men to start the fifth and with one out, hit another, and then gave up a run on an infield single to Zach Hoffpauir. Brant Whiting's fly-ball out scored another and after a walk, Dominic Jose's single to center scored two more.

In the blink of an eye, the score stood at 10–6 and the Cardinal had runners on the corners. Corbin had seen enough and brought in Ferguson, who walked the first man he saw before Tommy Edman filed out to right to hold the lead at four.

Those were tense moments for the partisan Vandy crowd. The Commodores failed to score in the middle innings, but Conde's seventh-inning single tacked on another run. Meanwhile, Ferguson settled down to fire 2 ⅔ scoreless innings and then Miller retired Stanford's last five hitters to end an 11–6 game. The Commodores were now one game away from going to Omaha for just the second time in program history.

"We just gave them too much early. Obviously, you can't give a team like Vanderbilt as many free base runners as we did," Stanford coach Mark Marquess said. "It's a credit to them. They got a couple of hits with people on base, which kind of broke it open early."

Any sort of celebration would have to wait another day. Quantrill pitched like a major leaguer, mixing his fastball with an off-speed pitch that befuddled Vandy all day on Saturday until Marquess removed him after 117 pitches before the eighth. Vandy had trailed just 2–1 behind Fulmer, who was clearly tiring in the seventh. Corbin waited too long to pull him and Stanford extended the lead to 4–1 on four hits in that inning.

"I spent a lot of time recruiting [Quantrill]," Corbin said. "I felt like he was a money guy."

Stanford's A.J. Vanegas, brought on to close, struggled terribly with his control. That helped the Commodores score two in the eighth and one in the ninth to tie. Vanderbilt was the visiting team that day, and Corbin brought Ravenelle in to throw the ninth in the hopes of getting to extra innings. Instead, Taylor socked a drive into the right-center-field bleachers, giving Stanford a 5–4 walk-off win.

"When [Stanford] walked off on Saturday night and hit that home run, I was thinking of everything in my mind that I was going to say in the dugout, and I'll never forget getting back into the dugout and the first guy to come in was Rhett Wiseman and then was Dansby Swanson. Almost in unison, they looked at me and said, 'We've got this, coach, don't worry about it.' . . . It pointed to how far this team had come, from February, from a mental standpoint," Corbin recalled.

As for Stanford, Quantrill had been the last great option on the mound at Marquess's disposal. On Sunday, Vandy rocked James Logan for five first-inning runs on a Conde single, Wiel's double, and singles by Wiseman, Norwood, and Delay.

Buehler, though, was unable to fool Stanford for long. The Cardinal plated four in the third, two coming on a tough error charged to Swanson on an infield bouncer that got by him. Corbin went to Stone to start the fourth, and although he struck out Brett Michael Doran to start the fifth, Ellison couldn't find the ball and Doran reached. He'd come around to score, but VU still held a one-run lead thanks to Reynolds's RBI single in the top of the inning.

On a weekend where nobody could stop the Cardinal for long, Stone, with help from an electric slider, did. Zach Hoffpauir doubled to lead off the fifth and though Stone walked Jose with two out, the Cardinal couldn't score. That would be the only inning in which he gave up more than one base runner. By the time his day was done, he'd finished the game with an 85-pitch, eight-strikeout outing. VU got four runs on five seventh-inning hits, and added two more in the eighth thanks to some shoddy Stanford defense.

When Hoffpauir popped to Conde, it was over 3:43 after it had started, 12–5 being the final score. VU players dog-piled Stone, the day's hero, on the mound once it was done.

"I knew they had a lot of lefties, but I knew if I could throw the breaking ball that looked like a fastball until the last second, then I could slow them down a little bit," Stone said.

Reynolds, another freshman, had been the weekend's offensive hero, with eight hits and three walks.

"I guess things just kind of went my way," Reynolds said. "Up and down the lineup, everyone was swinging well."

Omaha would be a new stage for Corbin's young team, but the first opponent would be quite familiar.

Heading west

The 2014 NCAA Tournament had taken more unexpected twists and turns than any in recent memory. Of the eight national seeds, just three made it to Omaha. Oregon State, the No. 1 overall seed, didn't even make it out of its regional, falling to the University of California-Irvine. Of the sixteen No. 1 seeds in regionals, only Vandy, Louisville, Texas Christian, Ole Miss, and Virginia had advanced.

The other three teams in Omaha were a Texas team that, at No. 2, had been under-seeded; the same third-seeded UC-Irvine team that beat OSU; and Texas Tech, a No. 2 seed that had won the Coral Gables Regional before disposing of fourth-seeded College of Charleston, the surprise winner of the Gainesville Regional. The Commodores were in a four-team bracket with Louisville, UCI, and Texas, with the winner playing the victor of TCU, Ole Miss, Virginia, and Texas Tech.

"I thought we had a good chance to do some damage if we pitched well," Corbin recalled. "At the same time, I thought we were in the toughest bracket there, too."

The thought of playing Louisville, Vandy's first opponent, made Commodore fans nervous. Not only was the memory of the Cardinals ending VU's 2013 season rather unsettling, but also there was the fact that when the two teams had played on May 6 in Nashville, the Cardinals had reached base 18 times against Buehler, Jared Miller, Kilichowski, and Stone in an 11–7 smacking of the 'Dores. The Cardinals also had ace Kyle Funkhouser, the All-America sophomore who had allowed a total of four runs in his last eight starts.

But Funkhouser was also prone to wildness, and it was clear from the beginning that the Commodores' hitters were willing to wait for pitches in the strike zone, even if that meant getting down a couple of strikes in the count.

Vandy's second inning started innocuously; Turner lined to center and though Wiseman singled, he was thrown out stealing. But Norwood walked and Coleman singled to right and Ellison walked, before Funkhouser unleashed a wild pitch into the vast foul territory behind home plate. A run scored and when Swanson ripped a double into the alley in left, Vandy had a 3–0 lead.

After Reynolds tripled in Swanson in the fourth, Vandy's lead stood at four. Fulmer had been terrific against the powerful Cardinals' lineup, but as happened in the Stanford game, Vandy's ace started to tire as the pitch count neared triple digits. Wiseman misplayed Sutton Whiting's fly ball to right into a run-scoring triple and Kyle Gibson later added a run-scoring ground out.

Louisville threatened again in the sixth after Fulmer hit Jeff Gardner with a pitch to lead off the inning, and with one out, Louisville's Corey Ray kept fouling off pitches to keep his at bat alive until taking ball four on the 11th offering.

The Cards now had the tying men on base and though Corbin had always been one to trust his starting pitchers, he was taking no chances in Omaha. He'd come to trust Stone as much as anyone on the staff, and when the freshman got a pair of fly–ball outs, that lead stood at two after six innings.

But Stone didn't have his best stuff on that Saturday night. Zach Lucas singled up the middle to start the seventh and with two out, Nick Solak singled him in. Corbin rolled the dice and brought in lefty Jared Miller, who'd struggled mightily in the previous six weeks, in the hopes he could get the lefty Gardner out. Instead, Miller plunked him on a 3–2 pitch.

Even though Ravenelle had failed against Stanford on the previous Saturday, Corbin had now made the big right-hander with the nasty slider his closer. It seemed like the right call at the time; Ravenelle had fly-ball tendencies and if there was a park that favored fly-ball pitchers, it was spacious T.D. Ameritrade Park, which not only had 375-foot power alleys, but that night, a 25- to 32-mile-per-hour wind that, depending on the inning, either blew straight toward home plate or toward the left-field foul pole.

In fact, that very wind had almost certainly taken a home run away from Vandy's Wiel and Louisville's Kay earlier in the evening, and maybe even one from Swanson as well. So when Louisville's Alex Chittenden hit Ravenelle's first pitch to right, it was an easy out for Wiseman and the Commodores kept that one-run lead.

Conde scored on a wild pitch from Kyle McGrath in the bottom of the inning, but as it turned out, Ravenelle didn't even need the insurance run. He got Louisville 1-2-3 in the eighth and though Gibson picked up an infield single with one out in the ninth, the right-hander struck out Cole Sturgeon looking and then got Solak to pop to Norwood in center.

It wasn't the prettiest win, but 3:51 later, VU was in the winner's bracket.

"It's a big win. These first games are difficult to play for a host of reasons, but I thought we managed it well," Corbin commented after the game.

The next opponent was UC-Irvine, which, thanks to ace right-hander Andrew Morales, had beaten Texas 3–1 earlier in the day. Corbin gave the ball to Beede, hoping his junior, who'd been drafted 14th in the first round by the San Francisco Giants two weeks earlier, could recapture the magic he'd flashed against Xavier.

It wasn't to be. A 1-2-3 first didn't translate into the second, where Beede began to hit and walk batters at an alarming rate. By the time he was out of the second, the Anteaters had four runs, though the lead stood at just two thanks to a first-inning RBI single by Wiel and a run-scoring squeeze bunt from Turner that scored Reynolds.

On Monday, after Beede still couldn't find his control in the fourth, Corbin pulled him for Buehler, who would be brilliant in 5 ⅓ shutout innings the rest of the way. Still, Vandy had to find some offense. It got just what it needed in the fifth, when Swanson and Reynolds led off with a double and a single, respectively. Conde grounded out to score Swanson and then Wiel ripped a game-tying double to left. A sacrifice fly from Norwood provided the go-ahead run that inning. Norwood added an RBI single in the seventh as the 6–4 lead held as the final.

The Commodores (11 hits) hit the ball better than the six runs showed, but the real hero was Buehler, who improved his record to 12–2.

"The game turned around when Walker came in. He pounded the strike zone from the minute he got in there to the minute he finished. Very impressive, very mature approach to the game," Corbin said afterward.

Vanderbilt was in the driver's seat in its half of the CWS bracket. UC-Irvine was eliminated by Texas, who would be the next opponent. A rested VU pitching staff would only need to beat the Longhorns on Friday to have two days' rest before the start of a three-game championship series on Monday, and should VU fail on Friday, it would get another chance to beat the Longhorns on Saturday.

But little came easy in 2014 for Vandy, and the Commodores were about to face one giant curveball before they'd see their first pitch against UT.

The birth of the unsung hero

Just hours before Friday's first pitch, which came at 2:09, Vanderbilt sent out a press release that simply read as follows:

"Vanderbilt third baseman Xavier Turner has been declared ineligible for a violation of NCAA regulations and will not participate in the remainder of the College World Series, effective immediately. Vanderbilt's baseball program and Department of Student Athletics are in NCAA compliance. The university, Department of Student Athletics and the baseball coaching staff will have no further comments."

The news was a bombshell, and threw Corbin and everyone for a loop. To further complicate matters, NCAA policy mandated that Turner be out of Omaha within 24 hours of the news (which Corbin had learned on Thursday morning), and that meant that Corbin also had to make travel plans for Turner. That included having Corbin's wife, Maggie, ride with him on the plane back to Nashville before she returned for the next day's game.

"We were supposed to have practice at 1 p.m. [Thursday], but then I knocked it back to about 4," Corbin recalls, "just so I could

Xavier Turner goes head-over-heels to make a play at Hawkins Field in 2014, with Vince Conde watching. (Mike Rapp)

make arrangements. Prior to getting dressed and taking off, I brought Xavier to the top floor of the hotel to really explain the entire situation to the kids, but also for Xavier to say, 'bye,' because . . . he was on an airplane out of Omaha [shortly thereafter]."

Teams don't usually release depth charts for baseball in midseason, and if they did, VU may not have even bothered to list another third baseman, since Turner had played in 64 of the team's 67 games, and had started 63 of them. Corbin had gotten the news the day before and surveyed his team as to who should replace Turner.

The answer was unanimous: his men wanted Tyler Campbell, who had once been an Oregon State commitment before flipping to Vandy during his senior year. Campbell came to Vanderbilt as a middle infielder, and one possibility could have been to move Swanson to third. But Swanson had been so dynamic at second, Corbin didn't want to mess with success there, and stuck Campbell, who had just 15 at bats in 14 games, there instead.

Campbell responded quite well to the challenge, going 2-for-3 and handling the only chance he had in the field flawlessly. Unfortunately, though, the rest of his teammates did not play so well that day.

Ferguson loaded the bases with his first seven pitches via a walk and two hit batsmen. After a strikeout, he got the potential 4-6-3 double-play ball he needed to end the inning, but a hard-hit ball from C. J. Hinojosa hit umpire Mark Uyl, stationed in front of Swanson. Instead of a scoreless inning, Texas, by rule, had a single and a run. When Madison Carter walked, the second run scored and Ferguson was pulled for Brian Miller.

Miller pitched as well as Corbin could have hoped, throwing a career-high 7 ⅓ innings, striking out eight, and giving up just two runs. But Texas's Nathan Thornhill was better, throwing eight shutout innings, and when closer John Curtiss came on to throw a scoreless ninth, the Longhorns survived with a 4–0 win. It was just the third time VU had been shut out all season.

"Much like Quantrill did for Stanford, we ran into a senior who had more to do with our non-success than anything," Corbin said.

The good news was that Vandy was back to having Fulmer ready to start the next night. The bad news is that Fulmer wasn't sharp, walking six men and giving up four hits in 4 ⅓ innings before coming out for Stone with the bases loaded and the game tied at 2. Texas's Ben Johnson grounded his first pitch to Campbell at third, and after a 5-4-3 double play, Vandy was out of the inning.

Wiseman knocked in a run with a double in the fifth, but Texas countered when Tres Barrera tripled to start the sixth and then came home on Zane Gurwitz's single. From there, Stone locked the Longhorns down in the seventh, eighth, and ninth innings, giving up just one base runner. But Texas's Morgan Cooper and Travis Duke were equally good, also keeping VU off the board in those innings.

Finally, Texas was on the verge of busting the game open in the tenth—or so it appeared for a split second. Wiseman was playing normal depth in right when Hinojosa blasted one to deep right-center against the black Omaha sky. Wiseman, though, gave chase, his hat falling to the ground, back turned toward home plate, and when he reached up with his glove

Dependable Brian Miller became Vandy's all-time saves leader. (Mike Rapp)

hand, the ball almost miraculously settled into the pocket of his glove.

The crowd erupted. A stunned Hinojosa stood at second, frozen for a second before tipping his cap toward Wiseman. Even Stone gave a brief fist-pump.

It seemed to take the air out of the Longhorns. Stone got Collin Shaw to ground to first, and though Johnson walked with two out, Stone fanned Barrera to end the top of the 10th.

With Curtiss on for a second inning of work, it looked like the game would head to the eleventh as Wiel grounded out and Norwood lined to center to start the inning. But Wiseman singled, Coleman walked, and Ellison was hit by a pitch. Suddenly, the bases were loaded and a walk to Campbell would mean a Longhorn elimination.

Campbell fouled off the first pitch and then took the next one, which was in roughly the same area, for a ball. The next pitch came and Campbell topped it to Hinojosa at short, where the UT shortstop charged and fielded it on the edge of the grass.

A split-second earlier, and there would have been another inning of baseball. With Stone at 72 pitches and most of the other good options other than Ravenelle burned, who knows how Vandy would have fared. Thankfully, Campbell's best attribute was his athleticism. The sophomore beat the throw at first by inches, and soon found himself getting mobbed in right field.

The Commodores, a team that some of their own fans had virtually written off two months earlier, would now be playing for a national title the next week. Corbin reflected on that afterward.

"This team has gone maybe deeper than anyone anticipated at the beginning of the season. But they have tremendous resolve. They've been in this situation so many times during the year, whether it's SEC weekends or the super regional and now they find another gear to move forward," he said.

With Virginia waiting, another gear was definitely needed.

Slaying the giant

An ideal championship team has several ingredients: elite top-end talent, depth, balance, and maybe most importantly, experience. Whatever else you want to add as a qualification, the Cavaliers had it.

On the mound, UVA had a dynamic rotation of Brandon Waddell (10–3, 2.45 ERA at season's end), Josh Sborz (6–4, 2.92), and most importantly, Nathan Kirby (9–3, 2.06), who was starting to get some buzz as potentially the top pick in the 2015 Major League Baseball Draft. If a starter faltered, Virginia coach Brian O'Connor had a terrific middle relief trio of Artie Lewicki (8–1, 1.31), Whit Mayberry (6–1, 1.60), and Austin Young (1–0, 1.75).

But what spoke most to Virginia's pitching staff was this: two weeks prior, the Cincinnati Reds took Nick Howard (2–2, 1.91) as the 19th pick of the first round. Howard, with 20 saves, had done a lights-out job as the Cavs' closer, but the Reds viewed the right-hander as talented enough to start at the MLB level.

As good as Vandy's staff had been, the Cavs, who would finish the season with a 2.23 ERA and 561 strikeouts in 626 innings, had better numbers. Perhaps more importantly, UVA hadn't lost in Omaha that year and therefore its staff was more rested.

"I felt like it was a Russia vs. U.S.A. hockey game, I really did," Corbin said.

And when the Cavs got hit, it helped to have a tremendous defense, which fielded .981 for the season, behind them. Virginia was terrific up the middle with Branden Cogswell at second, Daniel Pinero at short, and Brandon Downes in center. Behind the plate, UVA platooned Nate Irving and Robbie Coman, and the two held opponents to just 27 steals in 49 attempts all season.

"I thought they were the best team [in Omaha], at least the best team that we had seen in the tournament, and the best team that we had seen all year . . . there was no weakness," Corbin said after the season. "You looked at the pitching staff, you were thinking to yourself of how you were going to score runs because they got better as the game progressed, because they just went to one guy and went to another guy and the numbers were scary-good.

"Defensively, they had everything in place. They had an older guy at second base who was a hell of a player. They had an older guy at first base [Mike Papi] who could hit with anyone. They had the freshman version of Cal Ripken at shortstop and then they had a third baseman [Kenny Towns] who was just such a sound player and really was their best hitter in the tournament.

"They were in the national championship game for a reason, because they belonged. . . . I felt like towards the end of that tournament, we were too, but Virginia was from start to finish."

Virginia's lineup, one through nine, would be as good as the 'Dores saw all season. Cogswell, the leadoff man, had such a tremendous eye that he struck out 22 times all year against 42 walks. Cleveland had just taken Papi, who had that rare combination of terrific strike-zone judgment and home-run power, with the 38th pick of the draft. One spot ahead of Papi, Houston had nabbed left fielder Derek Fisher, who had a down year in 2014 due to a hamate injury, but Fisher was talented enough that many scouts had considered him the top available collegiate bat in the draft prior to the season. Right fielder Joe McCarthy had developed enough to hit between the two. From top to bottom, it was a lineup that could not only hit, but also one that taxed pitchers by working deep into counts.

At 52–14 with the No. 1 RPI in college baseball, the Cavaliers were an elite team on par with the teams Vandy had fielded in 2007 and 2011. Virginia was Las Vegas's favorite to win the College World Series before it started, and was still the favorite after Vandy emerged from the other side.

But as Corbin knew from experience, the favorite going in doesn't always win.

In the first couple of innings, Virginia certainly looked like the better team. Kirby blew through the first two innings without a blemish, striking out Swanson, Conde, and Wiseman in the process. In the meantime, the Cavaliers jumped all over Buehler for two runs on three hits in the first. When John La Prise doubled to start the bottom of the second, it looked like UVA was primed for more, but Buehler recovered to keep the Cavs off the board.

Vandy's third started harmlessly when Harvey, playing for the first time in ages, struck out. Kirby, who'd struck out 108 hitters against just 28 walks, suddenly walked Delay on four pitches. Campbell ripped a double off the base of the wall in left before Swanson walked on a 3–1 pitch. Reynolds grounded to Pinero at short and the Cavs had a shot for a force at second, but Swanson had gotten a good jump and beat the throw. Everyone was safe, a run was in, and now, the bases were loaded with nobody out.

Moments earlier, Kirby had looked like a guy poised to throw a no-hitter, but now, the Commodores had gotten in his head and his command completely abandoned him. Wiel walked on four pitches and then Norwood took a free pass on five. Vandy now had the lead, but Virginia had a chance to get a big out, or potentially even two, when Wiseman grounded sharply to Papi at first.

Papi had to make a split-second decision on whether to get the out at first, or try for the double play. While thinking it through, he lost his concentration and dropped the ball. Everyone was safe and another run was in, and that was it for Kirby, who came out in favor of Mayberry.

"I just couldn't find my release point. It hadn't happened all year, but it happened tonight," Kirby explained.

All of VU's eight hitters since Harvey had all reached. Vandy's DH got a second shot and hit a high fly ball to foul territory in right. McCarthy chose to make a play on it rather than let it drop, and all runners moved up a base as Wiel scored. The sacks were full again when Mayberry hit Delay with a pitch.

When Campbell bounced a double past Towns at third, the bases had cleared and Vanderbilt had an astonishing nine runs in the inning.

"We just kept the inning going with walks and timely hits, and Tyler Campbell's situation was so unique because not only does he hit a double, he hits one off the fence. That's not Tyler Campbell's game, but he did it [in Omaha] and the mere fact that he was able to re-cycle himself and hit another double, down the line, bases loaded, was just unbelievable," Corbin said.

A seven-run lead in T.D. Ameritrade Park, given the talent on Vandy's pitching staff, should have been easy to hold. But Buehler was sometimes prone to leaving too many pitches up in the strike zone where they could be hit, and that was the case that Monday night. When the Cavaliers rapped out four more hits in the third, the lead had been cut to 9–5, and since the UVA lineup was heavy with left-handers, Corbin went to Jared Miller to start the fourth.

Miller allowed leadoff singles to Cogswell and Pinero, but wiggled out of the fourth without allowing a run. In the fifth, Miller retired the first two hitters but yielded a triple to Downes, a walk to Cogswell, and a single to Pinero, and the lead was now 9–7. Meanwhile, Mayberry had settled in and kept the 'Dores off the scoreboard before giving way to Young with two outs in the sixth.

Vanderbilt would threaten in the seventh, with men at first and second with one out, but Rogers and Delay struck out. A one-out walk to Swanson in the eighth was erased on a double play.

But Vandy's Kilchowski had also done an excellent job in slowing Virginia after taking over to start the sixth. The Cavaliers went 1-2-3 in both innings, but singles from Cogswell and Pinero to start the eighth wound up plating another run and now, the Commodores clung to a one-run lead.

When Vandy went 1-2-3 in the top of the ninth against Young, Virginia had a chance to win. But Ravenelle came in and slammed the door, getting Towns to pop to short, La Prise to ground to short, and Downes to foul out to Wiel at first.

"Well, we're fortunate to win that game, for sure," Corbin said. "No one could have scripted that particular game and if anyone said they could, they're lying. I don't think you could have called a nine-run inning."

Vandy was now one game away from a national title. Beede had a chance to be the hero in his last collegiate game. The Commodores led 2–1 heading into the sixth inning of the second game when Papi led off with a single and McCarthy followed with one of his own on a hit-and-run. Fisher and La Prise both knocked in runs with ground outs and now, the Cavs led by a run. Downes then hit a rocket to center where Norwood raced to make a play, but the ball ticked off his glove for a triple.

That scored another run and by now, Beede appeared to be tiring, his pitch count exceeding 100 as he started the seventh. Three hits and an intentional walk to Papi later, Virginia now had a 6–2 lead as Corbin removed Beede for Bowden.

Meanwhile, Virginia's Waddell was brilliant, as the Commodores seldom threatened from the fifth on. The Cavs added an insurance run off Pecoraro in the ninth for a 7–2 win, setting up a winner-take-all game on Wednesday night.

"I didn't think we played that well. We didn't hit the ball, we didn't pitch as well, but I thought Tyler pitched okay . . . he just didn't get a lot of great [defense] behind him," Corbin said.

The good news for Vanderbilt is that it had a rested Fulmer ready, and the sophomore had the kind of competitive mentality that suited him well to get the ball on the big stage. Virginia countered with Sborz, a big right-hander with great stuff but sometimes erratic control.

The visiting Commodores jumped on Sborz in the top of the first as Swanson singled and then tagged up and took second on a heads-up play when Towns, his back to the infield, made a tremendous grab of Wiseman's fly ball near the stands at third. With two outs, he stole third and then took home when Coman's throw went into the outfield.

With Sborz having trouble with his command, Virginia's O'Connor pulled him for Lewicki to start the second. The Commodores wouldn't scratch against the right-hander until the sixth, when Norwood beat out an infield single to third and then took second when Towns's throw got past Papi. He took third on Wiel's groundout and then scored on Conde's two-out single to short.

Meanwhile, Fulmer had been terrific. There was a moment of anxiety in the second, when Virginia had runners on the corners with two out, but Fulmer fanned Downes swinging on a 3–2 pitch. The right-hander then coasted through the third, fourth, and fifth innings, getting the Cavaliers three-up and three-down in each.

But once again, Fulmer's pitch count started closing in on triple digits, which had been a danger zone for him recently. Sure enough, Coman led off the sixth with a single and with one out, scored on Pinero's single. After Pinero stole second and the 'Dores intentionally walked the dangerous Papi, Corbin went to Stone to see if he could work his magic one final time.

It didn't start well when he hit McCarthy to load the bases, still with just one out. Stone then got a huge strikeout of Fisher on a 1–2 slider down and away. The next batter was Pinero, who hit a low liner to Conde just inches off the ground that the normally sure-handed shortstop would usually turn into an out. Instead, it hit him in the heel of the glove for an error and Virginia had tied the game on an unearned run.

The Virginia crowd roared in approval. The Cavs could now break the game open at any moment. But again, Stone came back with his money pitch and when La Prise swung over the top of it, Ellison caught it as it grazed the dirt. The tie was intact.

Swanson was stranded at first after a one-out single, and though Downes led off the seventh with a single and took second on Coman's sacrifice, Stone fanned Cogswell and Pinero to end things there.

Virginia then went to Howard to start the eighth, and it looked like an uphill battle from there. Teams hit just .177 off Howard for the season, and the Cavs' closer had given up only seven extra-base hits in 35 ⅔ innings coming in. The best hope might be to walk and get a man over. Reynolds was up first, and he worked the count to 3–0 before lining to right. That brought Norwood to the dish.

Three years ago, Vandy's center fielder turned down nearly a million dollars from Toronto to come to Vandy. After two years of sitting on the bench in 2012 and 2013, followed by a struggle to start 2014—back on March 15, Norwood was hitting just .204—the right-handed hitter had finally started to come into his own down the stretch, hitting .375 in Omaha. That was a reason why, for the first time all season, Norwood was hitting cleanup that night. He'd already singled twice and walked and Howard knew he needed to be careful here.

"[Norwood] was seeing the ball well. He was checking off tough pitches. You could tell he had a very, very good routine going and his confidence was at a high," Corbin said.

The first pitch was an 82-mile-per-hour breaking ball that started in and buckled Norwood's knees. He had no chance and fortunately, it stayed inside and high for ball one.

Norwood stepped out of the batter's box, collected himself, and, perhaps prophetically, gave a token practice swing at an imaginary pitch around his eyes. The tension in Omaha was thick, and all that could be heard were a few scattered voices throughout the park. Howard then aimed a 97-per-hour fastball in the vicinity of where the previous one had gone, and it kept tailing in toward Norwood's shoulders as it reached the plate.

"With Howard's fastball and with Howard's success to the arm side, [Virginia] probably felt like that was a match. I can't blame them . . . that was going to be tough to turn around. But at the same time, late in the game, you don't want to get beat to the pull-side, because that's the shortest route out of the ballpark at T.D. Ameritrade. But at the same time, that was a very difficult pitch to hit, to put in play, let alone put over the fence," Corbin said.

Had Norwood laid off, it would have been ball two. Instead, Norwood went at it as if he knew exactly what was coming and got both arms extended and the bat head through the zone. A loud "whack" echoed throughout the ballpark as Howard jerked his head toward the left-field foul pole to follow the flight of the ball. About two seconds later, it had cleared the wall in left, a few feet over the fence and about twenty feet inside the left-field foul pole and into the Virginia bullpen.

Moments later, ESPN's Kyle Peterson said what virtually all fans on both sides were thinking: "What just happened never entered my mind when he came up."

Vandy fans were delirious. The Commodores hadn't homered since Wiel had done it against South Carolina on May 16, seventeen games ago, in a ballpark where just two homers had been hit between the eight teams in Omaha that year. Norwood rounded the bases and stomped home plate with his right foot, where his teammates greeted him.

"In my opinion, it was a great pitch. It just so happened that Johnny unlocked himself to get the barrel there and performed the right swing, with the right bat path, with the right swing, to center the ball. My only fear when it left the bat was that it was hit too hard, because if it was hit too hard, it created too much topspin," Corbin said.

"And I thought the ball was going to hit the top of the fence like it did with Dansby and Wiseman [earlier in the week]. But it didn't and I thought, *We got a break. We finally got a break.*"

Howard retired Wiel and Conde and Virginia's best chance was coming in the eighth, with the No. 3–5 hitters, Papi, McCarthy, and Fisher, due up. From there, it quickly went badly for Stone. Papi singled through the left side and McCarthy walked on four pitches. Corbin went to Ravenelle, and then Fisher laid down a bunt on the first pitch that moved both runners over.

As quickly as Vanderbilt had been in command, the advantage now shifted to Virginia. All Virginia needed was a base hit to the outfield to more than likely win the game. VU had its 7-8-9 hitters, Coleman, Campbell, and Ellison, due up in the ninth to face Howard; to that point the trio was 1-for-9 with three strikeouts and a lone single.

VU's middle infield was now back conceding a run. Ravenelle next hit Towns with a 2–1 pitch, which wasn't the worst thing that could happen since it put the double play in order. On the other hand, another hit batsman or a walk brought the tying run in. On a 1–2 pitch to La Prise, Vanderbilt got the ground ball it needed back to Ravenelle, who fielded the one-hopper and looked immediately toward home.

Had Ravenelle been a little quicker in getting the ball home, VU would have gotten a 1-2-3 double play but instead, Ravenelle took great care in making sure he delivered the ball accurately to Ellison. Vandy got the out at home but La Prise beat Ellison's throw to first.

It wouldn't matter. On the next pitch, Downes hit a bouncer to Conde's right at short. Conde calmly fired to Swanson, who had his foot firmly on the bag, and the ball hit his glove a few split seconds before a sliding La Prise's hand touched the bag.

Coleman walked to lead off the ninth, but VU couldn't get a runner past first. Now, it was up to Ravenelle to deliver a national title.

On a 1–2 pitch, Coman lined one hard toward right. Quickly, Wiseman sprinted over and speared the ball to his glove side about three feet off the turf, sliding to the ground just after he grabbed it. Out one was in the books.

Cogswell, perhaps the guy Vandy would have least preferred to face in that spot, was up next. But Ravenelle's slider in the dirt fooled him and once Ellison collected it and fired to Wiel at first, he too was done. The Commodores were now an out away from uncharted territory.

Pinero looked at a 94-mile-per-hour fastball on the outside corner, just above the knees, for strike one. Ravenelle tried the same pitch again, and just missed with a ball. On the next one, Pinero chased a 94-mile-per-hour two-seamer just off the plate and came up empty.

Ravenelle hadn't shown the freshman his best pitch, which was the slider. That pitch, at 86 miles per hour, was coming next. It came out of Ravenelle's hand looking like it was going to catch the outside corner. Pinero started his swing knowing he had to protect the plate.

His bat wasn't long enough. The only thing it would hit would be Ellison's mitt.

Ravenelle pumped his fist. Ellison tossed the ball aside and sprinted toward the mound. The Vanderbilt dugout emptied and dog-piled on the mound as fireworks went off behind the outfield, and a small haze of confetti hung nearby.

Vandy coaches and players grabbed Corbin and put him on their shoulders before returning him to the ground. Out near the mound, someone handed Beede the trophy, and after hoisting it momentarily, he turned and took it to Corbin, who lingered just outside the dugout railing. Beede handed it to him as the two embraced and the rest of the team filed over.

Eleven years earlier, six people watched as Corbin made his VU home debut. Now, over two million viewers were watching at home as Vanderbilt claimed its biggest moment in athletics history.

As VU play-by-play announcer Joe Fisher said, "Dreams do come true!"

Why this time?

Corbin had three truly great teams in 2007, 2011, and 2013. They were veteran clubs and were remarkable in that they had few weaknesses and were incredibly consistent. The 2014 squad was nothing like either of those in many ways; it had easily identifiable weaknesses for most of the season, and even threatened to not make the tournament at the season's midway point.

The only thing that you knew this team could count on before the season started was its starting pitching, and yet at the end of the season, it was the least-dependable commodity on the team. Of the team's ten games between the super regional and the College World Series, Vandy's starting pitchers registered one win, and those starters had a 7.12 ERA in 43 innings.

It's almost impossible to post those kinds of numbers in pitchers' parks, against elite teams, and still win.

And somehow, this was Corbin's breakthrough team.

Corbin believes the answer was in the way the team matured. He says that the team that wins in Omaha isn't necessarily the best team there, but the one that manages its emotions the best.

"The way we handled it, the way we got to Omaha, the way we handled the situation, was as good a team as I've ever been around. I've been there seven times now[7] and I thought this team handled everything appropriately," Corbin said. "They acted like a tourist for one day, which I gave them permission to do so, but I told them after that, this wasn't a business trip, this was a championship trip. A business trip is far different. A championship trip is something you go to and you intend to leave with the trophy, but you can only do that by being immersed in the small moments of the tournament, and that's what we [did].

"I thought the kids handled it so well. I thought they just channeled their emotions well because most teams lose not on their baseball ability, but how they handle their emotions, and they were able to manage their emotions perfectly."

The story goes a lot deeper than that, though. Corbin is arguably one of the finest coaches in college athletics today, but he's been introspective with regard to his flaws. Throughout his career, his temper and his lack of managing his emotions in the moment have at times gotten the best of him, and it didn't necessarily help his ball clubs.

The lowest point of Corbin's professional career came when Michigan beat the No. 1 Commodores in their regional in 2007 on that fateful Monday night when Alan Oaks broke the hearts of nearly everyone at Hawkins Field. That loss has haunted Corbin for years, and as if he needed another gut-punch, he got one not even 24 hours after Oaks delivered his.

"I remember losing in 2007, coach [John] Winkin from Maine was the regional rep and I've known coach Winkin forever. Maggie and I and he walked to breakfast that next morning, he's 80-something years old, he's gruff, I know he likes me, but at the same time he looks at me and says, 'Tim, you aren't ready to win this tournament,' Corbin recalled just over two weeks after his 2014

---

7 Corbin went six times as a Clemson assistant.

championship. "It was like a dagger in your heart when someone says that, but [he meant it as] an indirect compliment. Basically what he was saying was, 'You had a great team but you guys weren't ready. You just weren't ready to do that yet. It's too soon.'

"And I felt like punching him right there, but I knew what he meant. It's almost like, you've got to knock on the door several times before you can knock it over."

Seven years later, things had come full circle.

"When we go to bed at night, Maggie always reads and right now she's reading the Pat Summitt book to me a couple of nights ago and how [former University of Tennessee women's basketball coach] Pat Summitt won her first national championship twelve years into her career. She started reading off all these things that Pat Summitt had done and she said, 'The more I read this book, the more you have a long way to go before you're Pat Summitt, but your beginnings are so ironically close it's unbelievable,'" Corbin said.

"You've seen [me grow] in places, you've probably seen humility, you've seen frustration, but at the same time, when Maggie was reading all that, that was what I was seeing in Pat Head Summitt, this same fiery, frustrated, pissed-off coach who was mean to her team and didn't feed them on certain nights, but then became more loving, maybe more humble, just more knowing the older you got.

"I think that's what coach Winkin essentially was telling me, was that you've got to go through more experience as a person before you can start understanding what it's like to win at the highest level. And I didn't know that, but I do understand it now, and you probably do have to go through a lot of frustrations first before you can really taste this."

Now, the coach is trying to translate that maturity to his players.

"As many times as [Florida State coach] Mike Martin's been to Omaha,[8] I consider us very fortunate and very lucky. That's what

---

8 Martin has been a fifteen-time participant in the CWS and has never won it. The Seminoles' coach has been in the NCAA Tournament every year since his head coaching career in Tallahassee began in 1980.

ESPN's Kyle Peterson speaks with Tim Corbin in Omaha. (Jimmy Jones)

I told the team in the classroom, the very last thing I told them, I said, the one thing you should learn from winning a national championship is that it should make you more humble, because it's not a rite of passage to win this thing, but you should be humbled in the fact that you worked hard. It doesn't mean you're going to win it, but you were fortunate to win it and you're grateful for having the opportunity to win it," Corbin said.

As for Corbin, you can see he's also taken that lesson to heart, offering a brief quip when asked about how winning a title had changed things for him.

"I've got my picture up on the Waffle House bulletin board now—I've really taken off personally!"

EPILOGUE

Epilogue
The best I've covered

In eleven years, I had the privilege of covering the Vanderbilt football, baseball, and men's basketball teams, which included a lot of great
athletes. Here are the ones I feel were the best on the basis of their total
body of work at Vanderbilt. If an athlete's career had not concluded at
the time of publication, that player was not included in my rankings.

Football

1. **Jay Cutler, QB, 2002–06**
45 G, 710–1,242 (57.2%), 8,697 yds., 59 TDs, 36 INT passing;
453–1,256, (2.8 YPC), 17 TDs

When VU finally unleashed Cutler, he was the Southeastern
Conference's Offensive Player of the Year in 2005. Cutler ranks 11th
in all-time total offense and 17th in passing yards in conference his-
tory despite almost no supporting cast everywhere he looked. For fun,
I ranked the SEC's top 100 players of all time a few years back; I had
Cutler in the top 75 and in the context of his career, I think that's fair.

2. **Jordan Matthews, WR, 2010–13**
51 G, 262–3,759 receiving; 9–115 rushing, 25 TDs

For half his career, Matthews had no one to get him the ball
and the 'Dores other receiving options were shaky. But somehow,

Matthews is the SEC's career leader in receptions and yards, and led the league in both catches and yards as a senior, which made him a two-time All–American.

3. Earl Bennett, WR, 2006–08
35 G, 236–2,852 receiving; 20–44 rushing; 20 TDs
Bennett held the league's reception mark until Matthews came along. Other than his one year with Cutler, Bennett had no one dependable to get him the ball, but was still a first-team all-conference pick in all three seasons.

4. D.J. Moore, CB, 2005–07
37 G, 178 T, 13 INT, 1 FF, 4 FR, 22.8 KORA, 12.6 PRA
Easily the most versatile player in the last quarter century of VU football, Moore mixed in almost 300 yards for scrimmage and was an All-American player as a junior before turning pro.

5. Casey Hayward, CB, 2008–11
50 G, 198 T, 15 INT, 2 FF
I rated Moore higher for his versatility, but I doubt many would argue that Hayward was Vandy's best corner over the last 11 years.

6. Zac Stacy, RB, 2009–12
45 G, 581–3,143 (5.4 YPC) rushing; 46–415 receiving, 30 TDs
The underrated Alabaman ended his career as VU's all-time leading rusher, and also owns the school's top two single-season spots.

7. Wesley Johnson, OL, 2011–13
Vanderbilt coaches nabbed Johnson as the recruit they most wanted in the 2010 signing class. After redshirting, Johnson started every game of his career, didn't have a holding penalty until midway through his senior season, and played center, guard, and tackle all effectively. First-team All-SEC at left tackle as a senior.

8. Chris Marve, LB, 2008–11
49 G, 397 T, 30 TFL, 9.5 SK, 1 INT, 8 FF, 2 FR

Marve started as a redshirt freshman and then earned second-team All-SEC honors his last three seasons.

9. Moses Osemwegie, LB, 2005–08
44 G, 391 T, 31 TFL, 7 SK, 4 INT, 5 FF, 4 FR

Osemwegie was a tackling machine who was a first-team All-SEC player his last two seasons.

10. Chris Williams, OL, 2005–07

Williams mis-managed the classroom and didn't play until his third year on campus, and in three years turned himself into a first-round NFL pick as a left tackle.

11. Myron Lewis, CB, 2006–09
46 G, 170 T, 10.5 TFL, 5 SK, 10 INT, 4 FF, 2 FR, 26 PBU

A really solid corner who had a knack for the big play at critical times; was a second-team All-SEC pick for two years.

12. Jonathan Goff, LB, 2004–07
46 G, 317 T, 15.5 TFL, 6.5 SK, 3 INT, 3 FF

Highly regarded recruit took a bit of time to develop into a star, and then manned the middle for the Giants for a few years.

13. Andre Hal, CB, 2010–13
45 G, 133 T, 8.5 TFL, 6 INT, 2 FR, 31 PBU

Hal, a second-team All-SEC pick as a junior and senior, didn't register a lot of picks because teams preferred not to throw his way.

14. Kenny Ladler, S, 2010–13
50 G, 291 T, 11 TFL, 1 SK, 9 INT, 7 FF, 2 FR, 15 PBU

Highly regarded recruit contributed from day one, and played at an All-American level in 2013.

15. Reshard Langford, S, 2005–08
49 G, 247 T, 11 INT, 4 FF, 3 FR, 19 PBU
Never earned all-league honors but played well enough to get a short NFL stint.

16. Justin Geisinger, OL, 2001–04
Perhaps the strongest player over the last decade, Geisinger earned second-team All-SEC honors in 2004 and played briefly in the NFL.

17. Jovan Haye, DE, 2002–04
34 G, 149 T, 17 TFL, 10.5 SK, 1 INT, 4 FF
Converted linebacker had a monster sophomore year, earning second-team All-SEC honors; would have had better career numbers if he'd had some help.

18. Sean Richardson, S, 2008–11
49 G, 256 T, 18 TFL, 2 SK, 1 INT, 2 FF, 1 FR
Never was much against the pass, but was good enough against the run to earn an NFL roster spot with the Packers.

19. Jordan Rodgers, QB, 2011–12
299-535 (55.9%), 4,063 yds., 24 TD, 15 INT passing; 208–491 (2.4 ypc), 6 TD rushing
Wasn't accurate as a junior, but provided a spark with his legs. Improved that accuracy as a senior and led that 2012 team to a great year.

20. Rob Lohr, DT, 2009–12
50 G, 122 T, 31.5 TFL, 11.5 SK, 2 FF, 1 FR
Had a solid career, and was borderline dominant for the first half of 2011.

21. Pat Benoist, LB, 2006–09
41 G, 240 T, 17 TFL, 10.5 SK, 4 FF, 2 FR
Heady player who was a second-team All-SEC player in 2008.

22. Curtis Gatewood, DE, 2004–07
46 G, 110 T, 18 TFL, 10.5, 4 FF, 3 FR, 1 INT

Came to VU as a converted basketball player, played well at defensive end, briefly made the NFL as a linebacker.

23. Brian Stamper, OL, 2003–07

Long-time contributor who was a second-team All-SEC pick at right tackle in 2005.

24. Warren Norman, RB, 2009–12
243–1,317 (5.6 ypc) rushing; 20–218 receiving, 9 TDs, 25.9 KORA

The 2009 SEC Freshman of the Year was a dynamic playmaker in the return game as a freshman, and a pretty good running back, too. Knee injuries then took their toll, and his career had a premature end.

25. Tim Fugger, DL, 2008–11
46 G, 90 T, 20.5 TFL, 15 SK, 8 FF, 2 FR

Came to Vandy as a tight end, became one of the team's top playmakers as he earned second-team All-SEC in 2011.

Also considered: Chris Boyd, Marcus Buggs, Carey Spear, Brandon Barden, Chase Garnham, Kwane Doster, Ryan Hamilton

Baseball

1. Pedro Alvarez, 3B, 2006–08
170 G, 49 HR, 162 RBI, .349/.451/.658

Alvarez had two first-team All-American years and a third that (contrary to popular belief) wasn't a "bad" year, it was just an abbreviated season where his power was curtailed due to a wrist injury. His glove at third was inconsistent but average on the whole, and he had a tremendous arm. Bill James has a formula that estimates how many runs a player "creates" per 27 outs he makes (RC/27); I've run it for every one of Tim Corbin's teams and Alvarez, at 10.93 in 2007 and 10.86 in 2006, owns two of the top four single-season marks in the Corbin era.

2.   David Price, LHP, 2006–08
22–10, 3.22 ERA, 1.09 WHIP, 313 IP, 441 K

The National Player of the Year in 2007 left you with the feeling that you could be watching history in the making every time he took the hill. If the current rules for bat potency were in place, Price would have shaved at least a half run off his ERA. Had Price not been awful playing as poorly for about half the conference season as a sophomore, he'd have ranked first.

3.   Jeremy Sowers, LHP, 2002–04
23–16, 2 SV, 3.27 ERA, 1.15 WHIP, 339 IP, 327 K

The first real superstar of the Corbin era, the lefty combined brains with excellent command and a great breaking ball to be the kind of Friday-night starter that few teams had.

4.   Ryan Flaherty, SS, 2006–08
192 G, 20 HR, 169 RBI, .349/.424/.513

Tall, lanky shortstop with a pleasant personality, a good glove, contact ability, and extra-base power.

5.   Tony Kemp, 2B, 2011–13
194 G, 1 HR, 98 RBI, 177 R, .329/.424/.431

The SEC's 2013 Player of the Year was an on-base machine who made an remarkable transition from left field to second base—a position he'd never played—in the midst of 2012. He not only made that transition, but by 2013, highlight-reel plays were routine.

6.   Aaron Westlake, 1B, 2008–11
209 G, 42 HR, 178 RBI, .338/.434/.569

As a hitter, Westlake ranks only behind Alvarez as the best Corbin's had. His 11.39 RC/27 in 2011 is the best in his coach's tenure.

7. Sonny Gray, RHP, 2009–11
27–10, 6 SV, 3.18 ERA, 1.30 WHIP, 294 IP, 317 K

Location was the problem with Gray—he often fell behind counts and threw too many pitches to get into the eighth inning—but he was the best-fielding pitcher Corbin ever had and had an electric fastball and curve.

8. Mike Minor, LHP, 2007–09
22–10, 3 SV, 3.79 ERA, 1.21 WHIP, 304 IP, 303 K

One of the more polished left-handers in VU history ran into some bad luck—the WHIP is a bit out of line with his ERA—and suffered a bit in the rankings due to SEC ERAs of 5.00 in 2008 and 4.41 in 2009.

9. Curt Casali, C, 2008–11
208 G, 27 HR, 167 RBI, .316/.430/.502

I never thought I'd rate Casali this high, but he hit from start to finish and his teammates still rave about the his defense behind the plate and how that gave them confidence to throw him their breaking stuff.

10. Jason Esposito, SS/3B, 2009–11
196 G, 25 HR, 165 RBI, .330/.405/.514

Esposito and Dominic de la Osa had remarkably similar careers; both had all the tools and their performances fluctuated a good bit from year to year. Esposito had more value with the glove, which accounts for the higher ranking.

11. Dominic de la Osa, OF/SS, 2005–08
243 G, 46 HR, 188 RBI, .319/.393/.547

The school's all-time leader in at bats, RBI, and doubles, de la Osa was inconsistent but when he was great, the upside was the All-American campaign of 2007, which at 10.87 RC/27 is the third-best offensive year in the Corbin era.

12. Jensen Lewis, RHP, 2003–05
17–13, 11 SV, 3.01, 1.18 WHIP, 230 IP, 226 K

Affable lefty was available for wherever and whenever Corbin needed him. His best year (8–3, 2.62 ERA) came in 2005, which gets forgotten because it's the only year since 2004 that VU didn't make the NCAAs.

13. Grayson Garvin, LHP, 2009–11
14–4, 2.61 ERA, 1.18 WHIP, 162 IP, 157 K

The only knock on the SEC's 2011 Pitcher of the Year is that he had difficulties staying healthy, which limited his value.

14. Kevin Ziomek, LHP, 2011–13
19–9, 3.04 ERA, 1.18 WHIP, 243 IP, 241 K

Nearly played himself into the first round of the 2013 MLB Draft with a tremendous 11–3, 2.12 ERA as VU's Friday-night starter in 2013.

15. Connor Harrell, CF, 2010–13
248 G, 31 HR, 168 RBI, .288/.380/.471

Harrell was a streaky hitter and when he was on, you'd better not leave anything in the zone. Harrell's fantastic defense, though, never wavered a bit.

16. Brian Harris, SS, 2007–10
200 G, 16 HR, 107 RBI, .288/.438/.435

Harris got more out of his ability than any athlete I have ever covered at VU. He wasn't athletic but was steady enough to man short and play it well. In 2010, he set an NCAA record by getting hit by 37 pitches.

17. Conrad Gregor, 1B/DH, 2011–13
186 G, 9 HR, 115 RBI, .327/.444/.446

Every other hitter on the list provided more value with his glove, but how low can you rank a guy who had seasons of 9.4, 8.8, and 7.9 RC/27?

18. Mike Yastrzemski, ROF, 2010–13
253 G, 15 HR, 144 RBI, 176 R, .292/.397/.416

Could do a little bit of everything; he'd have been a center fielder just about anywhere else, but Vandy had Connor Harrell there.

19. Brian Miller, RHP, 2012–14
6-3, 26 SV, 2.31 ERA, 1.01 WHIP, 134 K

Had the most unorthodox pitching motion of anyone Corbin's ever had, as Miller slung the ball from the right side as if it were a forehanded Frisbee toss. It worked: he's the school's career leader in saves and had one really good year followed by two great ones.

20. Tyler Beede, RHP, 2012–14
23–14, 286 IP, 1.34 WHIP, 286 IP, 287 K

The erratic end to his career obscured how truly great Beede could be when he was on.

21. Ryan Mullins, LHP, 2003–05
18–12, 3.14 ERA, 272 IP, 1.24 WHIP, 223 K

Our memories of Mullins are a bit tainted because of the 2005 suspension, but let's not forget about that huge 2004 (9–3, 2.58).

22. David Macias, CF, 2005–08
204 G, 10 HR, 91 RBI, 169 R, .325/.428/.401

You always knew what you'd get with Macias: a consistent bat (RC/27s of 7.7, 7.1, and 6.4) and solid defense in center.

23. Spencer Navin, C, 2011–13
124 G, 7 HR, 58 RBI, .294/.426/.393

Either he or Jonathan Douillard was the best defensive catcher at VU, and his bat was underrated.

24. Warner Jones, 2B, 2003–05
174 G, 20 HR, 134 RBI, .341/.363/.505

Hit .414 in 2004, which won the SEC's batting title and made him a first-team All-American. If he hadn't battled wrist problems for most of 2005, he probably moves up a half-dozen spots on this list, and that's probably conservative.

25. Ryan Klosterman, SS, 2003–04
118 G, 11 HR, 47 RBI, .317/.396/.485

The Clemson transfer wasn't around long and had only had one good year with the bat (8.1 RC/27 in '04). His glove was also exceptional that season.

26. Anthony Gomez, 2B/SS, 2010–12
189 G, 3 HR, 135 RBI, .354/.383/.421

Few Commodores had the ability to put the bat on the ball the way Gomez did, and his defensive versatility made him a lineup fixture virtually his entire career.

27. Mike Baxter, OF/1B, 2004–05
121 G, 11 HR, 86 RBI, .345/.408/.493

Few realized how special Baxter's 2005 season was because it was the year VU didn't make the NCAAs, but RC/27 ranks it as the seventh-best offensive season since Corbin came to Vandy.

28. Cesar Nicolas, 1B/DH, 2001–04
182 G, 28 HR, 140 RBI, .306/.406/.508

Was Corbin's most legitimate power threat on that 2004 team that started his run of greatness.

29. Casey Weathers, RHP, 2003–04
13–4, 7 SV, 99 IP, 2.82 ERA, 1.17 WHIP, 128 K

Only threw 99 innings, but man, those were some spectacular innings.

30.T. Vince Conde, SS/3B, 2012–14
198 G, 12 HR, 120 RBI, .367/.364/.384

One of the most unlikely All-Americans in VU history (he was a third-teamer as a junior), Conde started every game at short in 2014 and was almost flawless in the field.

30T. Steven Liddle, OF, 2008–09
118 G, 10 HR, 79 RBI, .333/.418/.516

Almost forgotten because his career was brief and it didn't include a major role on any of Corbin's really great teams, Liddle had the ninth-best year in the Corbin era according to RC/27.

Also considered: Taylor Hill

Men's Basketball

1. Shan Foster, SG, 2004–08
132 G, 15.2 PPG, 59.5 EFG%, 79.1 FT%, 1.1 A/TO

The Louisianan with the high, arching shot remains Vandy's all-time leading scorer, and always had a knack for hitting the big shot. First-team All-American selection by *Basketball Times* in 2008.

2. Jeff Taylor, SF, 2008–12
134 G, 14.2 PPG 52.4 EFG%, 69.3 FT%, 146 STL, 60 BLK, 752 R

Taylor ended his career second on VU's career list in points, sixth in rebounds, eighth in steals, and tied for 10th in blocks. He is also the only player in VU history who was picked to the SEC's five-man All-Defensive team three times. So, why Foster ahead of Taylor? Because Taylor had a habit of disappearing at times and wasn't nearly as efficient from the field (or with the ball) as Foster was.

3. John Jenkins, SG, 2009–12
98 G, 16.9 PPG, 60.7 EFG%, 85.6 FT%

Jenkins offered little outside of shooting, but boy, was he ever efficient there. Jenkins averaged 1.5 points per shot compared to Foster's 1.38, but Foster was clearly better at everything else. Jenkins led the league in scoring his last two seasons.

4. Matt Freije, PF, 2000–04
121 G, 15.6 PPG, 51.2 EFG%, 78.6 FT%, 591 R

Freije was essentially asked to perform as a shooting guard while playing at power forward, and his efficiency numbers were hurt because for most of his career, he wasn't surrounded by other good shooters. Third-team All-America selection by multiple outlets as a senior.

5. A.J. Ogilvy, C, 2007–10
96 G, 15.3 PPG, 55.3 EFG%, 73.4 FT%, 640 R

Fans always downgraded Ogilvy because he was better as a freshman than as a junior, but per 40 minutes, nobody beat his scoring (23.9 PPG) and rebounding (10.4) numbers.

6.   Derrick Byars, SF, 2005–07
64 G, 14.8 PPG, 56.5 EFG%, 71.3 FT%, 1.39 A/TO

Byars' 2007 season in which he was named the SEC's Player of the Year may have been the most complete season posted by a Vandy player in the book's 11-year period. He was hurt in the rankings by playing just two years, plus the fact that his junior season was just okay.

7.   Jermaine Beal, PG, 2007–10
132 G, 9.5 PPG, 50.5 EFG%, 79.5 FT%, 2.1 A/T

Couldn't shoot well his first two years, but once that skill developed, he easily became the best point guard in the Stallings era. With the game on the line, you wanted the ball in his hands.

8.   Festus Ezeli, C, 2008–12
121 G, 7.7 PPG, 58.5 EFG%, 58.4 FT%, 543 R, 204 B

Never played a game of high school ball and as a result, had huge holes in his game (18 assists, 195 turnovers). However, he became a dominant defender and a dependable offensive player.

9.   Brad Tinsley, PG, 2008–12
134 G, 9.3 PPG, 53.4 EFG%, 83.8 FT%, 1.9 A/T

Finished tied for sixth in career free-throw percentage and once posted a triple-double.

10.   Corey Smith, SF, 2001–05
124 G, 7.7 PPG, 53.9 EFG%, 75.1 FT%, 96 S, 1.1 A/T

Good defender, tough-minded player, no great offensive skills but was at least average at everything.

Also considered: Mario Moore, Lance Goulbourne, Alex Gordon